Liv Kjørsvik Schei

THE SHETLAND STORY

Photographs by Gunnie Moberg

Drawings by Kari Williamson

B. T. Batsford Ltd, London

Acknowledgements

We are grateful for the warmth and hospitality that met us everywhere in Shetland while we were working on this book. We thank especially all those who gave generously of their time to advise and assist us in so many ways, and Norsk Faglitterær Forfætterforening for their support.

To us these islands are romance and adventure and a wonderful place to be. Through this book we hope to convey our love and respect for Shetland and her people.

Gunnie Moberg   *Liv Kjørsvik Schei*

ISBN 0 7134 5512 8

Typeset by Lasertext Ltd., Stretford, Manchester

Printed and bound in Great Britain by
The Bath Press Ltd., Bath, Somerset for the publishers

B. T. Batsford Ltd.
4 Fitzhardinge Street
London W1H 0AH

CONTENTS

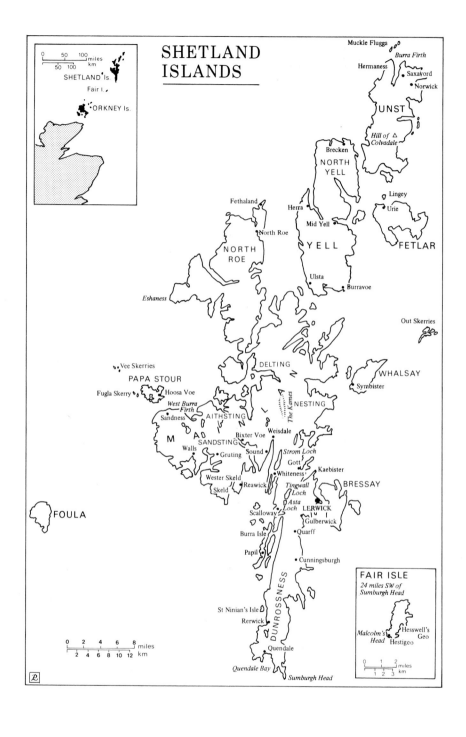

SHETLAND ISLANDS

0 50 100 miles
50 100 km
SHETLAND Is.
Fair I.
ORKNEY Is.

Muckle Flugga
Burra Firth
Hermaness
Saxavord
Norwick

UNST

Hill of △
Colvadale

Brecken

NORTH
YELL

Lingey
Urie

FETLAR

Fethaland
Herra
Mid Yell

North Roe

YELL

NORTH
ROE

Ulsta

Burravoe

Eshaness

Out Skerries

Vee Skerries

DELTING

WHALSAY

PAPA STOUR

Symbister

Fugla Skerry
Hoosa Voe

NESTING

West Burra
Firth

Sandness

AITHSTING

The Kames

M A D

Weisdale

Bixter Voe

SANDSTING

Walls

Strom Loch

Gruting
Sound

Gott

Kaebister

Whiteness

BRESSAY

Wester Skeld

Tingwall
Loch

Skeld
Reawick

Asta
Loch

LERWICK

FOULA

Scalloway
Gulberwick

Burra Isle
Quarff

Papil
Cunningsburgh

DUNROSSNESS

FAIR ISLE
24 miles SW of
Sumburgh Head

St Ninian's Isle
Rerwick

Malcolm's
Head

Hesswell's
Geo
Hestigeo

Quendale

0 1 2 miles
1 2 3 km

0 2 4 6 8 miles
2 4 6 8 10 12 km

Quendale Bay
Sumburgh Head

1 INTRODUCTION

Sometimes I tink whin da Loard med da aert,
An He got it aa pitten tagidder,
Fan He still hed a nev-foo a clippins left ower,
Trimmed aff o dis place or da tidder,
An he hedna da hert ta baal dem awa,
For dey lookit dat boannie an rare,
Sae he fashioned da Isles fae da ends o da aert,
An med aa-body fin at hame dere.

Shetlandic, Rhoda Bulter

During the uncharted centuries Shetland was the furthest north of the settlements on the fringe of the Atlantic. Some believed it to be Thule, the island at the edge of the world, discovered and described by an early Greek explorer. Certainly Agricola, the Roman governor of Britannia, must have thought so when he saw land in the north from the coast of Orkney. But 'despecta est et Thule'—seen was also Thule— was all the comment he had to make, apart from a vague geographical description. Why did he not try to land, where was his curiosity? The Romans were probably afraid of the great ocean with its wild uncharted seas, and their fear was the shield of the islands and their unknown people.

But the balance shifted, as it has done so often in Shetland history. With the coming of the Norsemen Shetland became a central part of a North Sea kingdom of widely scattered lands, bound to each other as much by a shared language and the same material culture as politically. After Norse power waned, Shetland was ruled successively from Copenhagen, Edinburgh and London. To the centre of power she was a distant outpost; to the North Sea community she remained an important crossroads and a vital partner. To understand later Shetland history it is necessary to be aware of this underlying conflict— even today the main issues in Shetland differ from those of mainland Britain.

Much of the remote rule was so negligent that the way to exploitation was left wide open. Perhaps this is why the Shetlanders regard the Norse period as their most lasting heritage, and the times before and after as of less consequence. After the takeover they lost their land and were at the beck and call of strangers. How free they really were under the Norse kings is difficult to say; what they do know is that afterwards they were tenants. A Shetland novelist writing at the beginning of the century, makes one of his characters say: 'We are not Scotch; we have never been Scotch; we will never be Scotch; we repudiate all connection with the Scotch.' Shetlanders will even today protest against being called Scots. But they also mind being spoken of as 'blown-away Norwegians'. They are Shetlanders and proud of it—and are very much their own people.

Shetland is still a very special part of Britain. But geographically the islands are no longer remote, even though they are closer to Reykjavik than to London! In the summertime the piers of Lerwick are packed with sailing enthusiasts eagerly comparing notes on winds and currents. Those of us who do not consider bobbing across the North Sea in a sailing boat the perfect holiday, are given a choice of

The latest car ferry, the P. & O. vessel St Sunniva, on her maiden voyage from Aberdeen to Lerwick via Stromness.

approach by modern means of communications. Car ferries arrive regularly from Aberdeen, Bergen and Tórshavn, and there are daily flights from mainland Scotland to Sumburgh Airport, south of Lerwick. In spite of an obvious lack of level land in some of the islands, most of them still have their own airstrip where the sturdy Loganair planes provide a reliable service. When they cannot land, nobody can!

Tourists flock to Shetland every summer for a variety of reasons, and amongst their numbers are anglers, ornithologists, botanists and geologists. Naturalists carrying binoculars can be seen everywhere and are jokingly referred to as a new and numerous species. Emigrants return from Britain or abroad to look for the land they once left, at a time when the future of the islands seemed bleak. Since they left Shetland too has been subject to time, and many things have changed in the last generation. The feelings of Laurence James Nicolson, who in his time was known as the Bard of Thule, will probably be shared by many of those who come looking for their roots:

> I walk where once I rowed a boat,
> a stranger and alone,
> and see with eyes of sad surprise
> That everything has gone.

Much of the change came with the oil business and the short-lived affluence it brought. The extent and benefit of this have been exaggerated. 'What can they do with so much money in a place like Shetland?' was a question asked in a BBC programme discussing the oil boom. This was at a time when prices in Shetland were almost twice as high as those in southern Britain, and people and traditions were threatened by oil and the sheer number of incomers. But Shetlanders are resilient, and money also provides the means to protect a threatened culture. The islanders have become strongly aware of their own cultural heritage, and many books have recently been written about subjects of local interest. It is perhaps true to say that change would have occurred even without oil, but it would have come at a less brutal speed. Nothing is gained without loss, but we cannot help mourning for the way it was.

Shetland, however, is still a romantic place. It is beautiful, damp and very windy. If you are willing to look for beauty where it is not obvious and get soaked to the skin while doing so, then Shetland is the place for you! The islands do not offer themselves, their history or their monuments to you—it is up to the visitor to go out and find them, and it is difficult at first to fathom the wealth of story and strife hidden among the heathery hills. Shetland takes a lot of knowing; no sooner do you think that you have grasped the picture than it splinters and turns into something quite different.

There are interesting sights to see and a variety of scenery. The scarred and furrowed coastline is awe-inspiring in places. Rocks and caves have been moulded into the strangest formations. Soft fields, lochs and endless moors stretch out before you. There are birds in overwhelming numbers, and spectacular sunsets against an even unbroken skyline. And yet the scene that will linger in your memory is more likely to be personal and subjective—perhaps a stack or a geo or birds in flight seen in the relief of sunshine and shadow, or blurred by mist and rain. Shetland is a place of individual experience, and either you feel its fascination or you do not.

Shetland is a land of paradox. It seems impossible that there has been so much bondage in a place that feels so free. There is a beauty that tears at you, and yet it is so often marred by buildings or construction work of breathtaking ugliness. The scenery gives an impression of strength and yet it seems so vulnerable. Suddenly you see why Shetlanders break their hearts over these islands and why those who left return when they can. There is a spiritual quality to the scenery that cannot be defined.

There used to be an unwritten rule in Shetland that whoever entered your home should be offered tea, and Shetlanders are still known for their hospitality. It is given with the natural dignity and good manners so striking in most Shetlanders, and especially in the older Shetland generation. They may seem reserved at first, but once they feel at ease with people, many Shetlanders turn out to be great conversationalists. And as so many of them have seen the world, they have a lot to say for themselves and are not easily impressed by strangers. They will treat them with courtesy, but will not set out to charm them in any way. Shetlanders do not need a facade; they are not on offer but are secure in themselves. They will tell you themselves that they are practical and pragmatic and open to new ideas. Others will describe them as dour and down-to-earth. And yet you do not need to have known a Shetlander long to become aware of the singer and dreamer in him. No wonder that music and poetry have such a rich tradition in the islands!

Shetland history as it has been told till now is full of myths. Her real history is very complex and so far nobody has attempted to write it. Perhaps it cannot be done. But it is also true that sometimes myths carry more of the essence of time and place than the facts as presented by the historian.

Here we have tried to tell the story of an island community, as seen from the outside. In all story-telling there is sleight-of-hand, and others will see things differently. A story must have a beginning, a middle and an end, said a wise man of old. We can only give you the middle part. The beginning of our story is lost in the haze of history, and thankfully there is no end.

2 NATURE

'Pray, Sir, where is Shetland?'
'Shetland is the name given to a group of islands in the Northern Atlantic, about 150 miles north of Britain.' (Eliza Edmondston, *Sketches and Tales of the Shetland Islands*, Edinburgh, 1856)

The young man who was thus asked the whereabouts of his home islands was incredulous and answered very stiffly. But that was in the nineteenth century, and today everyone will know that Shetland, or The Shetland Islands, in a position between 59° and 61° north latitude, make up the most northerly part of Britain. The group consists of about a hundred islands; the number depends on the distinction made between island and skerry. The total area is 1426 km² (550 square miles), and Mainland alone accounts for two-thirds of this. Back in 1861 there were 31,670 people living in 32 islands, and only some 3000 of them lived in Lerwick. Today the population pattern has changed: at the time of the 1981 census 23,130 people inhabited 17 islands, but two islands had only one family each. Lerwick's share had grown to 7255, and this tendency towards centralization is still marked.

Geology

Shetlanders both at home and in exile speak lovingly of their islands as 'The Old Rock'. It is an apt name, for the surface is mostly low and rocky, with little good farmland, and most of the rocks are very old. In fact the granite, schist, gneiss and serpentine are some of the oldest rocks in the world. The islands are situated on a ridge that separates the Atlantic from the North Sea. In geological features they resemble both Norway and the Scottish Highlands but differ from the volcanic Faroes.

The geological structure found in Shetland is primitive. The main framework of the landscape is formed by metamorphosed rocks, consisting mostly of mica schist and gneiss. On the surface of this core of old hard rocks were laid down basement beds of old red sandstone. These were followed by outpourings of lava which have formed several layers of igneous rocks. Narrow limestone bands crossed this landscape and relieved it of its monotony.

11

Faults in the western cliffs cannot hold out against the onslaught of the Atlantic. Erosion by the sea can be seen in many places, such as this gloup on Vaila, known as the Mammy Hole.

During the Ice Age the fringe of the great Scandinavian ice sheet covered Shetland, and this glaciation is responsible for much of the topographical detail. It made ice-scoured, wide and rather fertile valleys out of the limestone areas. It scooped out the hollows that have become the many small fresh water lochs especially found in Walls and Northmaven. It has given the Shetland scenery much of its rounded character. In a wall running alongside the road near the croft of Dalsetter in Boddam there is a boulder of laurvikite, a type of rock normally found only in the area just south of Oslo. It weighs about two tons and was moved across the North Sea by the ice sheet, as was also a large boulder on Bu Ness in Fair Isle.

Mica schists and gneiss crop out over much of Mainland, Yell and Unst, but the serpentine is probably the most interesting of the metamorphic rocks. The pier at Belmont in Unst has been carved out of this rock. There are large outcrops of serpentine in Unst and Fetlar—one has to go to Cornwall to find anything like them. But there are smaller outcrops in various parts of Mainland too, as in

Spiggie and Cunningsburgh and Northmaven. The old red sandstone is found in places like Fetlar, Bressay and Noss, as well as in Foula, Fair Isle and West Mainland. The igneous rocks are responsible for much of the fine rock scenery of North Mainland.

Faults in the western cliffs cannot hold out against the onslaught of the Atlantic. Erosion by the sea can be seen in many places, but perhaps nowhere more clearly than in the Grind of the Navir, where a gateway has been torn out of the igneous rocks. The land is losing out to the sea in another way too: Shetland is an area of depression, the land is slowly sinking in relation to the sea. About a century ago it was possible at low tide to cross on stepping stones from Muckle Roe to Mainland. When Lerwick harbour was being deepened, peat containing branches of trees was dredged up. Year by year the sea edges closer to cultivated land.

Attempts have been made to exploit mineral veins in the islands. Copper ore is found near Kibbister Ness in Dale Voe, at Copper Geo in Fair Isle and at Sand Lodge on Mainland, directly opposite from Mousa. For some time a mine was operated at Sand Lodge but it was never really a success and finally closed down in 1929. Around 1820 chromite was discovered in Unst by the geologist Samuel Hibbert. The deposits were found to be of marketable quantity and were quarried for more than a century. During the two world wars the chromite became important, as it was used to harden steel. Soapstone has been worked in Fetlar to make spinning whorls. Limestone used to be quarried for building purposes; today it is crushed and used to make the soil less acid.

Climate

The climate in Shetland is tempered by the warm saline water of the ocean current known as the North Atlantic Drift, a continuation of the Gulf Stream. It is a typically marine climate with slight temperature changes through the year. Winters are mild and stormy and summers are cool. In January the mean temperature is 4°C (39°F), which is about the same as in Edinburgh or London. But the moderating effect of the ocean also keeps summer temperatures at the fairly low average of 12°C (54°F).

Still there can be summer days that are warm and sunny, with a mirror-calm sea. Some summers have even been very dry. Because of the latitude it is possible to have 18 hours of sunshine in the long days of early summer. This is the time of 'the simmer dim' when day and night seem to merge imperceptibly in a muted light:

The day puts on a veil, the light is screened, and a landscape that, in fine weather, appears at noon to be almost infinite—in which long roads and little houses are luminously drawn—becomes small and circumscribed, and the hills and the shore, the sheep in the fields and the glinting sea, are visible, as it were, through a pane of slightly obscuring glass. (Eric Linklater, *The Dark of Summer*, London 1956)

Sometimes weather like this can go on for days, but very often a dense sea-fog seems to be the price exacted for a day of sunshine. It rolls in from the sea during the night and is like a sheet of white billowing wool that covers everything. At times the fog is low-lying, and we can watch it from above while still sitting in sunshine.

'The voar night comes creeping through the moss, the hairst night comes galloping on a horse' is an apt local description of the seasons. At the darkest time of winter there are only about six hours of daylight. With an overcast sky the darkness can be such that city-dwellers will have difficulty imagining what it is like. Sometimes the northern lights, Aurora Borealis, tremble luminously across the sky in waves of changing colour.

The air is more humid than anywhere else in Britain, and there is an average of 248 wet days throughout the year. Shetland is right in the path of a continual succession of low pressure systems which bring the familiar alternation between passing rain and hours or days of fine weather. This is the reason why people are always commenting on the weather. Still the annual rainfall is not large, only 1240 mm (49 in) as compared with 2108 mm (83 in) in Bergen, the nearest landfall east of Shetland. Owing to the low relief of the islands, rain clouds do not stay till they are empty, the way they do in Bergen, but pass on.

In the winter it snows on average 40 days a year. It usually does not lie very long. Before snowploughs became common, if it did settle, the snow would just have to cover the roads until *uplowsing*—the thaw—came. And there have been very snowy winters, with huge drifts, that are still remembered. In the vicious winter of 1947 the snow came in early February and lay for seven weeks. It is still known as The Long Snow. The blizzard back in 1887 was perhaps the worst recorded, as 17 Shetlanders lost their lives because of it. But such winters are exceptional, and generally there is very little snow for such a northern latitude.

The wind is the dominant climatic factor in Shetland. It seems to be always there, waiting to strike. When it is blowing a whole storm, known in Shetland as 'a stiff breeze', it is like waiting for a siege to be over. And yet, if you are properly dressed, to be out trying to fight the wind and the stinging rain can be an exhilarating experience. The sea, the sky and the bare landscape give a dimension never found in the sheltered valley. And gradually the wind will die down—it usually falls towards evening.

To a great extent the islands owe their fairly mild temperature also to the south-westerly and westerly winds coming from the Atlantic.

These are the prevailing winds as they have probably been at all times since the end of the last Ice Age. The northwesterly winds tend to bring rougher seas and bigger swells as they can sweep unimpeded right down from the Arctic. For eight months of the year the average wind does not fall below 15 m.p.h., and in the winter months it remains over 20 m.p.h. On average there are 58 days of gale a year. The highest wind speed was recorded at 177 m.p.h. (285 km.p.h.) at Saxavord in Unst in 1962. And yet it must be a comfort to us when meteorologists say that the Shetland climate was colder and rougher before, especially in the sixteenth and seventeenth centuries, and that the windstorms then were of a strength so far unmatched in our century.

Flora

In 1845 a young man named Thomas Edmondston from Unst published *A Flora of Shetland*. He died that same year, only 20 years old, in an accident while on a scientific expedition to South America. When only a boy he had discovered two rare plants in his home island: Arctic Sandwort (*Arenaria Norvegica*) and the Alpine Mouse-ear Chickweed (*Cerastium Arcticum Edmondstonii*). In Norway the Arctic Sandwort is a fairly common alpine plant, but the only other place in Britain where it grows is North Ronaldsay in Orkney. The Shetland Mouse-ear Chickweed is not found anywhere else in the world. Thomas Edmondston's sister describes it thus:

It has delicate white flowers, finely veined with faint sea-green. Its delicious perfume is as elusive and bewitching as its tints. It blooms on the most sterile ground exposed to bitter winds and salt spray. It lies low on the gravelly earth, opening its fragile coronal with a trust and courage that appeals to the human soul. When you take it in your hand it looks fragile enough to be blown to bits by a breath. (Jessie Saxby, *Threads from a Tangled Skein*, p349)

Thomas Edmondston found the Arctic Sandwort in the barren serpentine hill area north of Balta Sound, known as The Keen of Hamar. This has now been designated a *site of special scientific interest*, and you should consult the Nature Conservancy Council Warden before entering. Another place of special interest is the top of Ronas Hill with its arctic-alpine plants. Dwarf specimens of willows (*Salix herbacea*) are found there, and mountain ash grow in the cliffs nearby.

In a recent check-list of flowering plants and ferns found in Shetland there were 680 names. Of these, some 500 were considered native to the islands, and 15 of them cannot be found anywhere else. Admittedly, apart from Edmondston's Chickweed all of these are microspecies of the Hieracium, or Hawkweeds, an exceptionally variable and difficult group, popularly known as *Crux botanicorum*—the cross that botanists have to bear. Because of their irregular reproduction habits these plants are almost impossible to classify, and botanists usually solve this problem by steering away from them.

Perhaps the most striking visual impression of Shetland flora meets us in late spring and early summer when meadows and pastures are full of wild flowers. One of the first to appear is the Spring Squill (*Scilla verna*) which grows willingly almost everywhere and might be considered the emblem of Shetland. It is known locally by the unromantic name of 'grice ingan', pig onion, because pigs eat it. And yet it has inspired a local poet:

> Grice Ingans! Dat wis what da aald folk caaed dem,
>   Da peerie flooers at growes ower every broo;
> As Voar gengs by you see dem ida Norland
>   Sae tick dey're laek a mist o waarm blue.
> *Grice Ingans*, Vagaland

The pink thrift is called 'banksflooer' because it covers cliff edges and grassland along the shore. It adds vivid colour to the scenery. Daisies and pale yellow primroses also grow everywhere, and buttercups line the roads. Bright and colourful is also the red campion. It is of a type regularly found in Shetland and named *Silene dioica* (sub-species zetlandica). There are also eight species of orchids growing wild in Shetland, and some of them are a common sight in fields or by the roadside. The fragrant orchid is rare, but is found in parts of Unst. The heath spotted orchid has flowers varying in colour from white to deep red and is fairly common.

Orchids are often part of folklore, and the heath spotted orchid may have been used in Shetland for making love-potions. The local names often give a clearer idea of what the plants are like or what they have been used for. Thus the toxic fox-glove was called 'trowie gliv', the troll-glove, perhaps to frighten children away from it. Scurvy grass is a flowering plant which is quite common by the seashore. Its leaves contain vitamin C and were used in the old days to cure scurvy. Deep-sea sailors used to bring dried leaves along to eat on long voyages, and this plant is therefore known in Shetland as 'sailor's hope'. In the same way the small bogbean, growing near shallow fresh water all over Shetland, is known as 'gulsa girse' and was used to cure gulsa or jaundice in cattle. Wild flowers were also used to produce dyes.

On his tour of Shetland in the summer of 1774, the young Orkney minister George Low was walking across the hills on his way to Sandness when he came across a loch full of water lilies:

At some distance is Longa Water, where I found the *Nymphœa alba*, or Great White Water Lilly, Fl.Suec.470, in great plenty, the only time I had seen it in Orkney or Schetland, nor do I think it is to be found any where else thro'

The beautiful White Water Lily, Nymphaea alba, *Lunga Water, on the way to Sandness, West Mainland.*

them. The flowers very large, equalling a small tulip; the petals numerous, approaching to a full flower; the only instance that I know of this in our Island Catalogue. (*A Tour through Orkney and Schetland*, p119)

But Peter White, writing in 1883, points out that 'In a small loch at the base of Rooeness Hill, on the north side, is found the *Nymphœa alba*.'

Spring is slow in coming in Shetland, and the flowering season is about a month later than further south. Gardening is therefore a challenge, and requires careful planning. One of those to have succeeded in finding a balance between growth and climate is John Copland in his garden at Sullom, which he laid out in 1970. To give his plants the necessary shelter he has used drystone dykes and carefully-placed shrubs and trees. Another amazing garden in Shetland today is the nursery at The Lea in Tresta, which was made over a period of eight years by Rosa Steppan. She has experimented with ornamental plants from all over the world to find those best suited to the climate. Her collection includes old-fashioned roses, rare primulas and Himalayan poppies.

Woodlands

Trees are rare, and the overall impression given by the islands is of peat, mosses and heather, and fields in varying shades of green. When peat is taken for fuel, the hills become even barer. It was the sight of such denuded peat-hills that once made a visitor exclaim that he could see nothing but the skeleton of a departed country. The difficulty of growing trees is usually blamed on the combination of high wind force and salty air, but the sheep also nibble and destroy the young saplings, when they can get at them.

It has been pointed out that because trees grow on islands along the coast of Norway, they should grow in Shetland too. But Shetland trees are never in the lee of the wind, and additionally, Shetland collects more salt in January alone than any place on the Norwegian coast does in a whole year. The sea spray is carried over the whole surface of the islands by any storms that blow, and leaves are sometimes blackened even in the middle of summer. Despite this, decayed trunks are often found in bogs and river-beds. Windhouse Burn in Yell shows evidence of what must at one time have been a very extensive forest of birch-trees:

For a considerable part of its course the burn has, in the course of centuries, worn its way through the peaty ground until it has reached a harder bottom, so that in many places the banks are both deep and steep. For considerable distances the branches and roots protrude from the peaty sides. (*Old-lore Miscellany*, Vol. I 1907–8, pp91–2)

Cores of peat from West Mainland have recently been analyzed by the Faroese botanist Johannes Johansen using the latest scientific methods. The peat records the botanical development from the end of the Ice Age some 12,000 years ago. Trees were at their most plentiful around 5500 BC with large plantations of birch, hazel, juniper and poplar. From then on the climate seems to have worsened, and birch and hazel decreased. Through his pollen analyses, Johansen arrives at the year 3465 BC as the time of the arrival of neolithic man in Shetland.

By the time the Norsemen arrived there were still enough birch trees to become pointed out in place-names. In Northmaven there is a loch called Birka Water south of Uyea, as well as a hill known as Birka Vird near Gunnister Voe. Other native trees have had a precarious existence:

The mountain ash or rowan tree, the hazel, the honeysuckle, the hip-brier and willow are natives in many of the islets or holms in fresh water lochs. In any other situation, I believe, they could not exist for horses, cows and sheep browse upon and destroy everything that comes in their way when they are hard pressed for food. (Rev. John Bryden, *New Statistical Account of Scotland*, 1841)

Today wild hazel grows in only two places, and the other species do not fare much better. Attempts have been made over the last decade to save the native Shetland trees for posterity, but so far results have been rather discouraging.

Non-native trees like sycamore and horse chestnut were brought to Shetland by lairds and ministers during the eighteenth and nineteenth centuries. Trees were also planted around some croft houses. The best known garden from this period is perhaps the one that was planted at Busta House. It shows that many kinds of trees can grow to a considerable size if well enough sheltered. At Leagarth in Fetlar even quite exotic trees seemed to thrive at one time. In Kergord in Weisdale, probably the most sheltered area in Shetland, large scale planting was carried out at the beginning of this century. The area covers between eight and nine acres, and the trees are mixed conifer and deciduous, including such species as sitka spruce, mountain pine and Japanese larch, sycamore, beech and rowan. Kergord Woodlands have been proposed as a Local Nature Reserve by the Shetland Islands Council. The Shetland Amenity Trust has also carried out a project of planting and caring for trees.

Birds

— — we came, suddenly, upon a red-breasted merganser and her tiny young ones, which all squattered away into the water with a fearful plash, while the mother bird kept sailing round and round them till they got fairly out of distance. We had not, at the time, our guns with us, or they would assuredly not have escaped. (From the *Journal of Edward Charlton*, M.D., 1832)

Such a callous attitude from men calling themselves naturalists was not at all uncommon in the nineteenth century, indeed it persisted long enough in this century to help put an end to many vulnerable species. Among these is the erne, or sea-eagle, which was almost gone by the end of the century. In 1910 the last British pair nested on the Eigg, west of Whale Firth in Yell. They seem to have been fairly common in Shetland, and a place like Erns Hamar in Unst can tell us where they were found. Some time ago attempts were made to settle young ernes from Norway on Fair Isle, but they did not thrive. However, the Nature Conservancy Council has tried to follow this up by bringing in young ernes every year and rearing them in an artificial nest on Rhum. At least one of these has been sighted in Shetland, perhaps looking for a place to settle?

But Shetland birds have gained as well as lost through the changes that have occurred in the bird population. Small variations in the climate can affect the status of birds, although not all changes are explained that way. The most amazing development has been the spectacular spread of the fulmar, known in Shetland as the *maalie*.

The most amazing development has been the spectacular spread of the fulmar, known in Shetland as the maalie. *They are found everywhere along the coastline.*

Today they are found everywhere along the coastline, looking at a distance like strange white flowers. Until 1878 when twelve pairs were observed breeding on Foula, the fulmar was confined to St Kilda where it constituted the staple diet of the islanders. In 1890 an ornithologist visiting Papa Stour proudly reported sighting one fulmar there. Since then the birds have spread all over Britain.

The reasons for the spread of the fulmar have puzzled the ornithologists, but the explanation may be that because the fulmar feed on marine flotsam they go wherever they can find fish offal dumped at sea. Of course, wherever they go other birds will give them *lebensraum*; even formidable birds like the bonxies—the great skuas—and the greater black-backed gulls will at any cost avoid conflicts with the fulmar. This is because of the peculiar phenomenon of the stomach oil that the fulmar can bring up and eject at an enemy. Apart from its sickening smell it has a corrosive effect on a bird's plumage, and is thus a powerful weapon. Each bird yields nearly half a pint of this oil, which was used by the St Kildans for many purposes.

The bonxies were even in the early nineteenth century threatened by extinction because of their interest to collectors. In 1920 they were down to one pair nesting in Foula and two in Hermaness. Since then the bonxies have recovered and seem to be increasing in number all the time. There are now some 3000 pairs in Foula alone, and they

Hermaness, Unst. Today there is a total of more than ten thousand gannets in the colonies of Noss, Hermaness and Fair Isle.

have established many smaller colonies as well. Not everybody is happy about this increase, as they are cruel pirates who will hound to death other birds like kittiwakes and harry even gannets to force them to give up fish. Both these species have, however, built up their numbers greatly over the last few decades. The first gannet colony became established on Noss in 1911; today there is a total of more than ten thousand birds in the colonies of Noss, Hermaness and Fair Isle. There is also a small colony of gannets on Foula.

When the snowy owl decided to settle in Fetlar in 1967 it caused an ornithological sensation. It was first discovered by the well-known Shetland naturalist Bobby Tulloch. While walking across Stakkaberg in Fetlar in the company of European ornithologists he suddenly saw three large whitish eggs in a hollow. A pair of owls were busy trying to divert attention from their nest. They bred every year after that, until 1975 when the old male disappeared. To protect his territorial rights he had driven out other males, but it is hoped that some of the 20 young that were raised in Fetlar, will return there sometime to breed.

The area surrounding Stakkaberg was declared a Statutory Bird Sanctuary to protect the owls against too curious visitors. Another Fetlar visitor whose presence may be precarious because of the attention paid to it is the colourful little wader known as the Red-Necked Phalarope. For while today's naturalists bring cameras and binoculars instead of guns their sheer number can still cause harm to breeding birds. Many visitors also come to watch the birds during the migrating periods in spring and autumn. That is also the time to see the migrants that are just passing through.

As so many have discovered, Shetland is an ideal place for birds and birdwatching. Birds in their thousands return to the islands each year, and an estimated half a million seabirds of 21 different species breed there. This is perhaps because the wide range of coastal habitats caters to the nesting habits of different species. The many uninhabited islands make secure and secluded nesting-places. The best places to see the great variety of Shetland seabirds in their natural habitats are in the cliffs of Hermaness and Noss, which have been made into National Nature Reserves. Hermaness has had the added attraction of having as a summer visitor the black-browed albatross, which is rarely seen north of the equator. It was first sighted by a Swedish ornithologist. Each year the albatross has returned to the same ledge at The Point of Saito, to sit on his solitary nest right in the middle of a large gannet colony, waiting for a mate.

Although the seabirds are the most numerous there are in fact all of 65 breeding species in Shetland. One of these is the small bird known as the Shetland wren, *Troglodytes t. zetlandicus*, which is distinctive enough to be classified as a sub-species. It is rather larger than southern birds, with a dark reddish-brown plumage, flecked with brown beneath. It sings differently too, combining stridency of song with a different rhythm. There is an indigenous sub-species of starling as well, *Sturnus vulgaris zetlandicus*. Like the wren it is slightly larger, an intermediate between the European species and the Faroese sub-species.

Like the plants the birds also have their own characteristic local names. The red-throated diver is known as the raingoose because it keeps calling 'Mair weet! Waur wadder!'—More wet! Worse weather! The owls have been rare enough to be considered 'fey fuls'. The shag is known as the skarf, and was always surrounded by an aura of mystery. The Norsemen saw it as a troll bird that could change into a human being in a fairy-tale country far out in the western sea.

Wild animals

Perhaps because of the lack of trees there are no large land animals found in Shetland. However, rabbits are found everywhere. Myxomatosis was at one time introduced to get rid of them, but they have since recovered. Attempts have been made to bring in blue hare, but they have not really been successful. Because they turn white in winter the hares are quite conspicuous against the dark Shetland hills. The otter can still be found but are not so numerous as they once were. Stoats are common on Mainland.

Mus Thulensis is a sub-species of mouse peculiar to Foula. Its cousin in Fair Isle, *Mus Fridariensis*, has also developed characteristics sufficiently different to become classified as a sub-species. It is larger than Mainland mice.

Although all seals are known as selkies in Shetland, there is still a clear distinction between the common seal and the grey Atlantic seal. The common seal stays closer to the shore and is therefore known as tang-fish, tang meaning sea-weed. The more adventurous grey seal is known as haf-fish. A bearded seal was first recorded in Yell in 1977.

Common seals have lived in Shetland waters since the Iron Age at least, as seal bones have been found in middens at Jarlshof. They prefer to stay close to tidal streams and rips where fish is easily found. When playing about in pairs in the water they are truly in their element and are fun to watch. Because they are slow to move they seem helpless on a beach, at a distance even looking like large slugs. They look more at home when balancing on some outlying rock, and they will return time and again to the same places. While ashore they seem to lie and doze most of the time; all their social activities are carried on in the sea. They dislike the wind and look for a sheltered spot, and sometimes it seems as though the whole seal population gathers on the rocks. It may be that they cannot digest under water, and are ruminating on land:

This may be one of the reasons for those long periods of lazy basking on rocks or sandbanks or floating at the surface that are so characteristic a feature of the life of seals. It may be then that the internal organs really get to work and digest the food collected during the active hunting hours when the animal has been filling its stomach with prey. (Harrison Matthews, *British Mammals*, 1952)

There was a decline in the local seal population in the decades just after the last war, probably because of hunting. After protection was granted in 1970 the numbers increased to the point where now some 20 per cent of the British seal population can be found around Shetland.

Basking sharks used to be seen in the summer months, but have now become very rare. They like to stay in deep water under cliffs but are usually harmless unless they are provoked. Such an animal can be about 10 m (33 ft) long, and when it moves slowly along, raising and lowering its large body, with the tip of the tail nearly always visible, it makes a strange sight. It is not at all to be wondered at that people who saw it in the past thought they had seen a monstrous sea-serpent.

3 EARLY HISTORY

Shetland is rich in prehistoric remains, and because of isolation and a gentle land-use they have been left mostly undisturbed. It is marine erosion that poses the greatest threat to ancient historical sites in Shetland, as so much of the early settlement took place near the sea. During the last five thousand years the sea level has risen an estimated 6 m (19½ ft), and a great number of sites must have been lost. Other sites are still at risk. But sometimes the sea and the storm work together: Jarlshof emerged after a strong gale.

Sometime during the fourth millennium BC neolithic man reached Shetland in his quest for new land. By that time the settled life of the farmer had become a necessary alternative to that of the hunter and fisherman, and it was possible to base a living on the Shetland environment. The settlers would have brought their domesticated livestock with them. There is evidence that they grew barley. Later, in Norse times, oats were grown, too. The settlers were not primitive when measured by the yardstick of their own times. They seem to have come in great numbers, judging by their system of land division. The land was divided by substantial walls or dykes into large units which were then split up into separate fields. Some of the dykes, like the Finnigord in Fetlar, look rather like major land division boundaries.

Bronze Age
During the Bronze Age soils became impoverished through poor management, exhaustion and overstocking. There seem to have been climatic changes as well. Because of these interrelated factors large areas of Shetland became covered by blanket peat around 1000 BC. The peat has buried the ruins of early farms and partially preserved the landscape as it once was. This has made it possible to study early agricultural communities in a marginal area to an extent that is rare in Western Europe. Most of these early house sites were only recently recognized. The densest concentration of settlements, cairns, chambered tombs and field systems can be found in the area around Gruting Voe in West Mainland, but traces of very early agriculture can also be seen in other parts of Walls, at Dalsetter and around Mavis Grind.

A distinctive building style seems to have developed in Shetland. Some 160 house sites have so far been identified as belonging to the transition period between the Late Neolithic and the Early Bronze Age. They are oval-shaped and on average they measure $7 \times 4\frac{1}{2}$ m ($30 \times 14\frac{1}{2}$ ft). Houses of this type have been excavated at Ness of Gruting and at Scord of Brouster in West Mainland. They have thick drystone walls filled up with rubble and earth, which would have been kept damp by the water draining from the roof. This wetting was essential to keep the walls windproof, and is a technique also known in the Hebrides. Most of these early houses are found in high and rather exposed places, and this would suggest that the climate must at one time have been quite favourable.

The most striking of the houses is the large communal building at Stanydale, which was excavated by Charles Calder in the 1950s. It is about twice the size of any other house, but perhaps its most interesting feature is the roof. This was supported in the centre by two thick wooden posts. They were made of spruce, a tree which at that time grew only in North America and Scandinavia. As few traces have been found of everyday agricultural tools scholars have suggested that the house may have been a temple or some kind of village hall. It might have been the house of a chieftain. Nearby are three smaller houses of the common oval shape; there is also a system of field-walls as well as cairns of stones cleared from the fields. And of course, the surrounding peat banks may cover an even larger settlement.

Another structure that is special for Shetland is the kind of tomb that is known as the heel-shaped cairn. This type of chambered cairn takes its name from its floor plan, which quite literally resembles the heel of a shoe. These cairns are often built in prominent positions and vary greatly in size. There are large tombs on the island of Vementry and at Punds Water near Mangaster. To be buried in such a cairn may have been an honour for the chosen few, but there is no way of knowing on what basis they would have been selected.

Finds of bronze have been few but it is still true to say that Shetland had its Bronze Age, as many of the other changes brought about during this period are evident. Stone artefacts, burial practices, building styles and pottery change. Cremation became common practice. A new type of pottery known as 'beakers' became prevalent. The people who made it laid beakers in the tombs and cists of their dead. Towards the end of the period the burnt mounds came into use. These were places where meat would be cooked by dropping hot stones into a trough of water. More stones would be added from time to time to keep it boiling, the used broken stone forming the mound. One of the largest mounds is found at Vassetter in Fair Isle.

The late Bronze Age must have been a difficult time in Shetland, as environmental changes were making working and living conditions harder. There was a shift from crops to animals. Even so there must have been far more people than the land could support. The reason behind the obviously troubled times that were to come during the Iron Age in Shetland, is perhaps the intensified struggle for a share of meagre resources. Land had become precious.

Iron Age

The Iron Age is the term used by prehistorians to describe the period of cultural development that begins with the general use of iron. It reached Shetland about 600 BC. The most characteristic and most studied monuments of the Iron Age in Shetland are the numerous but enigmatic brochs. Some 75 sites have so far been definitely identified as brochs. Often the site can be recognized from the place-name, as it will contain elements like *brough*, *burgh*, *bur*, or *burgi*. The form *porrie* is used in Papa Stour. They are all derivatives of the Norse word *borg*, which means a castle or fortification.

Not all Iron Age structures in Shetland are brochs, but for a long time scholars were so preoccupied with them that odd sites were either believed to belong to other periods or explained as ruined brochs. The only site always to be recognized as different was the holm fort in Loch of Huxter in Whalsay. Although much of the stone has been taken for building purposes, there are still remains of a so-called blockhouse. The idea of the broch is believed to have evolved from this simpler structure. Most of the forts seem to have been built on inaccessible nesses or promontories. A spectacular site is Ness of Burgi near Sumburgh. The archaeologist Dr Raymond Lamb has identified all of 15 such promontory forts in Shetland and one in Fair Isle.

The broch structures are found in northern Scotland; there are, however, a higher proportion of them in Shetland and Orkney than anywhere else, and this has led many to believe that the idea of the broch evolved in the Northern Isles, probably in Orkney. Although the plan of the broch varies, it is still uniform enough to suggest that it is the idea of one master builder. Whoever designed them had quite advanced knowledge of building practices, as they are cleverly constructed. The brochs are circular drystone towers, and as assumed by the Norsemen who named them, they were probably built as fortifications. The brochs at Mousa, Jarlshof and Clickhimin are the best preserved specimens in Shetland.

Many theories have been put forward as to the possible purpose of the broch. Unfortunately the archaeological evidence is scant. In some cases sites were ruined by early amateur excavations, but as often as not sites have been robbed of stone over a long time. But it seems to be generally accepted that the brochs are defence structures. Dr Hugh Marwick, the Orkney historian, thought of the broch as an architecture of 'mortal fear'.

The brochs at Mousa, Jarlshof and Clickhimin are the best preserved specimens in Shetland. Here the internal wall face of Mousa shows scarcement ledges with ladder-like apertures.

Their construction has been connected with the Roman expansion in northern Europe, but the brochs were built long before this became a threat. Excavation of a broch at Bu near Stromness in Orkney showed that this must have evolved through many building stages from 600 BC, but most brochs were probably erected around 100 BC. It is known that Rome obtained slaves through slave chains in Britain before she became a Roman province, and the brochs may have been thought of as a defence against slave raiders. This idea was rejected by A. W. Brøgger, the Norwegian historian, who maintains that the number of the brochs and the enormous energy they represent are not in any reasonable proportion to 'so distant an effort of the Romans'.

The structure of the broch itself speaks against the idea of its being built to hide a local population for any length of time from some kind of external pressure. The very narrow entrance would not have made it possible to bring cattle into the broch. The broch could, however, house quite a few people and would need only a handful to defend it. The similarity to a medieval castle has led scholars to believe that the purpose of the broch may be dominance, and that the broch was:

essentially a castle, the private stronghold of a chief exercising hereditary authority over his dependants, and living in a state of chronic warfare with his neighbours. (W. Douglas Simpson, The Broch of Clickhimin, Viking Congress, 1950)

The fact that brochs are sometimes found in groups close together is another puzzling aspect. If the brochs are indeed the strongholds of a ruling aristocracy, then W. Douglas Simpson may be right in his belief that such a group of brochs represents a family compound where each heir would have his tower. Its size and strength might have been a question of pride and status.

One of the most interesting brochs in Shetland is the Broch of Clickhimin, just outside Lerwick. The water level of the loch was lowered in 1874, so that what used to be a small holm is now a peninsula. The site is striking, and it is not surprising to find traces of continuous occupation over a thousand years. During this long period it naturally underwent many alterations and evolved through several stages to meet changing social conditions. The broch was first excavated in 1861–2, but no account of the work was made, nor were any artefacts preserved. It was later surveyed by Sir Henry Dryden who made careful drawings of the broch as it then was.

The broch today presents a very different picture from when it was revealed by excavation. Most of the interior furnishings, including the central hearth, are gone. The broch is also considerably lower. In Dryden's drawings there were five windows above the entrance where there now are only three, and the upper stair has five steps where there used to be fourteen. The site therefore presented modern archaeologists with quite a challenge when it was re-excavated in the 1950s.

The site as we now see it serves to give us a composite picture of life as it was lived through the Iron Age in Shetland. It was first occupied around 700 BC by farmers who have left behind a small oval house. The site then was fortified in the earlier Iron Age before the broch was built. A massive stone rampart was built to encircle the holm. This stage also left behind the blockhouse now serving as a gateway. At a later stage the broch was built inside the existing fortifications. The stonework of the broch is of higher quality than the masonry of the rest of the site, and the shape of the broch seems also to have been dictated by the ramparts. An unusual feature of this broch is the fact that it has a second entrance. Most brochs have no other external opening than the ground floor entrance.

The broch later had a wheelhouse inserted within its walls, and new dwellings appeared outside as occupation of the site continued into the first millennium AD. An intriguing relic found on the site was the shard of a Roman vase, probably made in Alexandria round AD100. Another curious find is a footmarked stone. It forms a threshold at the end of the causeway, but it may have been moved there at a later date. Stones like this are believed to have been associated with inaugural ceremonies.

Another curious find is a footmarked stone at Clickhimin. Stones like this are believed to have been associated with inaugural ceremonies.

Dark Ages

The centuries before the coming of the Norsemen have been named the Dark Ages. In many ways life went on for a long time then as it had done in the Iron Age, with only imperceptible and gradual change. The term 'wheelhouses' is used for the houses built in the post-broch period. They are circular houses divided into rooms by radial stone piers which also served to support the roof. There is a well constructed wheelhouse at Jarlshof. Such a house may have been built into one of the old brochs or just outside it and would be made from the stone of the broch.

The name Picts is used generally about the people living in the Northern Isles and Scotland at the time. The land of the Picts extended from Shetland in the north to the Pentland Hills in the south, and probably some kind of federation held them together. For more than a century they subjected the northern flank of the Roman province to continuous guerilla warfare. Otherwise very little is known about them. The form Pict is supposedly from Latin *pictus*, painted, and refers to their alleged habit of tattooing themselves. To the Norsemen they were known as Péttar. Probably both the Norse and the Latin forms are distortions of an original tribal name.

On the whole there are fewer traces of the Picts than might be expected; this may be because the Norsemen later took over their sites and built new houses on them. A few place-names give us an idea of what became of them. Pettadale just south of Voe is today empty and barren. Pettadale Water and Burn in North Roe are also in a marginal area.

But the Picts were not the Barbarians the Romans tried to make them appear. Until they were overrun by the Norsemen they seem to have had an ordered and well-organized society. The monuments they left behind show that they were also a cultured people. These are the sculptured symbol stones—slabs of rock where the same patterns recur in new combinations. The earliest stones tend to show animals and abstract designs, whereas later slabs portray people and Christian symbols. The latter are known as cross-slabs and are the more common in Shetland. As local stone is used it follows that there must have been quite an artistic tradition in the islands. Some of the stones also had inscriptions in the ogam alphabet. These can be deciphered, but no key exists to the language found in them. Among the more interesting stones are those found in Bressay and in Papil, West Burra.

These stones have Christian motifs, and it is not surprising that they were found in old church sites. The Picts were christianized, but so far it has not been definitely established how their conversion came about. The Picts of the Scottish mainland learned about Christianity from St Columba of Iona and the missionaries who succeeded him, and at least one of these went north. But there are indications that the islanders also had ecclesiastical as well as artistic links with the Rome-inspired Christianity of St Ninian of Northumbria, as some of the symbols carved on the stones resemble Northumbrian illustrated gospels.

The name of the fourth century saint occurs in St Ninian's Isle. A monastic colony similar to the one in Bissay in Orkney may have been established in the island, but probably St Ninian himself never reached so far north. The hoard that was discovered during excavation of the chapel in St Ninian's Isle consists of 28 silver objects as well as the puzzling jawbone of a porpoise. The hoard is believed to have been hidden around AD 800, obviously to save it from Viking raiders. In the eighth century a very distinctive type of ring-shaped brooch was in fashion among the Picts, and no less than 12 examples were found on St Ninian's Isle. There were also eight silver bowls. One of these was imported from Northumbria, but the others were of Pictish manufacture.

The place-names also contain memories of other early Christians. There are nine known *papar* place-names in Shetland. Among these are Papa Stour and Papil Geo in the Isle of Noss. The name was used by the Norsemen about the Irish hermits they found both in Shetland and Iceland. The early Celtic Church was loosely organized and had monks rather than priests. An austere life in obedience to the Church and its tenets was an utter reality. It is this strongly eremitical aspect of their faith that makes them seek small islands and extreme marginal areas. The remains of their hermitages can still be seen in such awesome places as The Clett, a stack north-east of Fetlar, and on Burki Stack in Culswick. Some of the sites have produced relics of early Christianity, and many of them are known to have survived as churches or grave-yards for a long time.

The early Norsemen seem in part to have had an indulgent, rather humorous attitude to Christian practices. In Iceland the puffin is still nicknamed *papi*—evidently the settlers were struck by the similarity between the birds and the Irish hermits as regards both appearance and choice of habitat. On the Pictish cross-slab from Papil in West Burra a different carver seems to have added two strange-looking figures at the base of the stone. They are men with birds' heads, their prominent beaks rather suggesting puffins. Perhaps this carving represents some early Norseman's sense of humour!

All the prehistoric sites represent a rich cultural heritage that should be preserved and studied. There is a need for a thorough survey of the monuments of the different periods. Till recently, surveys and excavations have tended to be limited to special areas or types of monuments, but the appointment of a resident archaeologist has made possible a systematic study of Shetland prehistory.

4 NORSE TIMES

Norse settlers

The migrations from the Scandinavian countries during what has become known as the Viking Age have puzzled scholars, and have lately been the subject of a more reflective study, shorn of the extremes of romanticism or indignation. The Vikings became known to the world through the writings of their victims and enemies: the scribes of the monasteries who saw in them the coming of Antichrist or the judgement of God on his sinning people. The Scandinavians themselves learned about the Vikings from the marvellous stories and legends of the Icelandic sagas with all their larger than life men and women, and did not really understand how anyone could help admire their courage and cultural sophistication. After all, who would today remark 'the King has fed us well' when he saw tissue of fat on the arrow he was drawing out of his heart?

Viking raids seem to have begun in earnest in the last years of the eighth century, but there are many indications that ships must have crossed from Scandinavia to the Northern Isles long before that. Thus on linguistic evidence the form Péttar as a name for the Picts must have been adopted in Norse at the latest in the seventh century. The character of the place-names in Shetland does not preclude a first Norse colonization going back to about AD 600. Even in AD 98 the Roman historian Tacitus mentions maritime tribes in Northern Europe. Although some archaeological remains might be older, however, most of the early finds seem to date to around AD 800. The conclusion that may be drawn is therefore that though stray settlers perhaps established themselves in Shetland before the end of the eighth century, the main wave of colonization began then.

It also seems clear that most of the settlers in Shetland came from the Norwegian west coast, but there is no single or simple reason why the migration west over sea began. Population pressure at home has often been suggested; there was also a contemporary increase in iron production which made good tools and weapons possible. Still there can be no doubt that it is the remarkable sailing ships that hold the key to the Viking Age expansion. The ships were light, and even when loaded they only drew between 60 and 90 cm (2 ft and 2 ft 10 in). The *háfskip* used on ocean voyages would be broader in the beams and usually have a higher freeboard; they usually had one big sail that could be reefed when needed. They did not depend on wind and current alone, as they had oars fore and aft and could be rowed. Therefore they were fast and could land anywhere, even in extremely shallow water. Thus fortifications in strategic harbours could simply be avoided. The Viking raids were so surprisingly successful that it is no wonder this went to their heads completely, and more and more wanted to take part in this new venture.

In Shetland the incomers would not find rich farming land as in Orkney, but still it would be more or less the environment they were used to, with the added advantage that sheep and possibly also cattle could be outwintered. There was no timber, but stone for building was easily available. So far only two early Norse domestic sites have been closely examined: at Jarlshof in Dunrossness and at Underhoull in Unst. The reason why so few Norse farmsteads have been found is probably that most of them have been occupied continuously until present times. The settlers would have known what site they were looking for to suit their life-style best. They would have wanted easy access to the sea, a patch of fairly fertile land where grain could be cultivated, as well as pasture for their animals.

Excavations at Jarlshof have shown that early in the ninth century Norse settlers took over a substantial farm from the Picts. There they

Excavations at Jarlshof have shown that early in the ninth century Norse settlers took over a substantial farm from the Picts.

built a two-roomed longhouse that was 32 m (35 yd) long. Usually longhouses were some 20 m (22 yd) long and at least 5 m (5½ yd) wide, and the oldest examples would have semi-circular ends. Turf would be used to make the drystone walls windproof. There was variation in the number of rooms and also in the way they were furnished. The common pattern seems to have been a byre, a main living room with a central fireplace and a room for sleeping. Remains of houses built to this pattern can be seen almost everywhere in the Shetland countryside, as they remained common till fairly recently. In fact, houses of this type were characteristic of Norse settlements in general, and could be found also on the Scottish mainland, in the Hebrides, in Faroe, Iceland, Greenland and even North America. Strangely enough there is no example of such a house in Norway itself, probably because there timber and not stone would have been used as building material.

At Jarlshof the Norse incomers thus seem to have encroached on a population already firmly established. At Underhoull in Unst on the other hand, by the north shore of Burga Sand, a Viking longhouse is built on top of an Iron Age complex of a workshop and huts used for living quarters. The site would have been deserted before the Norsemen arrived, as several inches of soil separate the two building phases. The farmstead lies on the margin of a very fertile patch of land. The saving of land by rebuilding on earlier sites seems to have been a deeply ingrained habit with the Norsemen, and perhaps this was not so strange considering the meagre land resources they were used to having. Among the artefacts found is a toy quern which is interesting because it is an exact model of a full-scale one. It also gives a rather touching glimpse of day-to-day life in a pioneer family.

Such a farmstead would be basically self-sufficient for the necessities of life. Probably conditions did not change radically through the centuries to come. A small area of land would be walled in near the house and used to cultivate oats, barley and bere. Dung and ground shells would be spread on the land. Local soapstone could be used to make household goods. Hay-making was important, so that the animals could be seen through the winter. As the sheep could be left out over the winter they need not be slaughtered in the autumn, as they were in Norway. This left Shetland with more wool than was needed, which could therefore be sold to Norway in exchange for timber. Fishing does not seem to have been especially important in the first stages of settlement, but the farmsteads both at Jarlshof and Underhoull were close to good fishing grounds.

Norse rulers

On the archaeological evidence Shetland had a fairly large Pictish population just before the Norsemen came. What happened to them is an open question. They did not leave much trace in language or place-names, but there seems to be acceptable evidence that some of the Christian sculpture and the ogam inscriptions in Shetland may date from the period 800–1050.

A tenth-century date has long been proposed for the Bressay cross-slab with its Pictish inscription in ogam letters, which includes two Gaelic words, and one Norse, and has uniquely : between the words as in runes. A fragment from Papil which clearly resembles tombstones at Iona should also belong to that century. (Robert B. K. Stevenson, Christian Sculpture in Norse Shetland, Fróðskaparrit, Tórshavn).

There was immigration from Norway on a considerable scale, and according to the estimate of the Norwegian historian, A. W. Brøgger, there would have been a population of some 22,000 towards the end of the Viking period. As the number of people grew the township system of farming probably evolved of necessity. How this happened can be studied at Jarlshof.

In spite of being the nearest landfall from Norway and an important stepping-stone within the Norse geographical province, Shetland is hardly mentioned in the sagas. On the whole written sources are very sparse, but Shetland became a part of the Orkney earldom, and some references can therefore be found in the Orkneyinga saga. The earldom was at times ruled by more than two earls, and would then be divided between them. Thus after Earl Thorfinn the Mighty died c. 1065 his two sons Paul and Erlend became joint rulers, with Earl Erlend getting the northern and eastern part of Orkney. Shetland would also probably have been part of his share, and later this would have come to his son Magnus Erlendsson, the Saint. As pointed out by Dr Barbara Crawford, this explains why first St Magnus and later his nephew Rognvald could always count on support in Shetland.

The joint rule of the earldom was inherited by Magnus Erlendsson and his cousin and fellow earl Hakon Paulsson. The tension between them led to open conflict and the death of Magnus on Egilsay during Easter Week of 1117. The cult of St Magnus grew quickly, and it is an interesting fact that this seems to have happened mainly in Shetland.

In the very first statement about the pilgrimages of the sick to the tomb of the earl at Birsay it is said that men 'fared from Shetland and the Orkneys' ... and the very first miracle cited happened to a Shetland farmer called Bergfinn Skatisson who ... appears to have played a central role in publicising the earl's sanctity. If we turn to the Miracle Book (ON Jartegnabók) it is remarkable that of the dozen or so stories recounted ... all bar two were of healings to men and women 'from north in Shetland'. (Barbara E. Crawford, 'The Cult of St. Magnus in Shetland'. Essays in Shetland History, Lerwick 1984)

According to Dr Crawford there was at one time an important Magnus Church somewhere in north-western Mainland, and there are also several place-names connected with his name in that area. Against this background the fact that most of the miracle healings were taking place 'north in Shetland' seems significant, but so far the reason for this close association of the saint with one particular part of Shetland remains a mystery.

Some 20 years after the death of Magnus Erlendsson his nephew, the young Rognvald Kali Kolsson from Agder in southern Norway, decided to claim his part of the earldom from Earl Paul Hakonsson. He landed in Yell, where he was very well received indeed and 'went to feasts all over the land'. Earl Paul, on the other hand, did not want to go ashore in Shetland, as 'he did not trust the Shetlanders'. When Rognvald failed in his first attempt to win over Earl Paul, his wise old father Koll comforted him by saying that after all his mission had been worthwhile and much had been done if the Shetlanders were his friends!

The Orkneyinga saga describes an event that took place in Sumburgh Voe, at a time when Rognvald had become earl and was staying in the islands on his way back to Orkney, after a visit to Bergen. A poor old crofter was waiting for his mate to go out fishing, when a man in a white, hooded cloak came up to him and offered to do the rowing. They drifted right into the tide-race, and the crofter cried as he was sure they would drown. The stranger said: 'Be of good cheer, crofter, and do not weep, for he will draw both of us out of the tide-race who let us come into it.' And then he rowed right out again. The hooded man gave away his own share of the fish, but as he was walking away, he slipped and fell, and a woman who saw him laughed a lot at him. Ironically, the man said

> The Sif of Silk mocks my attire;
> but laughs at me more than she should.
> Few know an earl in fishing clothes . . .

This last line later turned into a proverbial saying. On the face of it the saga writer here evidently tries to illustrate the two sides to Rognvald's character—his kindness and his sense of fun, but there are clever undertones to this story with echoes both from Norse mythology and Christian belief.

Leading families in the Northern Isles rose against the Norse King Sverre Sigurdsson in support of another claimant to royal power. The *Eyjaskeggjar*, or island beardies, as they came to be called, seized and held large parts of southern Norway and spent the winter of 1194 in Bergen. They were taken by surprise and defeated by King Sverre in a bloody naval battle at Florevåg near Bergen in April of the same year. In the reprisals that followed in 1195, Sverre took Shetland away from the earldom and made it subject to direct rule from Norway. From then on Shetland was governed by royal officials as a 'skattland' which sent skatt, that is tax, and dues to the royal treasury at Bergen. All odallers paid skatt, but the crown also had income from the forfeited earldom estates.

Thus Shetland no longer looked south to Orkney, but came to look north to Faroe, as these two island groups for some time seem to have had more or less a joint administration. When the Apostles' Church in Bergen was completed in 1302, it had been built largely with rents from Shetland and Faroe. There are records of marriages between Shetlanders and Faroese, and of families owning land in both island groups.

Medieval Norway reached its flowering in the thirteenth century under strong and far-seeing kings, but in the fourteenth century the once so powerful Norwegian state sank into a decline. Many reasons for this have been suggested—such as the stranglehold of the Hanseatic League on all trade and the disastrous effect of the Black Death. The most probable underlying cause of all the difficulties, however, was the fact that natural resources were simply too meagre to sustain such a complex state in the long run. Thus apart from Orkney the whole Norse area was dependent on the import of grain. Then the old royal line died out, and in 1397 Norway ceased to exist as a separate kingdom when its crown was united with that of Denmark under Queen Margrete.

The political situation in Norway had a direct influence on conditions in Shetland. There are records of Scots invading Shetland both in 1312 and 1369, seizing the rents and arresting the royal stewards. The situation was not made easier by a strong power struggle within the Northern Isles. In 1379 three cousins laid claim to the earldom of Orkney before King Hakon Magnusson, who chose Henry Sinclair. One of the other claimants was Malise Sperra, who was named for his maternal grandfather, the Earl of Strathearn, Caithness and Orkney. It seems possible that he was later given some official status in Shetland by the King. *The Icelandic Annals* record that Malise Sperra was 'slain in Shetland with seven others by the Earl of Orkney'. This probably happened in 1391, and there is still a stone standing on the road from Tingwall to Scalloway to mark the place where he is supposed to have been murdered. A garbled contemporary account in an Italian letter maintains that around 1390 Earl Henry Sinclair won a victory over the King of Norway in Shetland.

It has been generally assumed that when Henry Sinclair was made earl of Orkney in 1379, Shetland would have been restored to the earldom at the same time. However, according to recent research by Dr Crawford it is probable that Shetland remained officially a separate entity. But the death of Malise Sperra opened the way to the financial dominance of the Sinclair family and the beginning of Scottish influence. Added to that the vain and severely debt-ridden King

Christian I ruled the kingdoms of Denmark, Norway and Sweden, which were still only loosely united. He was troubled by political risings against him and he also fell out with the Pope because he tried to have a notorious swindler appointed Archbishop of Trondheim. He seems to have been incapable of coping with anything but the affairs of the moment, and the mortgaging of land was a weak man's easy way out—and one which he had tried before.

Shetland was pledged to Scotland on 28 May 1469 for 8000 florins, as King Christian was unable to make up the sum to provide a dowry for his daughter in any other way. The Shetland document is almost identical to the contract which pledged Orkney for 50,000 florins the year before. The king pawned his royal estates in Shetland as well as the right to skatt from the odallers. From King Christian the Shetlanders received a letter admonishing them to be dutiful and obedient and pay their skatt to the kings of Scotland until the time might come when the islands could be redeemed.

5 IN SCOTLAND

Territorial claims

The time between 1469 and 1707 has sometimes been called the Scotto-Norse period of Shetland history. For some time to come the islands were in a position of seemingly belonging to two countries, with no clearly defined status. The Scots were determined not to let the pledge be redeemed, and in 1471 The Lordship of Shetland was annexed to Scotland, along with the Earldom of Orkney. It was stipulated at the same time that the islands could only be given away to a legitimate son of the king, but this was always ignored. Later kings of Denmark-Norway evidently considered the islands their legal territory still, as they made repeated attempts to pay the debt and get them back. To a great extent they were pressed to do so by their Norwegian subjects, who saw their interests in Shetland set aside. In their final attempts, during the conflict in 1640 between King Charles I and the Scots as well as in the peace negotiations at Breda in 1667, the Scandinavians were fairly close to succeeding.

Scotland largely followed the policy of feigned ignorance whenever they were faced with the demands of the more or less ineffectual Dano-Norwegian kings. That this was quite deliberate on the Scots' part can be seen from the register of the Privy Council of Scotland, the body which governed Scotland until the Union of Parliaments in 1707. This contains information on the various attempts made to raise with Scotland the question of redeeming Orkney and Shetland. Thus when in 1564 a trade delegation was going to negotiate an agreement with Denmark, they were instructed that if anybody should mention Orkney and Shetland, they must disclaim all knowledge of this question and 'gif na ansuer thairto'.

Trade links with Holland and Norway

For about a century the changeover to Scotland left little mark in Shetland. Communications with the Scottish mainland were poor, and in relation to the Scottish centres of government and trade Shetland remained remote and a land apart. The connection with Bergen remained close, but economically the ties with Germany and later with Holland were more important. The economy became tied to the Hanseatic League from the beginning of the fifteenth century. Direct trading within Norwegian crown lands was originally prohibited—it had to be carried on through the 'kontor' in Bergen—but as political power in Norway waned this prohibition was openly flouted. The Hansa merchants started making direct contact with people in Shetland, and this trade grew steadily throughout the next two centuries to the extent where the Germans virtually monopolized the export trade of the islands. There were merchants coming from most of the Hansa towns: Danzig, Bremen, Hamburg, Lübeck and Rostock. Ships usually left for Shetland in the early spring and returned at the end of August or early in September. The merchants would offer beer, salt and meal, as well as textiles, and in return they would buy among other things butter, fat, wool and feathers, but first and last they were interested in buying fish. Such great customers were they that demand for fish at times outran supply.

For a long time Shetlanders continued to look to Bergen as their natural centre of administration, commerce, and law. Probably the pledging to Scotland was considered a temporary arrangement—if thought about at all. Quite a few Shetlanders settled in Bergen to carry on their trade or craft. In order to be able to do so they would have to sign their names in *Bergens Borgerbog*, which is a list kept from 1550 onwards. It contains the names of many Shetlanders. Thus we find a 'Jacob Hjelt i borgermester gaard'—Jacob the Shetlander in the mayor's house—listed as moving to Bergen in 1593, and 'Christiern Joensenn, Hjelt' some years previously. So successful were these incomers that they proved a serious competition to the Hanseatic merchants. Therefore at one time furious merchants assaulted Orcadians, Shetlanders and mainland Scots carrying on trade in Bergen, and robbed them into the bargain. Twelve of the victims made formal complaints.

It is possible to see from the records just how important their competing trade was, and that the Shetlanders soon became involved in many different activities. They were often innovators in an area that too long had been dominated by the Hanseatic merchants, and they were a welcome element in many Norwegian coastal communities. Thus the potato is said to have been introduced on the Norwegian west coast some time before it reached Denmark from Germany, as it was brought there by way of the Northern Isles. In 1602 the only shipyard in Bergen belonged to Gjert Evertsen, who came from somewhere in the Northern Isles—people in Bergen did not always distinguish between Orkney and Shetland.

Many landowners held land both in Shetland and Norway to such an extent that it would be hard to say where they really belonged. Such a man was Lauritz Johannessøn Galt of Torsnes in Hardanger. His son Lauritz Galtung became an admiral and was later raised to the peerage. Another admiral with Shetland connections was Axel

Mowat of Hovland. His family died out in the male line when his only son was killed in a duel with Lauritz Galtung. Thus the Dano-Norwegian navy of the late Middle Ages got some of its most outstanding officers from the Hordaland district around Bergen, and many of them belonged to families that were equally at home in Norway and Shetland. This natural connection still exists to some extent in the coastal communities. Thus when the representatives of the small community of Øygarden took an independent stand on the Hordaland County Council, other members taunted them that they evidently would be happier as part of Shetland!

The Norwegian families owning land in Shetland were known locally as 'the lairds of Norroway'. Throughout the sixteenth century land transactions in Shetland seem still to have been dealt with in Bergen where the old laws were best understood. But in Shetland herself everything changed from the 1560s onwards.

Realization of Scottish power

There were Scots in Shetland before 1469, but they were few. The archdeaconry had long been held by Scots. They were appointed by the bishops of Orkney who themselves were Scots from the second half of the fourteenth century. This is not strange considering that in Norway the Black Death did not leave enough priests even for the cathedral of Trondheim. There was also rarely a minister of Shetland origin. Thus at first the church was the main cause of Scottish immigration. Some of the ministers came to pray and remained to prey, as one historian puts it. The powerful Giffords of Busta as well as the Cheynes of Vaila descended from incoming Scottish ministers who acquired a taste for land.

The Scots kept on coming during the sixteenth century; on the whole this is the period when they have the greatest impact on Shetland society. This is also reflected in the Shetland dialect—much of the Lowland Scots found in Shetlandic seems to be the language of the sixteenth century. Most of the incoming Scots were looking for land, and at the time there were few possibilities of finding that elsewhere. After the New World in the west was opened up Shetland was no longer so attractive, and immigration dried up. The Sinclair family had come before 1469 and had consolidated their position and become very powerful. Members of this family held the office of foud or chief magistrate for almost a century. Thus by 1600 Sinclair had become the most commonly used surname. Of course, the original Shetland families used patronymics and not surnames, and thus it is possible to tell that at the time roughly one-third of the population were Scots. Some of them came as traders, and there was a steady influx of specialists like lawyers and craftsmen. There were also those who came looking for adventure.

In 1560 the Reformation was carried out by the Orkney Bishop Adam Bothwell, assisted by Jeremy Cheyne who was archdeacon in Shetland. Perhaps the Reformed Church suited the Shetland psyche well, for the reform was entirely effective and Roman Catholicism disappeared. It was a peaceful and gradual change. Some practices, like the sign of the cross, survived for a long time, and Christmas Day has remained important. Shetland was never much affected by the Presbyterian–Episcopalian conflict which especially in Covenanting times tore mainland Scotland to pieces. On the whole there is no record in Shetland of religious intolerance or enthusiasm.

Mary, Queen of Scots, in 1564 granted Orkney and Shetland to her half-brother Lord Robert Stewart in perpetual feu. In 1568 she conferred the islands on her third husband James Hepburn, Earl of Bothwell, who was given the title Duke of Orkney. Bothwell fell out with and fled from the Scottish lords to his remote Duchy, hoping to find a refuge there. He was pursued by Kirkcaldy of Grange on the *Unicorn*, but through the skill of his pilot, Bothwell escaped while his adversary was made to look like a fool when his ship ended up on a rock outside the north mouth of Bressay Sound.

Lord Robert's position became strengthened. In 1568 he forced Bishop Bothwell to resign the Bishopric, in exchange for the Abbey of Holyrood, of which he was commendator. A 'commissioner' was appointed to take care of the spiritual aspect of the Bishop's duties. Thus from this time Lord Robert held the reins completely, as he had the right to all crown, earldom and church property in the two island groups, and could claim revenue from every man and woman there. He also became the chief magistrate and thus had extensive jurisdiction. Lord Robert wielded greater power in the islands than anyone had ever done before him.

In 1571 Lord Robert delegated his office as foud or chief magistrate of Shetland to his half-brother Laurence Bruce of Cultmalindie. The latter seems within a remarkably short time to have run foul of everybody. He was accused of every thinkable and unthinkable crime and seems to have abused his power in every way, such as tampering with weights and measures and filling up the courts with his own followers in order to obtain favourable verdicts. Thus any trumped-up charge would lead to the confiscation of land. Considerable evidence was collected and numerous complaints were drawn up against him. The uproar was great enough to bring two royal commissioners north to investigate. In the course of three weeks in February of 1577 they heard and recorded the opinions of some 760 persons from all over the islands. They met at Tingwall. Feeling was running high, and the Shetlanders expressed their indignation fearlessly. But this was the end of an old song, and not for another three hundred years would they speak up so articulately for their rights again. The complaints against

Bruce also give a detailed picture of Shetland life at the time.

Bruce went to jail for a while but soon returned to live off the fat of the land he had acquired. Some of his land was in Unst and there he built his stronghold, a very fine castle, at Muness. In an inscription above the door he admonishes his heirs to look after the building:

> Listen you to know this building who began
> Laurence the Bruce he was that worthy man
> Who earnestly his heirs and offspring prays
> To help and not to hurt this work always.

The building itself seems to have been wrecked rather early, but the Bruce estate prospered. In a charter from 1638 Andrew Bruce of Muness, the son of Laurence Bruce, turned over an estate of 1569 merks of land to his son. This estate represented about one-eighth of all land in Shetland and was the largest known grant of land ever made there. As landowners the Bruce family remained very powerful for a long time.

In 1581 King James VI made Lord Robert Earl of Orkney. This title had been annexed to the Scottish crown since 1471. Ten years later Earl Patrick Stewart succeeded his father. By 1592 he had built the house at Sumburgh that was named Jarlshof by Sir Walter Scott. Later he built his castle at Scalloway where the central court would meet after it was moved from Tingwall. This was still called the Lawting, and the old Law Book was used. The Scottish parliament had on more than one occasion acknowledged that the legal system of the Northern Isles was different, and Earl Patrick ruled accordingly within the framework of Norse law, but was quick to impose fines which most of the time would have to be paid in land.

Still the lot of the common man seems to have eased somewhat during Earl Patrick's days in power. He was out to catch bigger fry: the landowning families who had followed his father north and were busy extending their holdings and entrenching their positions of influence. To some extent he even seems to have protected the original inhabitants against them. He may have seen himself as the ruler of a semi-independent principality, or simply in the old role of an Orkney earl, as it was once played. This time the complaints to Edinburgh came from the Scottish landowners, Laurence Bruce of Muness among them.

Earl Patrick was imprisoned in 1609 and stood trial the year after. He denied few of the charges made against him. In 1615 he was executed in Edinburgh. King James VI of Scotland and I of England was eager to extend his authority; thus in 1611 he dissolved Parliament and ruled without it till 1621. He would therefore have feared a strong earldom. The Scottish Privy Council abolished the 'foreign laws' in 1611 and the old Law Book mysteriously disappeared. Norse law was replaced by country acts with elaborate rules for among other things

Earl Patrick Stewart's castle at Scalloway.

the maintaining of dykes, in the interest of 'good neighbourhood'. The dreaded office of ranselman was introduced, with wide powers to search houses and question people. In each parish there were ten or twelve such ranselmen, who reported to the bailiff. Thus the death of Earl Patrick, weak and vain though he might be, marked the end of an era. It was the last phase of independent political history in Shetland.

When Earl Patrick was removed from the scene power was effectively handed over to the Scottish landowners, and from then the fight was on among them to acquire bigger estates. According to Shetland tradition unscrupulous methods were often used to wrest the land from the original owners. In 1620 the Privy Council sent a commission to Shetland to investigate charges of 'multifarious oppressions and mal-practices' and they found that law and order were held in some contempt. Thus during the seventeenth century there seems to have been an element of social alienation between the majority of the population and those in authority. The old social order was breaking down without a new equilibrium replacing it. In 1694 The Baillie Court Book for Dunrossness shows as many as 20 cases of assault taking place in a community of 90 families.

In 1612 Orkney and Shetland had again been annexed to the crown, and crown lands were set to a series of tacksmen. In 1633 they were given as a life-rent tack to the Earl of Morton. For some time the Morton family were in or out of favour confusingly often, but in 1742 the islands were granted outright to the Earl of Morton who sold them in 1766 to Sir Lawrence Dundas, the ancestor of the Earl of Zetland, for 60,000 guineas.

Towards the close of the seventeenth century there were three powerful landed families besides Bruce of Muness with estates over 500 merks of land; the Mowats of Ollaberry held some 800 merks, mostly in Mainland, the Cheynes of Vaila owned 600 merks in the West Mainland, and the Sinclairs of Quendale held some 500 merks in the Dunrossness area. There were still odallers, or small freeholders, but their position was precarious. Their land was scattered and difficult to farm. This was true of the large holdings as well: the Bruce estate held only 765 merks at Muness; the rest consisted of pieces of land scattered all over Unst, Yell, Fetlar, Bressay and in six mainland parishes.

The end of the Scottish period saw 'the lairds of Norroway' ousted by Scots, and the only remaining economic link with Norway was the trade in boats from Sunnhordland. In the summertime the fishermen of the large Dutch herring fleets would buy fresh provisions from the local people, and Lerwick grew up largely on account of this trade. Added to that was the Hanseatic connection. Shetland might have left the Norse community of old, but she was still an important crossroads in a cosmopolitan world.

6 IN BRITAIN

Decline of trade

The beginning of the eighteenth century brought many national changes that seriously affected Shetland. Through the Union of Parliaments in 1707 Scotland became formally united with England, and the balance of power began to shift in earnest. Shetland became subject to a control more remote than before. In 1712 a high duty was placed on all imported salt, and this was one of the reasons that prevented the Hanseatic merchants from continuing their trade on Shetland.

By 1700 most Shetlanders making a living from the land had become tenants of Scottish landowners. Few of them farmed land that was valued at more than 5–10 merks. The Hanseatic merchants had for two centuries brought a modest prosperity to Shetland; by selling fish to the merchants the tenants could pay their rent in cash to the landowners and in good years even have something left over to buy more than the bare necessities. Many of the landowners also got extra income from leasing the sites where the merchants set up their bøds, or booths. The decline of the German trade therefore threw Shetland into economic crisis.

The changes brought about by the economic crisis were to exert a very strong influence on life in Shetland for more than a century and a half. Many of the prominent landowning families, such as the Bruces of Muness, the Cheynes of Vaila and the Sinclairs of Brough, went bankrupt. Their estates were bought up by the only people with capital, a group of Shetland merchants. The most powerful of them was Thomas Gifford of Busta. These merchant-lairds took up the fishing trade when the Hanseatic merchants left. When they wanted men to work the fishing boats they naturally looked to their own tenants. Crofts were divided again and again to provide more men for the boats. Getting a croft to work depended on willingness to fish for the laird, but with the size of the croft there was no real choice in any case. Early marriages were encouraged. From the middle of the eighteenth century the system of fishing tenures bound the crofter-fisherman and the laird to each other in mutual dependence.

The worst aspect of this system was that it made the tenants economic vassals, deprived of any independence or opportunity for initiative or means of registering complaints. The landlords' will became the tenants' law. It placed the tenants absolutely in the hands of the landmaster who could ... vary from the bullying tyrant to the genial master. As time consolidated the system, it is not to be wondered that the crofter-fishermen became submissive, even servile, accepting their lot as something pre-ordained. (John J. Graham, *Shetland and the Outside World 1469–1969*, p220)

Religion

Cultural and social conditions were changing too. The old Norn speech was no longer the recognized language of law and administration and thus had no status. 'Its passing diminished the cultural identity of the Shetland people, and as the eighteenth century opens we find them exposed and vulnerable' says John J. Graham. So few people were able to read and write that it was often difficult to find enough literate elders to form church sessions.

In 1700 Rev. John Brand travelled in the islands for a commission of the General Assembly of the presbyterian Church of Scotland. He saw much to criticize; he thought the people on the whole were ignorant of Christianity. The Church was poor both spiritually and materially, with slack ministers in derelict churches and manses. They had not yet stamped out all traces of Catholicism. Thus a woman in Nesting had born three malformed children though 'they knew nothing of Scandal they could lay to her Charge, but that she had lived soberly all her life'. However, it came out that she used to go barefoot every Sunday to the ruins of Our Lady's Kirk at Weisdale to pray for the health of her future children. The Rev. Brand seems quite shaken by such behaviour: 'If this be true, God hath Judicially Punished her'.

During the eighteenth century law and social order seem to have been restored, and to a great extent this came about through the efforts of the Presbyterian Church, which became really effective. Shetland had some strongly individualistic ministers who ruled their parishes with a firm hand. The elders of the church session also wielded considerable power, but according to John J. Graham they had many social responsibilities too:

They looked after the church finance and fabric, they were community bankers offering loans to those in need, they administered poor relief, looked after lepers and other unfortunates, provided some help for motherless children, fostered orphans, supervised local schools, ran small libraries, and were in general the only organised body operating within the parish.

The old Scottish Presbyterianism, as to some extent also Methodism, was based on Calvinist doctrine and organization. It was a cold, strict and hard religion with no warmth, as can be seen from Shetland churches. Bleak, bare and brownish they do not appeal on an aesthetic level, but serve effectively as reminders of the seriousness of life. Their

Uyeasound Church, Unst. Somehow these cheerless churches do not tally with the warm and outgoing character of the Shetland people.

interiors are no more inviting. People do not seem to take pride in their local church the way Scandinavians usually do. Somehow these cheerless churches do not tally with the warm and outgoing character of the Shetland people, although the style of the church may have been inspired by a reaction to Catholicism.

Population growth and progress

In 1755 there were 15,210 people living in Shetland. During the next century the population grew steadily, so that by 1851 it had more than doubled. There were many reasons for this growth. People no longer died from small-pox, as this disease was effectively stopped by inoculation. Earlier epidemics seemed to recur with a frightening regularity of some 20 years, and most of them took a very heavy toll. The population of Foula was almost wiped out at one time.

An important factor in the island economy was also the increased cultivation of the potato, which rapidly became a staple food, along with fish. Still in the years between 1780 and 1850 there was famine once every four years on average, as this was a period when survival depended completely on the success of each year's harvest and fishing.

Any expansion in Shetland was checked at the end of the eighteenth century by the coming of the Napoleonic Wars. For the first time Shetlanders had to pay a heavy price for becoming British. Every able-bodied male in sight was captured by the press-gang and forced to join the Royal Navy. Out of a total male population of 9945 in 1801, as many as 3000 served in the war.

Even in 1806 Dutch and Danish coins were more common in Lerwick than British money. But access to many markets was closed, and it became difficult to sell fish. The severe weather of the period caused bad harvests, so that for many reasons the years of the Napoleonic Wars were bitter times indeed for Shetland. The survivors of the war, however, came back as seasoned men who did not fit into the old simplistic social structure of tenant and laird. Whaling ships from Peterhead, Dundee and Hull called regularly in Shetland to take on local men. The lairds tried to stop them from going, but without success. A new class of small, independent merchants grew up, and these meant competition for the shops run by the lairds. Yet people had grown used to having a long-term credit with the lairds, which worked as a kind of social security system. Ministers would grumble that this mutual dependence, known as the Truck system, between laird and fisherman-crofter caused improvidence and lack of initiative.

The effects of over-population were becoming noticeable from the 1830s. There were also a number of setbacks in the fishing. The so-called Potato Famine of 1846–7, owing to a crop failure from blight, therefore hit Shetland seriously, and helped make the 1840s one of the most difficult decades in her history. A side effect of the Potato Famine was the building of metalled roads all over Shetland, which thus got a proper road system by way of relief works, as the pay was one pound of meal a day. Therefore these roads have come to be called Meal Roads. Most of the work was done by the women while the men were away at the fishing, and the roads were well-built. But they very often seemed to lead nowhere, and local people said such roads only served to wear out their rivlins—the soft leather shoes usually worn at the time—so they preferred the heather.

In 1835 the only road in Shetland was a five-mile stretch in Lerwick. When the Meal Roads were finished in 1852 there were 176 miles of road. Other communications improved as well. The penny post was greatly welcomed and started an avalanche of letters and newspapers through the mail. In 1858 the first regular all-the-year-round steamer service began, and it became easier to ship cattle and ponies out of the islands for sale in the South.

A maximum population was reached in the middle of the nineteenth century. It remained fairly stable until the 1870s when it began to drop markedly. In the two decades between 1861 and 1881 more than 8000 people emigrated. This meant the loss of one quarter of the people.

In 1872 a Government commissioner called William Guthrie came to Shetland to investigate the working of the Truck system for a report to Parliament. He asked some 17,000 questions, but the tenants answered cautiously. Guthrie found that 90 per cent of the total acreage was owned by 32 people, and that most Shetlanders were the tenants of these landowners. If they did not fish for the landlord or for a merchant of his choosing they might have to leave their holdings. Guthrie wrote in his report that 'It has been so much a habit of the Shetlander's life to fish for his landlord, that he is only now discovering that there is anything strange or anomalous in it.'

The Crofters' Act of 1886 gave the crofter-fishermen security of tenure and made it possible to escape from debt-bondage. Yet it did not solve the problem of Shetland's economic structure, with too many people living off meagre resources. An arable acreage of some 50,000 acres just could not support a population of rather more than 30,000, and emigration went on unchecked. It was the rise of the herring fishing in the 1880s that reduced the decline in the next two decades. Thus in 1884 as many as 337 first-class decked herring-boats were Shetland owned. Some 300,000 barrels of herring were cured in Shetland then, and this gave work to more than 7000 islanders. There was also much profit ending up in the pockets of Lerwick curers and merchants.

Shetland was quietly going through an economic and social revolution and casting off the oppression of the past. Culturally there were changes too. Education became compulsory for children between 7 and 14, and the school-year was extended to 40 weeks. Many came to look down on all the old ways as backward, thus endangering the whole native culture. This was seen clearly by Laurence Williamson, the Yell crofter and scholar, who wrote in 1892:

This is a transition time as never was before. The old Northern civilisation is now in full strife with the new and Southern one, and traditions, customs, which have come down from hoary antiquity, are now dying for ever. The young don't care for their fathers' ways. I mean what was estimable in them. The folklore and family traditions and picturesque stories yield fast to the *People's Journal, Glasgow Mail, Ally Sloper's Half Holiday* and such like.

After 1911 the herring fishing suffered a series of setbacks from which it never really recovered. The number of men taking part in this fishery decreased rapidly, but the coming of the First World War drew attention away from a failing herring industry. Shetland's strategic importance to Britain became obvious. The Tenth Cruiser Squadron was stationed at Swarbacks Minn. It consisted mainly of former Atlantic liners that were fast enough to run from submarines and overtake other German ships that had to be kept away from the Atlantic. Lerwick became a coaling base for this operation. These activities led to a temporary boom during the war. But Shetland paid a heavy price for her war effort: 600 men were lost, largely at sea. In the United Kingdom on the whole the casualty rate was 1 out of 45, Shetland lost 1 out of 32 men.

In the two decades between the wars communications with the rest of Britain were improved. In the 1920s the 'North Company', or more correctly the North of Scotland and Orkney and Shetland Steam Navigation Company Ltd, had half a dozen ships. Their flagship was the *St Magnus*. All their ships sailed the route Leith–Aberdeen–Kirkwall–Lerwick. Still the economy stagnated, and Shetland became known as a Distressed Area. The herring fishing had been relied on too much as a keystone of the economy. Amenities like mains services for electricity and water that were taken for granted everywhere else in Britain, were lacking. But the decrease in the population slackened, perhaps because there were fewer chances of emigration.

The 1939–45 war repeated the history of the First World War. Of a male population of some 9500 about 4000 served, mainly in the Royal Navy or the merchant fleet. Air warfare was a new factor of the Second World War, and Shetland had her first enemy attack on 13 November 1939. Three 'action stations' of the R.A.F. were established, at Sumburgh, Scatsta and Sullom Voe. After Norway fell in the spring months of 1940 it was believed that Shetland would be invaded next. Somehow the belief has persisted in Shetland that the Germans had promised Quisling, in return for his support, to win Orkney and Shetland back for Norway. According to a private communication from Dr Magne Skodvin, who has studied the German occupation of Norway during the last war, this idea has no foundation in fact.

During the war the islands became a refuge and a base for Norwegians fleeing from home, and old bonds of kinship were rediscovered. On the whole troops outnumbered civilians and many adjustments had to be made. During the war years Shetland was thrust into the twentieth century; later modern oil development has seen to it that she has stayed there.

7 THE SHETLAND BUS

'No one can realize our feelings when we saw the Shetland islands low on the horizon, islands which were not only the land of freedom but of kinsmen.'
Captain Årstad of Royal Norwegian Navy.

'They were haemly folk, the Shetlanders!'
Ingvald Eidsheim, Captain of the *Hitra*.

For Norwegians who lived through the Second World War the name of Shetland is etched in memory. It became a symbol of freedom and hope at a time of humiliation and defeat. For those who grew up after the war the story of the Shetland Bus already has the remote heroism of a saga, but for those who were in the thick of things at the time it was real enough, even if the sense of adventure also played an important part.

The Norwegian escape

Germany invaded Norway in a surprise attack in the early hours of 9 April 1940. After having lived at peace for more than a hundred years the Norwegians were at first mentally unprepared for a war where they had to fight tanks with hunting rifles. But even before Norway officially capitulated to the Germans on 7 June, the first boats had left the western coast between Molde and Haugesund, to head west over sea. On board were people who wanted to carry on the fight outside the country; some were British citizens escaping from what was now enemy territory. The route to Shetland was the shortest; it was also a route already well-known to many fishing boat crews. The towns of Bergen and Ålesund were to become the main lines of connection.

In Ålesund the young lawyer Harald Torsvik and his friends early began to help people escape to the west. Gradually several such export groups, as they were called, were formed. They worked independently of each other. 'To take the Shetland Bus' became an idiomatic expression for escape. In Shetland this will have a double meaning, as the Dutch fishing boats that used to come for the herring were known as 'busses'—from the Norse word *búza*, a big wide ship. To take the Shetland Bus was the way out for the resistance fighter when he felt his cover was about to be blown. It was also a voyage to adventure for the young man, but for many this was a voyage with no return.

Boats were bombed and shot at or sank in storms. Still the wish to go spread like a fever, especially among the young, and all kinds of boats, even kayaks, were used. How many tried and failed we will never know for sure. There is a story that even two little boys began to row across, but they grew tired, so after a while they went ashore to ask whether they still had far to go to get to Shetland!

All the escape stories differed, but some of them were no less than miraculous. Boats were overcrowded, blankets were used as sails, and the compass was either lacking or of little use, the way it was on board the *Traust* from Utvær in the Sognefjord. When the *Traust* was far out in the North Sea she was sighted by a British aeroplane; the skipper painted on a foresail in big letters: 'Shetland?' and the aeroplane showed them the way.

Not all the escape stories were success stories. The $8\frac{1}{2}$ m (28 ft) long *Kantonella* left Haugesund on 20 February 1941 with nine men on board. Storms raged in the North Sea, and they must have fought hard and long before they were wrecked off Mid Yell during a violent night one week later. They were buried in Mid Yell churchyard, and every 17 May, the Norwegian National Day, the Shetlanders put flags and flowers on their grave.

During the first year of the war as many as 40 boats left the Ålesund district with some 600 passengers on board. In some of the small coastal communities there were hardly any young boys left. The Gestapo called Ålesund 'Kleines London' and sent their best people to the town to unravel the operations and put a stop to them. The fishing boat *Mars* came from Shetland with the sole purpose of bringing Harald Torsvik to safety, but he refused to go. Torsvik's group was arrested in the spring of 1941. The Germans had then given up the hope of winning the Norwegians for their ideas, and during the autumn of 1941 their attitude hardened. When the Torsvik group stood trial at a German military court in Oslo the verdict was therefore given beforehand—five of them were sentenced to death. After the sentence had been passed an extraordinary incident occurred: the President of the Reichsgericht rose, crossed the floor to where Harald Torsvik was seated and saluted him. The clerk of the court was openly crying. The novelist Knut Hamsun sent a personal plea for mercy to Adolf Hitler; he had none to give. The sentence was carried out on 26 November 1941, and the location of their graves, today, is unknown. Many more death sentences followed.

From the highest authority in Berlin came the order that the traffic to and from Shetland must be stopped. The watch which was already kept on the coast was strengthened to make it more difficult to get out. When a young boy disappeared his father or other family members would be arrested in reprisal. As time went on there was also a shortage of seaworthy boats. But the Germans' best move was infiltration. When the *Viggo* was stopped before it sailed, there were two informers on board. Most of the passengers and crew were summarily shot. What the Germans called 'Feindbegünstigung', assisting the enemy, was punishable by death.

The full attention of the Gestapo was then centred on Bergen. Through the infiltration of agents and by sealing off the city they managed to roll up the illegal organization known as the Stein group. Some 200 people were arrested and submitted to severe torture. Among them was the young radio operator Ingebrigt Valderhaug, who had been back and forth to Shetland, and operated direct under S.O.E. (Special Operations Executive) in London. He was caught red-handed with a transmitter in his hide-out in an old ladies' home, and has become famous for saying that two hours with the Gestapo was like 20 years in a Norwegian jail. He was executed along with many others.

The German campaign to stop the North Sea traffic culminated in the assault on the fishing village of Tælavåg on the island of Sotra outside Bergen. In the spring of 1942 a Gestapo officer was shot and killed there by two men brought over from Shetland. They belonged to the Norwegian Independent Company No. 1, popularly known as the Linge company, which was specially trained in Scotland for missions to occupied Norway. This incident made the German Reichskommissar Joseph Terboven say about the Norwegians: 'If they will not love us, we shall at least teach them to fear us!' And he vented his fury on Tælavåg which was levelled with the ground. The male population was sent to concentration camp in Germany, where 31 of them died, while women and children were interned. After the war this was the first place in Norway to be rebuilt.

The export groups had all been torn to pieces and the reprisals were effective; operations quietly died away. The traffic *from* Norway was over. The story of the Shetland Bus is a tale of two countries. It began in Norway but it continued in Shetland, and the military traffic from there increased in scope until the end of the war.

The British link and Lunna
As time went by Lerwick filled up with fishing boats that were in more or less of a seaworthy state. There was a need for vessels to keep open the communication lines between Britain and occupied Norway, in order to land all kinds of equipment as well as fetch and bring agents and saboteurs. In seaworthiness the Norwegian fishing boats were second to none, even if they were slow, and they had the great advantage of being able to move about in coastal waters without being suspicious. The greatest danger lay in their being discovered outside the legal fishing limit. The boats therefore came and went at night, protected by darkness.

The special unit that was formed for the link had a quite unique status. To begin with it was wholly under British command, organized by Major L. H. Mitchell, who was an army officer. He was later joined by Captain A. W. Rogers, a Royal Marine. The now so famous writer David Howarth, who was then a sub-lieutenant in the Royal Navy, became responsible for maintenance and the day-to-day operations at the base that was established at Lunna in East Mainland. This base was to take over the running of the fishing boats to the Norwegian coast. In his bestseller *The Shetland Bus* Howarth gives a fascinating picture of how they try to find their way in this indirect form of warfare. They had no experience to build on, and they often felt like boys playing at war.

It was an added difficulty that although the officers were British, the men who had to do the job behind enemy lines were Norwegians, with little or no military training, but used to relying on their own judgement and making their own decisions. It was difficult for the officers to accept that they could not join the missions because their very presence would have endangered them all. Nor could they give an order and expect to have it followed, as they had no power behind their commands. If the Norwegians did not want to follow order, they could just get up and leave, as they were civilians. All orders therefore to be explained and justified. This took time, and required a mental adjustment from the officers.

The base of Lunna was ideal for the purpose. As headquarters the men used Lunna House, an old manor dating from *c.* 1660. The whole

The first headquarters of the 'Shetland Bus', Lunna House, an old manor from c. *1660, now a hotel.*

parish of Lunnasting at one time belonged to the Hunter family. The men from there were famous for their prowess at the haf fishing, and 'never spaek o' da Lunnasting men' became a familiar saying. Lunna House had room for 35 men, and the Norwegians used to joke that the King of Shetland must have lived there. It seemed to them a romantic place, straight out of one of Sir Walter Scott's historical novels. Yet its best point as a base was its location: on a narrow isthmus with good harbours both in the east and the west. Moreover, it was secluded, and to avoid attention was essential.

The first mission successfully operated from Lunna in August 1941, before dramatic events in the autumn; even in September came disappointment and setbacks when the *Vita* was captured by the Germans in the Trondheim area and all on board were arrested. In October the *Siglaos* was attacked by planes and the young Nils Nesse killed. When he was being buried in the little churchyard at Lunna, it was uncertain what had happened to the crew of the *Nordsjøen*, who had gone to lay mines somewhere on the northwestern coast of Norway. They had in fact run into hopeless weather, and their boat sank. After a hard return journey wandering their own country as outlaws, they stole a fishing boat, *Arthur*. At the Lunna base they had been given up for lost, when on the evening after Nesse's funeral there was the unmistakable throb of a Norwegian engine, and the *Nordsjøen* crew was back.

The crews of the fishing boats had, in effect, two enemies: the Germans and the elements. In a particularly violent November storm the *Arthur* and the *Blia* were struggling to keep afloat. The *Arthur* had been to the Florø area to deliver arms and was on the way back to Shetland again when the motor failed. The crew drifted helplessly for five days, attacked by planes and losing one man to the sea when he was washed overboard by huge waves just north of Unst. Eventually, however, they made it. The *Blia* was also on her way back to Shetland, after having completed a mission on the island of Stord, with 36 escapees on board. Being only $16\frac{3}{4}$ m (55 ft) long, and heavily loaded, the *Blia* did not stand a chance in such weather. Years later a bottle was found in Hafrsfjord near Stavanger with a letter inside it. It was probably from a resistance man who was on the *Blia* when she sank, and it begins: 'We are sinking. Tell my wife and children farewell— help them.'

The Lunna base was a lonely place and life ashore often became monotonous for the crews. All communication with the outside world was difficult. As time went on it became evident that the base should be moved, as their actual isolation became a threat rather than an advantage once the Germans knew where they were and could wipe them out by sea or air at a stroke.

At the same time there was a bitter political strife at the highest level between the Norwegians and the British about control of the base. The Norwegian authorities in London felt that the crews were being sent on irresponsible missions like the mine-laying expedition of the *Nordsjøen* by officers who had no real knowledge of the conditions. By way of compromise all the men started wearing Norwegian naval uniforms to give them the protection of military status in case they were captured. But the crews themselves wanted to retain their independence so that they could freely decide whether to go on a mission or not.

Scalloway and Leif Larsen

During the summer of 1942 the base was therefore moved to Scalloway. This was on the wrong side of Shetland for going to Norway, and despite its sheltered, natural harbour, the waters off this part of the coast were difficult and dangerous. However, Lerwick was already taken up by naval units, and the co-operation with Jack Moore and his marine engineering firm, William Moore & Sons, weighed heavily in favour of Scalloway, as efficient maintenance had become essential. The Prince Olav Slipway was built at Moore's workshop to repair the boats of 'the Shetland gang', as they were called in Norway. It could take boats up to $33\frac{1}{2}$ m (110 ft) in length. The slipway was opened in the autumn of 1942 by King Olav, who was then the crown prince.

At the same time as the base was moved to Scalloway it came under Norwegian control and the crews were enlisted in the navy, with a commander in charge and a lieutenant as second in command. From then on the unit was officially termed the Norwegian Naval Special Unit (N.N.S.U.).

One of the most ambitious plans made at the Scalloway base was to sink the German battleship *Tirpitz* while she lay at anchor in the Trondheimsfjord. After the sinking of the *Bismarck* this was the only battleship left in the German navy. The plan was known as Operation Title. At the end of October 1942 the *Arthur* was fitted out with two torpedoes of a new type known as Chariot. According to plan two men in diving suits would sit astride each torpedo and steer them quite close to the side of the *Tirpitz*. There the warhead of the torpedo would be detached and secured to the target with magnets, the time fuse would be set, and the crews would be able to disappear as quietly as they had come.

At first everything went accordingly. The torpedoes were hidden on deck under a load of dry peat, which was nothing unusual on the west coast. When they were approaching the Trondheimsfjord the torpedoes were fastened underneath the boat, ready for use; as they went up the fjord, however, they ran into an unusually choppy sea that proved too much for the towing wires. Both torpedoes were lost. This was a hard blow after all the effort that had gone into the venture. The *Arthur*

Jack Moore, Scalloway. His marine engineering firm, William Moore & Sons, provided efficient maintenance and repairs for the boats of 'the Shetland gang'.

was scuttled in the mission and the crew had to make it across the border into Sweden. During their escape run Able Seaman Robert Evans was taken prisoner and later shot by the Germans. The killing of Evans was a serious charge against Admiral Dönitz at the war crime tribunal in Nürnberg.

Skipper of the *Arthur* was Leif Larsen, the legendary figure of the Shetland Bus. The sea was his life from his youth, but colour blindness prevented him from joining the navy. Instead he became skipper of a coastal steamer and got to know every voe and holm of the fjord

59

country. He came home from the Winter War in Finland in April 1940, just in time to join up when the battle of Norway began. Leif Larsen was said to carry both chart and compass in his head, and his qualities of leadership soon became evident in Shetland. He was the first skipper to be elected by the vote of the men and, in all, he made 52 trips to Norway.

Perhaps the most dramatic trip that Larsen made was his mission to Træna in Nordland in March of 1943. After the Soviet Union became involved in the war, North Norway had become more interesting to the Allies, and a resistance group based in Træna was established. The *Bergholm* with Larsen as skipper had delivered arms and equipment to the base and was on her way back to Shetland when she was attacked by two German planes. Six of the eight men crew on board were hit; the young Nils Vika died of his injuries while they were in the lifeboat trying to get to shore. After rowing for four days they reached the Ålesund area and some time later they were picked up by a motor torpedo boat sent over from Shetland to find them.

Even before the war was over Leif Larsen had become a legend and a symbol of the Shetland Bus. When he was appointed a sub-lieutenant in the Norwegian Navy he also became eligible for the Distinguished Service Order, the highest distinction given to a non-British officer. With his 11 distinctions he is the most highly decorated Allied naval officer of the Second World War, but he is the first to point out that he took part in a joint effort. A modest man, he has worn his distinctions only once—when he was pressed to do so for his luncheon with General Lord Montgomery of Alamein.

The operations, however, took their toll. In the winter of 1943 a number of the missions failed, and in all 24 members of the unit of some 60 men were lost. One mission to end in disaster was that of the *Brattholm*, a big whaler, which left Scalloway on 24 March with a crew of six and five passengers for Toftefjord on a small island north of Tromsø. The idea was to land the passengers there to serve as organizers and instructors for local resistance groups. But things went badly wrong and they were surprised by the Germans, who opened fire. Of the 11 men who had been on board the *Brattholm* only one made good his escape. Hunted by the enemy, Sergeant Jan Baalsrud somehow made it through snow, ice and extreme cold across the border into Sweden where he collapsed and lay unconscious for a week. His survival story was told in another of David Howarth's books, *We Die Alone*.

Many factors made it clear that the time of the fishing boats for missions to the Norwegian coast was over. There was such a shortage of fuel in Norway that few boats of any size were active along the coast, and the Shetland boats therefore became very conspicuous. The Germans had established a fine-meshed control net around the coast of what they called *Festung Norwegen*—Fortress Norway—and the boats were vulnerable.

Still it was obvious that the traffic should go on as the communications were essential. In the autumn of 1943 the unit therefore received from a naval base in Miami in Florida three small American submarine chasers. They were named *Hessa, Hitra*, and *Vigra*, and were under the command of Petter Salen, Ingvald Eidsheim and Leif Larsen. Each boat had a crew of 26 men; of these three were officers. They were fast and efficient and gave the crews more freedom of action than the Shetland Bus men were used to having. It was a great day when the submarine chasers arrived in Scalloway.

On 17 November 1943 the first subchaser left Scalloway on a mission to Norway, with the flag flying openly. During the last years of the war the boats carried out 114 such missions. Apart from one incident when a Canadian plane mistakenly opened fire against the *Hessa* when on the way back to Shetland, these trips were mostly uneventful and there were no casualties. And even if these missions could be dramatic they became a kind of routine patrol. Agents, arms and equipment were landed, refugees were taken on board and brought to Shetland. Ingvald Eidsheim on the *Hitra* held the speed record: 25 hours to the Norwegian coast and back.

Today it is natural to ask whether the rewards justified the human outlay? There is no simple answer to such a question, but an effective defence of the strongly-indented coastline of western Norway tied up many men and resources that the Germans sorely needed elsewhere. The combined operations launched from Shetland at Christmas of 1941 against Reine in the Lofoten Islands and the strongly fortified Måløy, took the Germans by complete surprise. Captain Linge was killed while trying to storm enemy headquarters in Måløy. He was the leader of the legendary Linge Company, which carried out so many behind-the-lines operations in Norway. These commando raids, as well as the constant pinpricks made by the Shetland Bus, had convinced Adolf Hitler that it was in Norway that the allied invasion would come: 'Norway is *das Schicksalgebiet* [the area of destiny] of this war.' Gradually the Festung Norwegen was built, until the whole western coast was full of gun sites. Constantly, new divisions and more coastal artillery were sent to Norway. When the Allies invaded Normandy in June 1944 as many as 340,000 Germans and a large part of the German Navy were stationed in Norway with little chance of getting out.

To Norwegians the psychological factor was of great importance: there was a life outside occupied Norway. Large quantities of arms and technical equipment were landed. When the Germans capitulated in May 1945 there were 60 illegal radio stations transmitting, and most of them had got their equipment from Shetland. In addition, when the Resistance marched forth out of hiding they were carrying guns brought across the North Sea.

In the winter of 1982 a Russian submarine was grounded just outside the Swedish naval base of Karlskrona, and the pictures of it made the front pages of the world press. A surprising consequence of this was that Norwegian journalists discovered the wreck of the submarine chaser *Hitra* half submerged on a beach close by the grounded submarine. Captain Eidsheim went to Sweden to identify his old ship, which by now was a miserable sight. The wreck was brought home again and funds collected both in Shetland and Norway made it possible to restore the boat almost back to the original. Spare parts and the original engine from the sister ship *Vigra* were found. The restoration work was lovingly carried out in a small shipyard in Leirvik on Stord, taking almost five years and costing nearly half a million pounds. The ship was launched on 8 May 1987. Escorted by four Norwegian motor torpedo boats, the *Hitra* later returned in style to her former base at Scalloway, and was given a warm welcome. The vessel is today a floating naval museum and a memorial to The Shetland Bus and the men who ran it.

8 PEOPLE

Life wis an auld sweet fiddle tune,
Fur da buitless boy wi feet brunt broon,
Bi sun an sea an siftin saand,
Ida gjeos an voes o da Simmer Laand.
Jack Renwick, *Da Simmer Laand*

Although this verse nostalgically describes those childhood summers when the sun seemed to shine all day, it also conveys some of the magic of a northern summer. There is an exhilarating feeling of space and freedom of movement. Shetland is irresistible on a hushed summer day. But life has to be lived at other times of the year too, and in the northern world where settlement in many places was marginal, it was often simply a question of survival. Material culture must adapt to the climate and to economic conditions. Any study of life as it was lived in Shetland until quite recently gives an impressive picture of man's ability to make use of his environment. Knowledge was evolved over a long period of time and handed down from father to son, from mother to daughter. The origins of traditions were lost in time so that customs and beliefs sometimes persisted long after the reasons for them were gone.

Turfing and harvest
Summer was often spoken of as the six months of never sit down as there was work to be done around the clock. Among other things the year's supply of peat had to be got ready, and this work took up much of the summer. The bluish kind of peat was most sought after as it would burn as fiercely as any coal. The banks were flayed and cut in April or May, as the weather permitted. It was very important that there was no frost after the peat was cut. It would still be quite sodden then, and if the moisture froze and expanded, it would make the peat crumble. The back-breaking task of flaying and cutting was men's work. Raising and turning the peat could be done by women or children while the men were away at the fishing. When the peat was dry enough the children might cart it home in a wheelbarrow. The women would also carry the peat home in a kishie on their backs, with their hands left free for the knitting.

Life wis an auld sweet fiddle tune,
Fur da buitless boy wi feet brunt broon,...

Without the peat life in Shetland would have been untenable through the centuries. It was an unwritten law that everybody could take peat for their own needs. Because fuel was abundant there was perhaps never the same grinding kind of poverty as met with in urban areas. A good fire could be had whenever it was needed; indeed it rarely went out in summer or winter. 'This is an old fire, it has never been out in my lifetime', said a crofter in Foula. When he died in the 1960s, his house was left empty. As the roofs in the old houses were mainly built with turf, they would soon fall apart if the fire went out.

The corn-cutting was done with scythes, and was another task for the men. The women and the children would gather the corn together in sheaves which later made up stooks. There was a long and patient process involved before the corn was turned into oatmeal or beremeal.

Without the peat, life in Shetland would have been untenable through the centuries.

In a growing season with favourable weather a good tattie (potato) harvest could be had, and this would make all the difference. With some meal, salt herring, dried salted whitefish and enough potatoes to see them through the year, a family would never go hungry.

Yet it took only one night of storm sometimes to destroy the harvest and a whole summer's work; fish was then looked to as an essential substitute. The men were working 'da haf' from May till about the middle of August, when of course all the fish caught went to the laird's factor. But whenever their other work permitted they would 'geng tae da Eela'. This was fishing for young saithe, which were known as sillocks in their first year and piltocks in their second. This fish was usually plentiful in a tideway or in the broken water of a tide-rip, and the best time to catch it was in the early evening, around sunset. August was the best month for piltock fishing, when every house would be festooned with fish hung up to dry.

Fishing

In the autumn and winter it was more common to fish from the craigs, where both women and men would work patiently till they had filled 'da bødi'—a large deep basket made of dried dock stalks. They would take the insides of limpets to chew and spit out as bait. However, in the 1930s an old man in Unst complained to the folklorist Einar Seim that the young people were becoming too grand to chew limpets. But in hard years the piltocks seem to have been all they had in the way of food:

65

—in September (1804), when in some of the meanest cottages, I enquired what they generally had for breakfast? they answered, 'Piltocks'. What for dinner? 'Piltocks and cabbage'. What for supper? 'Piltocks'! Some of them declared they had not tasted oat-meal or bread for five months. (Patrick Neill, *A Tour through Orkney and Shetland*, p92, Edinburgh 1806)

Most people had a boat or at least a share in one, as it was essential both for transport and for fishing. They were between $2\frac{1}{2}$–6 m (8–20 ft) in keel and pointed at both ends, and looked like the Norwegian yoals, which is not surprising as until fairly recently the keels and boards were often imported ready-shaped from Sunnhordland. This type of boat in fact seems to have survived longer in Dunrossness than anywhere else; the boats were taken good care of in the old days and would have long lives—50 years was not unusual. When not in use the boats would be drawn up on a beach, preferably a pebbly one, as the iron-shod keel would slide more easily then. Sometimes skids, known as 'linns' and made from the ribs of a caaing whale, were used to draw up the boat.

Houses

All over Shetland today there are abandoned townships where once there were thriving little communities. From a distance just a green patch of land can be seen and as you get closer the ruined houses become discernible. In some of these places the tenants were evicted, in others they left of their own accord. A township usually consisted of five or six crofts and would be known by names like the 'Toon o' Vollister' or the 'Toon o' Beosetter'. The lives of the people living there were interwoven with the land and the sea, their simple communal living depending on a combined effort.

When a new house was about to be built, stone for the walls was always easily found, but constructing the roof sometimes caused problems. In former times the wood for a roof and partition of a small house was often brought over from Norway ready-made, a house where this was used would be known as a *stock-stove*. In essence the style of building had changed little from the Norse longhouse over a thousand years. All houses were curiously alike, built, as they were, to the simplest pattern:

The cottages of the tenantry are low, covered with turf, and then scantily thatched with oatstraw. They are divided into two apartments; the outer and larger one is used for all common family purposes; the fire-place, without a chimney, is near to one end, and several beds or sleeping-places, each enclosed like a cupboard, are at the other. These dormitories serve as a partition from a small panelled room, where the heads of the family repose—it has a window and chimney, but no grate. (Eliza Edmondston, *Sketches and Tales of the Shetland Islands*)

There was a coziness to the Shetland home:

There are bulky sea-chests, with smaller ones on top of them; chairs, with generally an effort at an easy one; a wooden bench, a table, beds, spades, fishing-rods, baskets and a score of other little things, which help ... to make it a domus. The very teapot, in Zetland always to be found at the fireside, speaks of home and woman, and reminds one of the sobriety of the people ... (From the report of Dr Arthur Mitchell, a Poor Law commissioner)

Thriftiness was a necessary virtue, and things were not thrown away as one never knew when they might come in handy. This ingrained attitude to material things is probably the explanation for all the derelict cars so much criticized today by visitors, but many an old banger is used for practical purposes—such as a hen house!

Social customs

On the whole the division of labour between men and women followed very strict rules. For the women there was a kind of enforced equality: with the men and the young boys away at the fishing or whaling or in the Merchant Navy they very often had simply no choice but to do the men's work as well. And always there was their weary makkin, with the needles known as 'wires' and the knitting belt ever at the ready. They knitted and knitted—because they were used to it, but first and last because they had to for economic reasons. 'Lass tak dy sock' was the refrain of the young girl's life—she was expected to knit at least enough to get her own clothing in exchange from the shop. Much of the daily crofting work as well as household affairs were left to the care of the women. Families were large, and the lying-in period after childbirth was usually the only relaxing break a married woman ever had.

The croft and the sea had to provide the food they needed, and in the summertime they also had the luxuries provided by 'da koo idda byre' (the cow in the byre). When hot water was poured onto buttermilk, known as bleddik, it would coagulate into a kind of cottage cheese called kirn-milk. The liquid then remaining was known as blaand, a very refreshing drink with a slightly sharp or acid taste. It improved by keeping for a few days, and would along with bere bannocks make up the simple faerdiemaet (provisions) of the haf-fishermen. There were also oatmeal cakes known as burstin-brunnies. This name probably derives from burntstin (burnt stone), as the oats were dried with heated stones. Oatmeal was also used for porridge, a staple fare. If taken in true Shetland fashion, the porridge and the milk would be in separate bowls. Porridge was also made from sooins: home-ground meal was soaked in water until it fermented; the rather acid sediment from this was called sooins and used for porridge or pancakes. Fresh meat was rarely available, but the salted and dried

67

mutton known as reestit, boiled with potatoes, neeps and cabbage, was always a popular meal. Fish could of course be served in many ways. Kiossed heeds were fish heads or small fish which had been rolled in a cloth and left in an airy place to become gamy. Unfortunately, none of these old dishes are ever available in Shetland restaurants today!

After a busy summer of almost plenty, life quietened down over the winter. If the harvest was poor, then the winter had to be struggled through somehow. With a little more luck and a successful harvest it was possible for the crofters after working full-stretch all summer to hibernate for a while on their winnings! It would be the time for the old social custom of 'gyaain aboot da nicht' to visit each other. People would gather round the low-lintelled fireplace in the living-room during the long winter evenings. The darkness of the crowded room would be broken only by the light from the peat fire and the kolli lamp, but there would be music and games and stories. From sunset on Saturday until sunrise on Monday was *helie* and then only the most essential tasks would be performed.

There was no room for social distinction in the old township. Land use was based on strict equality. Sharing and complete co-operation were necessary. Anyone who had social pretensions, who boasted or was too pompous for his own good, would soon be deflated by the understated, cooled down, but slightly malicious form of Shetland humour known as skyimp. At its best it can be very subtly ironical, as in an old verse from Unst:

> De vaar e gooa tee
> When sona min guid to Kadanes:
> han kan ca' rossa mare
> han kan ca' big bere
> han kan ca' eld fire
> han kan ca' klovan di taings

'It was a good thing that my son went to Caithness: He can call rossa *mare*; big *bere*; eld *fire*; klovan *di taings*.' To be using Scots words would evidently be considered a kind of affectation.

Winter would also be the time for a wedding. It would always be held on a Thursday. The belief that the choice of day could affect an event seems to be very old. For the Nordic peoples the Thursday had a very special status and was as important as the Sunday. It had a magic quality: one could break the power of the trolls by doing the same thing on three Thursday nights running. Nobody can win over someone who was born on a Thursday. It was the best day for a wedding. It was the day chosen for the opening of the ting session both at the Allting and the Gulating. Of course it was the day of the god Thor, who was the protector of life in all its aspects.

A wedding would be attended by both young and old, and the

young couple would go around inviting everybody. After the wedding they would take cake and wine to the people too old to come. Music was very much a part of the festivities, and the dancing would go on all night; in Whalsay tradition is said to demand two nights of dancing and ten gallons of whisky! The dances were all reels, and the bride should dance with every man who was able to stand up with her.

Three couples are required to make up the figure of a Shetland Reel. The bride dances the first 'turn' with the bridegroom. Then they 'run' through the figure 8 and she 'sets' to the married man. After dancing with him, and a 'run' thereafter, she sets to the best man. Finally, she returns to her own man. Meanwhile he has been dancing with the 'mairéd womman' and the best maid. That is called the Bride's Reel. (Jessie Saxby, *Shetland Traditional Lore*, p124, Edinburgh 1932)

The Norse system of name-giving lasted quite long in Shetland. A man would add -son to his father's name, a woman would use -dotter, later -daughter. Such a name is known as a patronymic. In a small community it is a simple and convenient method of identification, and it is used in Iceland to the present day. Its drawback is a modern one: it is a system that causes havoc in any records and makes it very difficult to trace a family tree. Because of the shifting patronymics Shetland settlers in Bergen can rarely be followed past the first generation.

But even in a small community there might be several ending up as Olaw Laurenson or Rasmus Magnusson, and a further identification became necessary. A place-name was therefore added: Olaw in Flattabustare, Rasmus in Ocraquoy and Magnus in Howkenasetter. This remained the custom until sometime in the nineteenth century, when a registration of family names served to 'freeze' most of them, and the names ceased to have an individual connection with places or persons. Many fine old Scottish names were also kept alive through this custom, as Shetland records will show us: Laurence Erickson, Thomas Harraldsoun, Marete Svensdotter, Marion Colbeinsdotter and Agnes Mawnisdotter. The custom lasted longest in the more isolated districts, and James Manson of Foula is reputedly the last Shetlander to have been named after his father, Magnus Robertson, who died during the First World War. Surnames ending in -son still remain characteristic of Shetland, and we find names like Johnson, Laurenson and Thomason.

The old Christian names became Scotticized or disappeared altogether when ministers refused to christen children with names they considered pagan. Thus Olaf became Oliver which also could be shortened as Olie; and Sigurd was turned into George, although it remained Sjurdi when spoken and seems sometimes to have been allowed the written form of Shuard. It is difficult to understand the logic behind changing Hakon into Hercules, the hero of Greek legends, as he was definitely pagan. Perhaps the custom was started by a minister who loved the classics; in any case anyone burdened with such a name was always known simply as Hakki. Biblical names became very common. Magnus was always allowed as it was a saint's name. Another popular name that somehow survived was Tirval, from Torvald, in spite of being connected with the Norse god Thor. Today this name somehow conveys the typical, sometimes even the caricatured, Shetlander. There is an old saying: 'We're a' Tirval Shuardson's bairns' which expresses a feeling of equality. Of course, Shuardson also became changed into Stewartson, and then into Stewart.

Girls' names seem to have fared a little better. Inga, Hilda, Osla, Freya and Sinnie have always been very popular. Osla is a version of the Norse name Aslaug, and for a long time it had to be written as Ursula, the name of a fourth century German saint. Sinnie already was the name of a saint, as it was short for Sunniva. But only ignorance of its origin could have let the name of Freya, the Norse goddess of love and fertility, pass muster!

Celebrations and festivities

Perhaps the greatest annual event is Up-Helly-Aa which is held in Lerwick on the last Tuesday in January. Months of planning and patient community work culminate in one colourful outdoor spectacle—the burning of a Viking galley. The ceremony takes place in the early evening, and the flames of the torches show up strikingly against the dark winter sky. The long procession of brilliantly dressed guizers follows in the wake of the great galley, while the band plays the Up-Helly-Aa song. When the site of burning is reached *The Galley Song* is sung. Then a bugle is sounded and the guizers throw their flaming torches into the galley. And while the longship which has been worked on lovingly for so long burns and blazes the guizers sing *The Norseman's Home*. After that the festivities go on all night in private halls. The festival is repeated on a smaller and more intimate scale in places like Unst, Bressay, Yell and Northmaven. There the Up-Helly-Aa is celebrated more as a friendly family event where everybody takes part, with children also dressing up as Vikings and having a wonderful time.

The particular form of the festivities has evolved over more than a century, making the festival into a very special Shetland event, but perhaps today it is possible to perceive the traces of old beliefs in the modern fairy-tale trappings?

Shetland was slow in accepting the new Gregorian calendar, Lerwick adopted it in 1879 and people in Foula have not really done so yet! In the old calendar Christmas fell on 5 January. It was known in

Perhaps the greatest annual event is Up-Helly-Aa in Lerwick. The long procession of brilliantly dressed guizers follows in the wake of the great galley.

Shetland as Yule—a common Nordic word—and the festivities used to last for the greater part of a month, as they would begin early. Originally the word Yule was used for the pagan feast celebrated at the time of winter solstice to mark the end of the agricultural year. Beer-making and guizing and bonfires were among the cultic customs. But Yule was a frightening time too—the powers of darkness grew stronger. The *oskurei* or *jolerei*, demons or dead who found no peace, thundered on fast horses through the sky. Tar and beer barrels were the only known protection against them. These myths are known in several other countries too, such as Scotland, Ireland and France. Up-Helly-Aa was for a long time celebrated on 29 January to mark the end of Yule, and the name is said to derive from Uphalliday—the end of the holiday. It was also known in the old days as Twenty-fourth Night. Around the middle of the nineteenth century Lerwick celebrations turned quite rowdy. Men in guizing outfits would make a bonfire of tar-barrels, after having marched along Commercial Street. Then they would make a round of friends' houses. The tar-barrelling was prohibited from 1874, but it turned out to be difficult to stop it and instead was organized more safely.

There was a strongly romantic Nordic revival towards the end of the nineteenth century, and it was perhaps unavoidable that the festival would somehow become tied in with the Vikings. The first galley was burnt in 1889. The singing came after that. The first song to be used was *The Norseman's Home*, which has also been known as

The Hardy Norseman. It has come to be thought of as the Shetland anthem. The author of the lyrics is unknown, but the tune was used for an unofficial Norwegian anthem for 100 years. Written in anger by a Norwegian student in Copenhagen when he learned that his country would not be allowed a university of its own, the song was at one time prohibited but proved impossible to suppress, and became the Marseillaise of Norway.

A permanent committee of 17 members is in charge of the festival. A guizer jarl, who is really a master of the ceremonies, is elected. Each year they choose as their main theme a new character from history or saga, and who this is going to be is a closely guarded secret. Their costumes are ingenious and beautiful, if not perhaps always strictly realistic. Only the guizer jarl and his squad dress as Vikings; the hundreds of other guizers dress up as anything that takes their fancy. Each squad usually consists of some 20 men. The most important aspect of the Up-Helly-Aa festival, however, is perhaps that of people of different groups and ages making a communal effort and celebrating together. It is also a lesson in self-discipline, as any squad that does not behave according to the rules laid down is not allowed to take part the following year. While the Up-Helly-Aa is a wonderful spectacle for a visitor to watch, it is definitely not a tourist event.

Leaving and returning
The Shetlander's love of home has become legendary:

To such an extent is this feeling carried, that, in the case of girls in service in the south, it often brings on a disease known to the faculty as *Morbus islandicus*. There is no other symptom than a gradual dwindling away, and the patient herself is often unaware of the cause of her illness, the only remedy for which is immediate return to the dearly beloved *Old Rock*. (John R. Tudor, *The Orkneys and Shetland*, p176, 1883)

But over the years there was often very little choice; people were compelled by economic reasons to leave. There were many partings as family after family set out to make a new life somewhere else. Many men joined the merchant navy and sailed the seven seas for most of their adult lives. They were rarely home and became unwilling exiles. Others emigrated to Canada, Australia and New Zealand, where they could find living conditions somewhat similar to their own.

A Shetlander in Wellington, New Zealand, first got the idea of gathering emigrants from all over the world for a large reunion. The

The Guizer Jarl and his squad march along Commercial Street early on Up-Helly-Aa morning, giving the Lerwick people their first sight of this year's ingenious and beautiful costumes.

In Out Skerries, John Henderson has, since 1980, thrown over 150 bottles into the sea. His wife Anna shows letters from his many 'bottle pals'.

first *hamefarin week* was arranged in 1960 and was a great success: emigrant Shetlanders were welcomed back, and celebratory events took place all over Mainland and the islands. The hamefarers came at a time when the community was gaining confidence in itself; for the first time in a century the flow of emigration was drying up and there were even people coming back to settle. The 1985 hamefarers found more change still and for some today's Shetland was very different from their own nostalgic memories.

Radio Shetland arranged a theme tune competition for Hamefarin '85 and received 18 entries. Juries all over Shetland awarded points for each tune. The winner was *Da Hamefarin* by Jill Slee Blackadder, whose song aptly expresses the spirit of the Hamefarin:

> Dey'll be Sinclairs an Syversons an Johnsons an Jamiesons,
> An Mansons an Malcolmsons at wir Hamefarin,
> Watsons an Williamsons an Hughsons an Herculesons,
> Dey'll aa be here in Shetland, bairns, tae hae a spree.

Dey'll be coming fae America, Sooth Africa, Australia,
An Saudi Arabia tae wir Hamefarin,
Alaska, Spain an Canada, New Zealand, Scandinavia,
Dey'll aa be here in Shetland, bairns, fae ower da sea.

Yet the Shetlanders who stayed at home are not the proverbial country cousins. The interest in people and the world around them is still there. In Out Skerries, John Henderson has thrown over 150 bottles into the sea with letters requesting the finders to write to him. Replies have come from people living all around the North Sea, and a lively correspondence is the result. Many of his new-found friends have come to see him, and one summer the Hendersons set out to Norway to visit some of them. In the old days a man might have been at Davis Straits or off to the whaling in South Georgia without ever having been further south in Britain than the Pentland Firth. Indeed, Shetlanders were once so numerous along the seaways of the world that they were sometimes spoken of as North Sea Chinamen.

There is an element of skyimp also in the story of the old Shetlander who listened patiently to a tourist telling him of the delights that could be had in Aberdeen, before he said dryly: 'Maybe so, but it's not a patch on Rio, or Macao, come to that ...' A Foula man who had been taken south by the film crew to see the première of *The Edge of the World* was asked by a journalist what he thought of the marvels of London. 'Muckle da sam as hit wis da last time I saw hit', was the reply. Shetlanders have roamed the world, and staying in their home islands is a positive choice, because to them it is the best place to be.

9 FOLKLORE

Through popular tradition it is possible to glimpse the survival of a mythical way of thinking going back far into antiquity. Folk tales imaginatively express a people's attitudes and social values. In many of the stories told there may also be cores of historical truth so distorted as to take on the vagueness and elusiveness of the fairy tale. A people's popular tradition will also reflect its way of life. To the inhabitants of an isolated valley the mountains will mean mystery and often fear. In Shetland folklore the sea is the place of mystery—inscrutable and full of creatures who may be benevolent but who more often are hostile and malign. Mountain and sea alike can never be mastered; it is man who must bend to their terms.

There was an old belief in Shetland that the tides were caused by a monstrous sea-serpent who lived near the edge of the world and would need six hours to draw in his breath and another six hours to let it out again. This is probably a version of the Miðgarðsormr, the serpent which in Norse mythology lay in the ocean outside Miðgarðr, the inhabited world. It was one of the most terrifying monsters threatening mankind, and the god Thor himself tried to fight him. Thus a story from the Edda survived in Shetland long after it was forgotten in the Scandinavian countries.

Lines are blurred between myth and reality in the lore of the sea monsters. The *brigdi* was the monster the Shetland fishermen feared the most. It was described as a huge flat creature with fins, today believed to have been the basking shark (*Selache maxima*). The brigdies were known to pursue the haf-boats. The fishermen took to carrying axes for protection against these creatures, but the most effective way of getting rid of them was to throw a piece of 'lammer', amber, into the sea.

The *sifan* was the Loch Ness kind of monster, with humps and a long neck. It seemingly had no evil intentions but inspired fear purely through its size and its looks:

It was one hundred and fifty feet long. It had a huge head covered with barnacles as large as herring; a prodigious square mouth, with whiskers— probably of seaweed—seven or eight feet long, and of a bright green colour . . .

The sifan *was a sea monster with humps and a long neck. It seemingly had no evil intentions but was terrifying because of its size and its looks.*

This description was given in a sworn account by the six man crew of the fishing boat *Bertie* of Lerwick. In June 1882 they had been fishing for two days south-east of Fetlar, and their hold was full of fish. They were just hauling the lines when they saw the monster heading straight for the boat. They fired at close range and threw ballast stones at it, but this only served to infuriate the creature, which followed them for three hours. In May 1903 a similar monster was seen by the crew of the fishing boat *Adelong* when fishing off Scalloway. It ruined ten of their nets.

The legend of the mermaid reached Northern Europe rather late, and this may partly explain why stories about them were rare in Shetland. Yet the belief in them may have grown when a sixern crew in 1833 insisted that they had caught one, having found her entangled

The njuggle *was especially dangerous after sunset. He was a vicious water creature bent on enticing people into the water by all possible means.*

in their lines off the island of Yell. They drew her into their boat and removed the fish-hook which had caught her. Arthur Edmondston of Unst discussed the episode with the skipper and said later that not one of the six men doubted its being a mermaid. He dismissed the usual explanation of 'optical illusion' and thought it quite impossible that Shetland fishermen could make such a mistake.

The *njuggle* was a twin of the Norwegian nøkk of so many folk tales, and was found in rivers and lochs. He was a vicious water creature bent on enticing people into the water by all possible means. He could disguise himself as a stick of wood or a human being, but mostly he appeared as a fine horse, looking so peaceful and tame that people were tempted to ride him. Once the rider was seated on his back he would plunge into the water. When the njuggle roared it was said that he was waiting for his victim and that somebody would drown. Being especially dangerous after sunset, the njuggle was used effectively both in Norway and Shetland to scare children away from the water.

Legend has it that some brave young men in Tingwall captured a njuggle and chained him to a standing stone near the road from Tingwall to the Lochs of Asta; the marks are still there today. Nuckro Water in Whalsay and Njugals Water near Tingwall were thought to be haunts of the njuggle, as the names show.

It was only a Finn who could safely ride a njuggle. The Finns are a recurrent theme in Shetland folklore, although they are shadowy and hard to define. To some extent they are confused with the seal folk, and may have much in common with the huldrefolk in Norway. They live close to people and can at times be helpful.

...sea monsters are for the most part called Finns in Shetland. They have the power to take any shape of any marine animal, as also of human beings. (Tudor, *The Orkneys and Shetland*, p167)

There are place-names in Shetland referring to them: Finnigord or Finjigert in Fetlar and Finnister in Nesting. The Finn element has been explained in many ways. In Norway the name originally meant the Lapps as well as the Finns, and in Scandinavian popular usage the name Finns still refers to the Lapps. One explanation rather commonly met with is that the Finns were Lapp people brought over as slaves by the Norsemen. They were short and dark, and in the popular mind the stories about them would merge with the legends of the Picts.

There are place-names, however, in Sweden and south-eastern Norway compounded with the word 'Finn', in places where there has never been any Finnish or Lapp settlement. On a small holm near Sjernarøy in Rogaland are the remains of a large prehistoric stone wall which is locally called Finnborg. In the same way Lund Cathedral in the south of Sweden was according to popular tradition built by a giant called Finn.

Most stories of trolls and giants in Fetlar were connected with the prehistoric stone wall known as Finnigord or Finjigert—the Finn fence—that divides the island. According to tradition the fence was built overnight when the farmer at Kolbinstoft promised to trade his best cow for it. When he woke up in the morning the fence was there and the cow was gone. Where the fence ends at Houbie near the Broch of Tresta in the south of Fetlar there is a cave where the troll used to live. In the north of Unst there is a prehistoric fence ending in a cave called Da Haljer o' Fivlagord. Fivl is an old Norse name for troll, and when both Finn and Fivl are used to describe the builders of the same kind of fence it seems a logical conclusion that this is because they meant the same thing to the people

For a long time anyone who looked odd or acted strangely might be spoken of as a 'Norway Finn' who could 'dø mair dan maet himsel'—

do more than feed himself. Sometimes just a reference to the Finns could have healing power, as in this charm used to get rid of toothache:

> A Finn cam ow'r frae Noraway
> Ta pit tøthake awa,
> Oot o' da flesh an' oot o' da bane'
> Oot o' da sinin an' inta da skin'
> Oot o' da skin an' into da stane,
> An' dere may du remain.

The belief that Finns knew magic and sorcery is very old in northern cultures. It is found in Beowolf, the oldest English epic, where 'Finna land' is used to denote a supernatural place. As late as the twelfth century Norwegian church laws specify the punishment to be meted out for 'believing in Finns or troll women'. The fact that the Finns had another culture and spoke a completely different language would of course enhance the feeling of strangeness and fear of the unknown, and perhaps explain why an ethnically descriptive word acquired a mythical meaning. There is no reason to believe that the Finns were ever in Shetland.

The original trolls were quite different from the Finns and the later trows. In Norway they were usually big and coarse, but occasionally some were quite small. They hated people, whose presence would make them roar 'I smell Christian blood!' Giant and troll had much in common. They were mountain creatures who could both be turned to stone if surprised by the sun. The giants survived the longest in Unst and in the Scalli Hills between Aithsting and Weisdale. They are linked with so many stones that it is no wonder they died out! At Wester Skeld two stones stand where giants out to plunder were surprised by the rising sun. The boulders in the Ve Skerries were thrown there by a giant called Atla. In Siggershoull, a hill north of Colvidale in Unst, lived the giant Sigger. He once went to the top of his hill to fetch a boulder he wanted to use as a stepping-stone to his favourite fishing place, because like all giants he hated getting his feet wet. His wife jeered:

> Oh, Siggie, Siggie, mony an ill stane
> Is lain upon dy riggie.

This so infuriated the giant that he started chasing her but slipped and fell, with the stone on top of him. There he still stays, as no man has been able to move 'Sigger's Stane'.

The trolls are remembered in place-names like Trolladale and Trollhoulland. They grew smaller, acquired human characteristics and became known as trows. The trows lived in hills or mounds or on lonely moors. Shetland trows were great music lovers and for that reason they so forgot themselves while dancing to fiddle music at

Haltadans in Fetlar that they did not see the rising sun, and were turned to stone. And there they still are, in a circle of low stones, with the fiddler and his wife as the two stones in the middle. People who passed a green knoll at night might be surprised to hear wonderful music, and through an open door they could see the trows dancing. With the Shetlanders' natural love of music it would be hard not to enter, but it was important to stick a knife over the door as a precaution: steel as well as the Bible was dreaded by the trows. Otherwise one might find oneself staying with the trows for years that felt like minutes only, as the sense of time was all changed.

Altogether it was better to follow the old advice: 'Never meddle wi' da trows', but there were some who could not avoid their company, as the story of the Fetlar crofter, Bjørn, shows. He was riding home one night on a grey mare with a roan foal behind when near the Smugga a voice called him:

> Du, at rides da gray
> An' rins da red;
> Tell Tona Tivla
> At Fona Fivla
> Is fa'en ida vjelna vatna.

When he came home he excitedly told his wife what had happened. A small 'trowie boddy' rushed out of the byre crying that it must be her child who had fallen in the water. In the byre she had been milking a cow, and in her hurry she left behind the silver cup she had been using. Anything belonging to a trow was believed to bring good luck, and Bjørn and his wife proudly displayed the cup. But the story does not end there: some time later the local minister came visiting, recognized it as a communion cup that had disappeared, and took it away with him.

Another variant was taken down by the Shetland writer J. J. Haldane Burgess and takes place at Stakkaberg in Fetlar:

> Du at rides da ridd an rins da grey
> Geng haem, an inta da byre, an say:
> Varna, vivla, tail a tivla
> Is faain i da fire an brunt her.

Again a trow who had been milking a cow, rushes out exclaiming: 'O care an düll! dat's my bairn at's faain i da fire!' In her hurry she forgets her brass pan. This remained at the farm for good luck, and was every night filled with food, until one night when they forgot to do so and the pan mysteriously disappeared.

On the face of it these tales are variants of a local Fetlar theme as they often refer to places there. But the Faroese linguist Jakobsen found another variant in Foula. This seems to prove that this is old Shetland tradition. But this is in actual fact one of the wandering stories that are in essence the same from one culture to another, with only the details adapting to time and place. One of the tales that the Norwegian folklorist P. C. Asbjørnsen collected around the middle of the nineteenth century, takes place on a farm somewhere north of Oslo. A wedding feast is being held there, and a boy who is bringing the food is going as fast as he can by horse and sled, when a voice calls to him:

Hør du, kjøre du åt Eldstad fram,	Listen you, if you are going to Eldstad,
så sei henni Deld	then tell Deld
at Dild datt i eld.	that Dild fell in the fire.

When he arrives at the wedding and repeats what he heard, one of the wedding guests cries 'Oh, that's my child' and rushes out as if she were crazy. When in her hurry she loses her hat, they can all see that she is trowy. However, folklorists point out that this story was told as early as AD 100 by the Greek writer Plutarch. Of course, there are no trows in Plutarch's story, just mysterious voices.

Some of the magic we hear about in the sagas is used benignly by women who knew how to use herbs in healing and were respected for their knowledge. Magic was also practised by the god Odin until it occurred to him that it was not quite seemly for men to be associated with it; the goddess Freya therefore took over his role. Since then magic has been mostly regarded as a female domain, and women have certainly paid a heavy price for it. There were no sharp dividing lines in the popular imagination between trow, Finn and witch, or *heksi*, as she was called in Shetland Norn. In mediaeval theology there was no distinction either, and all magic was considered heresy and the Devil's work, for which there was no mercy.

Witchcraft was a complex system without clearly defined tenets: to accuse someone, therefore, became an easy means of destroying an enemy. The charges were often so preposterous that it is incredible to the modern mind that they could actually be believed. Until the beginning of the seventeenth century it was possible in Shetland to clear oneself of such a charge if five friends helped swear one's innocence. This was known as the 'saxter aith'—the oath of the sixth. From that time, however, clearing oneself became harder and the charges more unbelievable. In 1644 Marion Pardone from Hillswick was burned at Scalloway. Disguised as a porpoise she had allegedly swum out to sea and overturned a fishing boat so that the crew drowned. No witnesses had seen a porpoise near the boat, but even so the charge against her was upheld. In all there were some 20 charges, and even on the way to her trial she was accused of evil dealings:

You being then more than sixty years old and coming from Breckon to Hillswick, when you were to be arrested and sent to Scalloway to suffer for the previously mentioned crimes, were seen to converse on your way with the devil who appeared to you in the likeness of two corbies [carrion crows], one on either side of you and going and hopping along with you to Hillswick. Robert Ramsay overtook you and challenged you about the corbies, why they kept so near you. You said they were aware you carried bread on you, and that made them follow you, for you had thrown crumbs to them—which was only a lie made by you, concealing the truth. (*The Shetland Book*, 1967)

Another sinner was Luggie of Kebister who would boast of his prowess as a fisherman—the fish he caught was not just big, it was already cooked for him! Given the times he lived in, his fate was sealed.

Most of the stories of witchcraft are not dramatic, but tell of cream which will not turn into butter because it has been 'wranged' by the old woman on the small croft nearby, of the best cow that mysteriously has no milk, or of the hens that will not lay. It was all known as 'taking the profit'. A woman who suspected that her farm animals might be exposed to witchcraft might go through long and complex rites to protect them. There were also those who made a living as wise women and were expected to put on a show to live up to their reputation. Consequently, when charges of witchcraft were brought against them, they found them difficult to deny.

Fantastic stories would be told about the peat-fires in the long winter nights, of trows and witches, Finns and sea monsters, and they would not lose in the telling. Probably they were only half believed in, but much of the tradition had come down through the centuries and therefore they were often accepted unquestioningly.

10 SHETLANDIC

—no isleman now can use the tongue
Of the bold Norseman from whom their lineage sprung.
                    Sir Walter Scott, August 1814.

Trowe wir minds wir ain aald language
still keeps rinnin laek a tøn.
                            Vagaland.

Shetland speech is soft, even and slow. Although not dramatic like Shetland itself, it is expressive and rich. Two other languages have formed it, Norse and Scots, but there are traces of Dutch and German, and today the influence from modern English is very strong. Thus the language reflects history.

As Sir Walter Scott tells us, the old Norse language 'Norn' had given way to an Anglo-Scots speech when he visited the islands in the summer of 1814. Before then Norn had been the main language of the islands for almost a thousand years, after the language of the Picts disappeared practically without trace.

Early Norn history
In *Diplomatarium Norvegicum* we find the oldest surviving document from Shetland. It is a letter from the lawmen of the islands in 1299 about a purchase of property where they think incorrect information has been given:

'Allum eim monnum sem þetta bref sia eða heyra senda allir lagþngis menn at Hiatlandi Q.G. ok sina—' (To all those men who see or hear this letter all the lawmen of Shetland send God's and their own greetings—.)

This letter fulfils the requirements of the time both in language and form.

A letter from Unst in 1465 is, in spite of a rather slapdash style, also written in pure Norse:

'Ollum monnom theim som thetta breff sæ ædher høra sendher Andres William son q.g. ok sina kunnikt giorandhe medh thesso mino vpno brefue at jak hafwir selth beskedelik man Symon Hognason eina mark brenda j jordh ...'

(To all those men who see or hear this letter Andres William son sends God's and his greeting and wants to make it known with this my open letter that I have sold to modest man Symon Hognason land for one burnt mark [i.e. in pure silver] ...)

This is written in a language which is rather different from that found in the letter of 1299, having developed along exactly the same lines as the language did in Norway in the Middle-Norwegian period after 1350. That this should be so is not surprising—after all Shetland was the Norse area most closely connected with the mother country.

When indeed Danish became the written language in Norway, it was also, therefore, accepted as such in Shetland. A letter of compromise from 1586 is written in this language, but interspersed with a number of Norse and Scots expressions:

'Anno 1586 paa thenn fierde dag December wore wy effther skriffne y Gerde y Redeførd sogenn thet er att sige Willom Monssønn till Gerde laurettis mand y Ønyst ...' (In the year 1586 on the fourth day of December we the undersigned of Gerde in Redeførd parish that is Willom Monssønn of Gerde lawman in Unst ...)

Written Danish would be rather different from the language spoken in Shetland, and therefore Scots might not seem so much more alien.

After the changeover in 1469 the pressure from Scots began to come quite quickly through the two power centres, the Church and the courts. In order to progress in the new order of things it became necessary to know Scots. The earliest document in Scots is from 1525 and deals with church matters. Probably Scots was the only written language used from the beginning of the seventeenth century. Court records covering the trials under Earl Patrick are extant from 1602 and written in Scots, with a few Norse words here and there. When Swinna Petersdottir had to appear before the Lerwick Session in 1732, she let them know that they were not fit to be elders and had 'clags of dirt at their tail'. This, being an old Scots expression of disparagement, indicates that spoken Scots had long been in use in the southern part of Shetland. The story of the minister Magnus Manson who became known as Magnus 'Norsk' suggests that this was true even a century earlier. In spite of his Shetland name he could not speak Norn, so that when he became a minister in Unst in 1593, he had to go to Bergen to learn Norwegian so that his parishioners could understand him. For in the North Isles and in the outer islands such as Foula and Fair Isle Norn lived on as the spoken language until some time in the eighteenth century, and Magnus Manson's congregation in Unst understood no other language.

Norn was never studied while it was still a living language, and therefore there are many questions that will never be answered. There are only chance statements from travellers or people who have experienced the language for short periods of time. Many of them are

Scottish ministers. Common to most of them is that they do not have the necessary qualifications for understanding Norn and judging its status. Yet their stories do convey a general impression of what happened to the Norn language. About 1680 the minister of Dunrossness James Kay relates that in the southern part of his parish most people are incomers from Scotland and their language is 'mostly the same with the Scottish ... yet all the natives can speak the Gothick or Norwegian tongue ... by reason of their commerce with the Hollanders, generally they promptly speak low Dutch.' The inhabitants of the northern part of the parish, on the other hand, are with few exceptions old Shetland families who all 'can speak the Gothick or Norwegian language and seldom speak other among themselves; yet all of them speak the Scottish tongue both more promptly and properly than generally they do in Scotland.'

But it was only a question of time before Norn would give in to the pressure in other parts of Shetland as well. In 1733 Thomas Gifford of Busta, who was Steward and Justiciar Depute of Shetland and one of the big landowners, wrote thus:

The ancient language spoken by the inhabitants of Zetland was that of the Norwegians called *Norn*, and continued to be that only spoken by the natives till of late, and many of them speak it to this day amongst themselves, but the language now spoken here is English, which they pronounce with a very good accent; and many, especially about Lerwick, speak Dutch very well, having had frequent occasion to converse with the Dutch people. (*Historical Description of the Zetland Islands*, p28)

In 1774 the young Orkney minister George Low travelled around in Shetland and also visited Foula, which long was the last bastion of Norn. He wrote that there were some who still knew Norn on the island, but that the Norse language was the speech of the last generation and would be entirely lost by the next.

None of them can write their ancient language, and but very few speak it, the best phrases are all gone, and nothing remains but a few names of things and two or three remnants of songs which one old man can repeat and that but indistinctly. (*A Tour through the Islands of Orkney and Schetland*, Kirkwall 1879)

The old man referred to by Low was William Henry, a crofter at Guttorm in Foula. He sang a ballad in Norn for George Low, who being a Scotsman did not understand what he heard. Low therefore wrote down its 35 stanzas the way it sounded to him. He called it *The Earl of Orkney and the King of Norway's Daughter: a Ballad*. It is also known as the Ballad of Hildina, and Low's original manuscript is kept in The Advocates' Library in Edinburgh. William Henry was unable to read or write, but he had an exceptionally fine memory. The composition of the ballad shows that Henry himself must have had a fairly good understanding of what he was singing.

Low put much effort into his difficult task. He made some obvious mistakes like splitting up words or lines, and for a long time the text was considered the unreadable remains of a dying language. In 1900 the Norwegian linguist Marius Hægstad made a careful study of Low's original manuscript. He had then for many years been intrigued by what he called 'the linguistic riddle of the Hildina Ballad'.

From Low's text, 7th stanza	*Hægstad's version:*
In kimerin Iarlin	In Kimer in Iarlin
U klapasse Hildina	u klapa se Hildina onde kidn;
On de kidn quirto	'Quirto vult doch fiegan vara
Vult doch, fiegan vara moch	moch or fy din?'
or fly din.	

In English this would be: 'In comes the Earl and kisses Hildina on her cheek; "Who would you want dead, me or your father?"' Through his linguistic analysis Hægstad found a strangely intact language. Of the 260 words used in the ballad, all may be Norse; this, however, is disputable, as not all of Low's handwriting is equally legible. Another Norwegian scholar, Sophus Bugge, was able to reconstruct the ballad the way it probably was when it was composed. This is the same stanza in literary Norse:

Inn kemr hann jarlinn
ok klappar ser Hildina undir kinn:
'Hvárt vilð pu feigan vera
mik eða föður þinn?'

This is the Lord's Prayer as Low took it down from an old woman in Foula:

Fy vor o er i Chimeri. Halaght vara nam dit. La Konungdum din cumma. La vill din vera guerde i vrildin senda eri chimeri. Gav vus dagh u dagloght brau. Forgive sindor wara sin vi forgiva gem ao sinda gainst wus. Lia wus eke o vera tempa, but delivra wus fro adlu idlu for doi ir Konungdum, u puri, u glori, Amen.

In this text we find six Anglo-Scots words, but two of these are part of the final blessing. This was not used in the Norse version of the Lord's Prayer, and has evidently been added later, owing to Scottish influence.

As time went by the Church grew stronger and education became more common. The church and school language was based on an English Bible translation, The Authorised Version of 1611. A survey from 1826 made in seven of the twelve Shetland parishes shows that 76 per cent of all people over 8 years of age knew how to read. As Bible texts were used for much of the reading practice, it follows that English became the language of literacy. The same thing happened in Scotland as well. But the fact that Shetlandic was under double fire from both Scots and English may have somewhat neutralized the effect. For it is a fact that, although the language the Shetlanders used among themselves could no longer be called Norn, it was a very distinctive medium—a Shetlandic tongue. In 1939 Christian Pløyen, the Danish government representative in Faroe said of it:

The language in Shetland is now exclusively English, but mixed with many words of Norse origin, and which I would not have easily understood, if I had not known the Faroese tongue. ... The dialect is, moreover, different, and in some parts of the country, was very difficult to understand. It is not only the foreign words that make the Shetland tongue difficult to make out; there is besides a peculiar accent, a rising and falling of the voice, which is by no means unpleasant, and which the Faroese also employ when they talk their own dialect. (*Reminiscences of a Voyage to Shetland, Orkney & Scotland*, Lerwick 1896)

It was this similarity in accent and words which made the Faroese Jakob Jakobsen want to study Shetlandic. Ever since he was a child he had been used to talking to Shetland fishermen when their boats put into harbour on Faroe, and he was struck by the ease with which he as a Faroese could understand them and communicate with them.

Jakobsen and his study of Shetland Norn

Towards the end of the nineteenth century there was an aura of romance over the study of Nordic language and folklore. Saga translations had given the northern peoples a heroic past, and they gloried in it. Around 1880 the restoration of the Faroese language began in earnest. It was a demanding task, as very little had been done before. Jakob Jakobsen (1864–1918) at first intended to take up this work, and his first scholarly work is a collection of Faroese words. But during this work Jakobsen became interested in finding out what had happened to the old Norse language in Shetland—a place which was often mentioned in Faroe as a horrifying example of what lack of linguistic awareness could lead to.

Therefore Jakobsen went to Shetland in the summer of 1893, and he was warmly received:

Everywhere I have met with the greatest interest and sympathy for my project; they seem to have waited a long time for some Nordic linguist to come in order to rescue the remnants of the old 'Norn' or 'Norse'. (From a letter to the Tórshavn newspaper *Dimmalætting* in August 1893)

Originally Jakobsen intended his visit to be for three months, but he stayed for two years. Before he left he lectured on his work, and his audience was thrilled to hear his perfect Shetland pronunciation. In 1897 he defended his doctorate thesis 'Det Norrøne Sprog på Shetland'— The Norse Language in Shetland—at the University of Copenhagen.

This was a landmark in Nordic philology. It was never published in English, but parts of it were included in the English edition of his Norn dictionary *Etymologisk Ordbog over det Norrøne Sprog på Shetland* which was his life's work. When he died, he had reached as far as *w*. He did not have the time to write the introduction which he had all thought out and knew would be the most important work he had done. His dictionary was translated into English by his sister and published in two volumes in 1928 and 1932 and called *An etymological dictionary of the Norn language in Shetland*. It became a standard work, of great importance also for Norwegian language research. For a long time it was a collector's item, selling for hundreds of pounds. When Shetland Folk Society in 1984 decided to reissue the English version, at a reasonable price, it was therefore a welcome effort.

Jakobsen's work was in part funded by the Carlsberg Breweries in Copenhagen, but all his life he struggled to make ends meet financially. When at last he might have had a university appointment, he died before he could take it up. His work, however, came in the nick of time as nobody spoke the old language anymore. The common spoken language was close to Lowland Scots, both regarding vocabulary and forms. But Jakobsen still saved for posterity thousands of words of Norse origin, as well as fragments of rhymes, riddles and proverbs in Norn. His sources did not always themselves understand the material they gave him—the last survivals of Norse language and tradition. 'The more I study this poor maltreated language and try to forge the fragments together, the stronger I feel its strong affinity to my own tongue, and the stronger the bitterness towards the Scots and the English, who have systematically hindered its growth and development' (from his letter to Dimmalætting).

He discovered that although the spoken language at the time was close to Lowland Scots both in vocabulary and grammar, it still contained a number of everyday words and expressions left over from the Norn. The pronunciation as well as the accent was also distinctively Scandinavian in character, but this speech was changing character even then. The pressure from English was great, and many Scots words and expressions were also becoming obsolete.

To some extent the Norn vocabulary in the Shetland dialect was closer to Norwegian than were Faroese and Icelandic. It varied from district to district, but on the whole it had most in common with the dialects of south-western Norway, especially the dialect of Vest-Agder. There were also words that could be traced back to Primitive Norse, the language spoken 100–700 AD. Some words had also retained an older meaning than they had in the other Scandinavian languages. And in the use of the old Germanic prefixes bi- and ga-, the Shetland language was on an earlier level than the classical Norse of the Icelandic sagas.

The Norse element was surprisingly rich. It survived mostly in words used for daily life and work, and especially in names for concrete and visible things. The name for a category of things might be Scots, but the name for the separate object would still be Norn. This was especially true of words denoting furniture, farm animals, boats, fishing tools and the weather. While Scots words would be used for the houses themselves, the Norn was kept in *glug*, *lem* and *tørilaft*—small window, trap-door and loft. In the same way the old-fashioned furniture would be *langsede*, *stab* and *krak* for long seat, a wooden block to sit on and a foot-stool. Nicknames and pet names, the use of special words and expressions lived on. The choice of words was often quite wide; thus cod and saithe could be described very precisely through a variety of special names.

Perhaps the strangest thing Jakobsen found on his wanderings from one district to another was the old sea language. The fishermen in Shetland believed like the fishermen in Faroe and in western Norway that there were many words and names one must not mention while fishing at the haf. In Shetland this sea language was richer than anywhere else, even if there was a certain touch of humour about it when Jakobsen wrote it down. Instead of the taboo words, the dangerous words, only noa words, or haf-words, lucky words were spoken. When Sigurd in the heroic lay in *The elder Edda* killed the dragon *Fáfnir*, he would not tell his name to the dying Fáfnir, because the dragon's words would be all the more powerful if he cursed his enemy by name. In the same way the truth of things must be kept hidden from the evil forces lurking in the deeps, otherwise not only the catches of fish but even the lives of the fishermen were in danger. The sea language was therefore quite unlike the language spoken ashore, and it could also vary from one boat crew to another.

The sea language has roots far back into early Norse times, with words and kennings taken from *Alvíssmál*, a lay from The elder Edda, which tells how things were called in the languages of the gods, the elves, the dwarves and the giants. In the sea language the sea was known as *djub*, *mar*, *log* or *holåst*. Alvíssmál tells us that the dwarves called the sea *djúpan mar*, the elves called it *logr*, and to the giants it was *álheimr* or *álost*. Common to the words of the sea language was that they had fallen out of use even before they had been replaced with Scottish words. Therefore this secret speech also had an aura of something fateful and wondrous—but did the evil forces understand only Scots?

Among the haf words we find these: *de opstander*, *beniman*, *predikanter* for minister, *de opstanders bjorg* for manse and *de bønhus* for church. There are also many variants for wife: *de frau*, a loanword from Dutch, and *de kuna* were both used in Unst, and *de hospera*, from the Norse word *husfreyja*, in Fetlar. A young boy who did not use the right words or show enough respect for them could be sure of getting a box on the ear from one of the oldtimers in the crew.

Words of great interest to linguists thus led a shadowy existence. Without Jakobsen's zeal they would have been lost for ever. The same is true of the children's rhymes and lullabies he found. They are distorted and must have been completely without meaning to the mothers who used them to sing their children to sleep, but perhaps that gave them a certain magic:

> Klapa klapa søda
> boksina skolena bjøda

In Foula the old way of greeting each other was still remembered: *Goden dag*, and the reply: *Goden dag til dora!*

Even today Shetlandic is a composite language, formed by the changing influences the islands have lived through. Not much serious research has been done on it since Jakobsen, who saw it as his ultimate task to save Norn elements for posterity, but did not really concern himself with Shetlandic as an integrated whole.

Shetlandic today

From a Scottish point of view Shetlandic is especially interesting; it has been described as the most distinctive and individualistic of all Scottish dialects. The Scots that was adopted was the official language of the courts and government offices in Edinburgh, and visitors from time to time would remark on the strangely correct Scots spoken by the Shetlanders, a language of the seventeenth century from the so-called Middle-Scots period. It would be an interesting task to study the Scots element to see how it had been affected by Norn. There are still some words in use that have long ago been forgotten in Scotland, such as:

> *knap*—to speak in an affected way
> *deer*—to make an impression
> *grøflins*—on all fours.

It is especially important to study the German and Dutch elements before they disappear from the language completely. There is much cultural history in this vocabulary, as in the expression 'I didna wirt haea stør'—I didn't have a penny. *Stør* is the Dutch coin *stuiver*, which was much used in Shetland in earlier centuries. Older English and even French have also left their mark and help make Shetlandic such an expressive medium: 'Kum dee wis in—come your ways in.' 'Wait du, till I get me habuillements aboot me—wait till I get some clothes on.'

And even today there are many words and expressions that will seem familiar to a visiting Norwegian: *stoorawind*—a strong wind, *mareel*—a phosphorescence of the sea, *voar*—spring. Idiomatic expressions like *wi dat sam*—at once, and *geng husamilla*—to go from house to house with gossip, will make no sense to an English speaker but have equivalents in Norwegian. The practice of making new variants of verbs by adding prepositions or adverbs is also similar in the two languages:

> ta tak aboot—to secure crops against bad weather
> ta tak aff—to take aback
> ta tak at—to go ahead
> ta tak in for—to speak in support of
> ta tak til—to cry.

And these are only a few of the ta tak-combinations.

But Shetlandic is not the same in all parts of the islands. It is possible to distinguish between several variants that all have developed in different directions concerning vocabulary and pronunciation. Thus Whalsay speech comes the closest to modern Norwegian in pronunciation, especially in the vowels *a* and *e*. Most of the time a Shetlander will be able to tell where another islander hails from. It is possible to divide the local speech into three main dialect groups: south, west and north.

All speech in Shetland has 12 vowels, apart from the dialect in Fair Isle, with 11, which on the whole resemble the Scots vowel sounds. But stressed vowels before *l, d, n* are often palatalized. This is considered a Norse characteristic, as it is not found in the dialects of the Scottish mainland. In Norwegian we find palatalization as far south as the Sognefjord. The vowel *o* is in many words pronounced like the Norwegian ø-sound, as in 'møld' for earth or mould. So strong is this Norse ø-sound that it also colours words of Scots or English origin, so that 'curious' becomes *cørious*, and 'been' becomes *bøø*n. On the west side of Shetland this sound is not so clear; it often becomes the diphthong *øy*.

The division east–west also concerns the consonant sound *kw–wh*. On the west side these two sounds combine, so that both 'quite' and 'white' are pronounced *kwite*. 'Where' becomes *kwere*, and 'when' turns into *kwen*. When a word begins with *kn*, as in 'knife', the sound is often fully pronounced. The English sound that perhaps causes Norwegians most despair, the voiced sibilant in the beginning of words like John or general, is unvoiced in Shetlandic. But the most striking characteristic is perhaps the pronunciation of *th*, which becomes *d* or *t*. This means that unvoiced th as in 'thing' becomes *t*—ting—and voiced th as in 'brother' becomes *d(d)*—bridder. Therefore a Shetlander would say: 'Im tinkin didis waur wadder dan der haen sooth—I think this is worse weather than they're having in the south'. The division does not affect th as a final sound.

Besides 'you' in polite speech Shetlandic uses 'du' as a familiar form, which is gaining ground all the time, especially among young people.

This form takes the third person singular of the verb in the present tense: du is, du comes. The Scots use of -s in the plural form of the verb still lingers: 'Da bairns comes hame neist week'. And in the same way as in the Orkney dialect the verb 'to be' is used instead of 'to have' to form compound tenses of the verb: 'I'm written'. This may possibly stem from Norse usage.

Much has been lost on the way since Jakobsen collected his material. Many words that not so long ago were common and correct are unknown by the youngsters of today. This has many causes. The Shetlanders no longer go to the haf in sixerns, and words for this and similar occupations die out because there is no longer any need for them. Moreover to talk 'correctly' or 'properly' was for a long time to speak English—until quite recently Britain totally rejected the use of dialects. It was in fact not until the 1960s that the Shetland dialect became accepted and respected. This may have come about because the improved economy in Shetland at the time gave a feeling of identity

One of those who have felt the conservation of Shetlandic as a challenge is John J. Graham. In The Shetland Dictionary *he has tried to give a picture of the dialect he himself knows from Mainland.*

and assertiveness. Then in 1977 came Radio Shetland where the dialect is spoken most of the time. Local writers have used the dialect to great effect. It is ironic, perhaps, that status of the language has finally been achieved when so much can no longer be saved.

One of those who have felt the conservation of Shetlandic as a challenge is John J. Graham, former head master of Anderson High School in Lerwick. In an article in the New Shetlander he says of the Shetland he grew up in: 'Culturally we grew up in two worlds and got the worst of both. On the one hand our linguistic training in school was artificial and inhibited, while on the other we came to view as socially suspect our native speech and traditions.' In *The Shetland Dictionary* he has tried to give a picture of the dialect he himself knows from Central Mainland.

A drawback all dialects have in common is that the written image is lacking, and all attempts to reproduce local pronunciation correctly only make the task of the reader more difficult. But people in Shetland today are culturally aware and want to hold on to their linguistic identity. Shetlandic is genuine and immediate. This version of the 23rd Psalm also shows how beautiful it can be:

> Da Loard's my hird, I sanna want;
> He fins me bøls athin
> Green mødoo girse, an ledds me whaar
> Da burns sae saftly rin.
>
> He lukks my wilt an wanless sowl,
> Stravaigin far fae hame,
> Back ta da nairoo, windin gaet,
> Fir sake o His ain name.
>
> Toh I sood geng doon Daeth's dark gyill,
> Nae ill sall come my wye,
> Fir he will gaird me wi His staff,
> An comfort me forbye.
>
> My table He has coosed wi maet,
> Whin fantin gød da fremd;
> My cup wi hansels lippers ower,
> My head wi oil is sained.
>
> Noo shørly aa my livin days
> Gød's love sall hap me ower,
> Until I win to His ain hoose
> Ta bide fir evermore.

Translated by John J. Graham

11 PLACE-NAMES

Lingey, Daaey, and bonny Hascosay,
Oxna, Papa, Hildasay and Hoy,
Samphrey, Bigga, Brother Isle and Orfasay,
Magic names that even time cannot destroy.
A Hundred Shetland Islands, B. Tulloch.

The great majority of Shetland place-names are of Norse origin. The spelling often differs wildly from the pronunciation; indeed the spelling may seem to have been dictated by the whims of the cartographer, as the same name is spelled differently from one end of Shetland to the other. Still, the place-names that must seem so bewildering to many visitors, are often easily understood by Scandinavians—they can even today tell what a place must be like just from seeing the name.

There is no poetry in the Norse place-names, but there is a kind of beauty in their logic and precision. They give quite matter-of-fact descriptions of scenery, fields and topographical features, as the old language would have elements to express the most minute variations. There were for example some 20 words for a hill of different shapes or heights, and coastal features could also be very specifically described. Thus the place-names were useful symbols of identification. Historically some of the nature-descriptive place-names go far back into antiquity, as Germanic tribes settled in Norway even before the Bronze Age and lived there undisturbed by the great migrations that disrupted the place-name traditions in continental Europe.

There are possibly more than 50,000 place-names of Norse origin in Shetland. Although these do not all date from the earliest settlement period, it is obvious that the first settlers were faced with quite a task of name-giving. However, they had a stock of names and compound elements ready to draw on; thus a place-name like Lerwick, from the Norse *leir-vik*, would be the natural name for a bay with a bottom of clay or mud. There are numerous names from the same root in Norway, the best known being Leirvik on the island of Stord in Sunnhordland. For that reason many places within Shetland have also been given identical names; thus we find Gruting in Fetlar and in West Mainland for a stony area, from the Norse *grjót*, for stone, as well as Sandwick in Unst and in South Mainland, used to describe the same topographical feature, a wide sandy bay. In some cases a place-name may have been given for nostalgic reasons to remind the settlers of the place they left behind. Although this seems relatively rare, it may still be the reason why Voss from the Norse *Vors*, the only name of its kind in Norway, has also been found in Unst.

The place-names prove the logical assumption that most of the settlers came from the west and south-west coast of Norway. Elements like *gil*, ravine, and *skáli*, hut, as in Leascole, Grindiscol, were specifically Norwegian. Some elements common to the Scandinavian countries occur in a form that was only used in Norway: *bakki*, slope, in Bakka, Backlands, and *klettr*, a cliff or rocky bank, in Clettnadal, Stoura Clett. A few elements can also be pinpointed to specific areas in Norway; *drangr* is typical of Agder in southern Norway.

Some of the Norse words have acquired an 'Atlantic' usage: their meanings differ in Norway and the Norse settlements in the west. This is true of *stakkr*, *drangr*, and *grind*. Thus Ramnastacks in Shetland are high rocks sticking up out of the sea. Stack has come to mean a high, steep skerry in the west, whereas in Norway it was used of a haystack. Drangr was in Norway a solitary rock or mountain peak; in Shetland it came to mean a steep offshore rock, like The Drongs in St Magnus Bay. A grind in Norway means quite literally a gate in a fence, but in Shetland and Faroe it is also used more figuratively of a narrow bay between cliffs or a narrow isthmus, as in Grind of the Navir and Mavis Grind. Also in Shetland an isthmus that was so low and narrow that boats could be dragged from one end to the other was not called a *drag* as it was in Norway, but a *hvarf*, from which have derived Easter and Wester Quarff in South Mainland.

Place-names are often important historical signposts to events taking place hundreds of years before or to the institutional history of a region. Loch of Girlsta becomes a significant place when recognized as Geirhildarvatn, the loch where Hrafna-Floki's daughter Geirhild drowned *c*. 870, when on the way to Iceland with her father. Hrafna-Floki Vilgerdsson has come down in history as the man who gave Iceland its name. The names ending in -ting tell us that the old legal system prevailed in Shetland as in other Norse areas: Delting from the Norse *Dalaþing*, Lunnasting from *Lundeiðsþing*, and Nesting from *Nesþing* are names used for local assemblies. A charter from 1321 tells us of another, *Rauðarþing* in Northmaven.

Place-names can also teach us about an earlier way of life. This works the other way too—knowledge of the cultural background is a key to understanding names that would otherwise perhaps remain obscure. Thus Tøvakoddi refers to the striking of wadmel to make it firmer; it is a rounded stone by the shore, washed over by the tide. Saltness is a headland where seawater was boiled to extract salt, and

Kalliness was the name given to a place where one called to the opposite shore to be ferried across.

The Norwegian historian Peter Andreas Munch was the first scholar to take an interest in Shetland place-names and to realize what valuable historical material they represented. Munch never went to Shetland, but he had a wide range of historical knowledge and an almost intuitive insight into the etymological meaning of a name. He methodically studied the names found in old rentals and charters and in that way he was also able to throw some light on Shetland history in the late Norse period. The result of his research was published in the 1850s.

Thomas Edmondston of Unst included in his 'Etymological Glossary of the Shetland and Orkney Dialect' a chapter on the origin and meaning of some Shetland place-names. He knew Munch's work but does not always agree with him.

The work was carried further in the 1890s by Jakob Jakobsen, the Faroese linguist. He had the advantage on Munch that he stayed for some time in Shetland and heard the local pronunciation of the names, but he did not have Munch's historical knowledge. His work on Shetland place-names was published in Copenhagen in 1901; the English edition The Place-Names of Shetland came in 1936, but has been out of print for years. The late John Stewart of Whalsay did valuable work on the place-names of Fetlar and Foula, as well as on Shetland farm-names in general. Although his work was, for a long time, difficult to obtain, the Shetland Library and Museum published some of his work as Shetland Place-names in 1987.

The study of place-names can be fascinating, perhaps because so much is still guesswork and leaves room for the imagination. The name for Shetland itself appears in a confusing variety of spellings over the centuries, and has caused much discussion among scholars. The form consistently used in the Icelandic sagas is Hjaltland, and this has become accepted as the Norse name. It has been used in Iceland till the present day, whereas the form Hetland is common in Faroe and in West Norway. 'Hjalt' meant the cross-piece of a sword between the hilt and the blade. Jakobsen suggested that this word might refer to the shape of Mainland, but many scholars have cast doubt on this theory.

The Norwegian historian A. W. Brøgger points out that the Icelandic literature was written down in the thirteenth century but that the name for Shetland is written quite differently in documents from that period. The oldest of these documents, written in Latin at Westminster in 1221 by one of Henry III's clerks, refers to one Nicolaus, archidiaconus Heclandensis. Nicolaus also went to Rome, where the pope's clerk refers to him in 1226 as archidiaconus Ihatlandensis. The modern spelling appears as early as 1289 in a letter from King Eirik Magnusson in

Bergen to the English king, introducing his envoys, among them *Thorwaldum de Shetland*. The first letter known to have been written in Shetland comes from all the lawmen *af Hiatlandi*, and is dated 1299. Thus none of the early sources use the name Hjaltland, but of course the saga writers may have known of an earlier usage. Brøgger suggests that the name is pre-Norse and refers to Inse Catt, the islands of the Catt-tribe, mentioned in early Irish sources. The name was analogous to Inse Orc for Orkney. The Catt-name would probably have been pronounced chat. The -land element is of course Norse.

The fact that both Orkney and Caithness are named for prehistoric tribes who lived there seems to give added weight to Brøgger's theory. But, of course, it all remains conjecture.

In the sixteenth century the Scots used the form Yetland. At that time the printed form of y in Scotland was z, and this confusion resulted in the inaccurate form of Zetland. This name was used for a long time in official quarters and survived in Zetland County Council, but has now fortunately been dropped. The Shetlanders hope that the plural form 'The Shetlands' will also become redundant as they do not accept it.

Most of the other island names end in -ey, although this element today appears in a variety of spellings. The word 'isle' is a fairly recent corruption.

Mainland	from the Norse *Meginland*.
Unst	the Norse form was *Ørnist*. Ønyst appears in a letter from 1586. Other forms are Ønstr, Jemist, Aumstr, Anst. As it is difficult to know the original form it also follows that the meaning remains obscure. Munch guesses at Ørn + vist, the abode of the eagle, but the name may be a Pictish survival.
Balta	from the Norse *Baltey*, perhaps from a man's name Balti, meaning bear.
Uyea	from the Norse *Ey*, island, an incredible distortion.
Haaf Gruney	from the Norse *Hafgrœney*, the green island in the sea. There are also Sound Gruney near Yell, Gruney near North Roe, as well as Grunay in Out Skerries.
Yell	from the early form *Jala*, which even in Norse times became Jela. The Scottish form Yeale turned into the present form Yell. The name has by most scholars been considered a Pictish survival, but the Norwegian scholar Per Hovda points out the similarity, both in name and natural features, between Jeløya in

	the Oslofjord, Jelsa in Ryfylke, and Yell. Hovda thinks the names derive from an old root el-/ol- for 'white' and refer to wide sandy beaches.
Linga	from the Norse *Lyngey*, heather island. There are numerous islands of this name in Shetland, the largest being West Linga near Whalsay.
Urie Lingey	from the Norse *eyrr*, coarse sand mixed with stones. When used of a small island this name often indicated a place used for holmgang.
Hascosay	the earliest known form is Hafskodzøy, from 1480. Munch believes the original form to be *Hafskotsey*, from hafskot, spray from the sea.
Fetlar	the earliest form is *Fœtilør*, Føtilar is used in a document from 1490. Fetlar was first used in 1558. The name seems to indicate the Norse plural form in -ar. Fetlar was always spoken of as the Est Isle and the Wast Isle. In Norse *fetill* means a band or strap.
Samphrey	from the Norse *Sandfriðarey*. This name is known from documents from 1512. Sandfriðr is a woman's name.
Bigga	Munch suggested that the original name may have been *Bygðey*, an island with something built on it. There is a Bygdøy in the Oslo basin.
Orfasay	from the Norse *Orfyrisey*, a tidal island, from the same root as Orphir in Orkney.
Brother Isle	from the Norse *Broðurey*, as suggested by Munch.
Lamba	from the Norse *Lambey*.
Little Roe	from the Norse *Rauðey Litla*, the little red island.
Gluss Isle	the island was mentioned in 1490 as *Glimsey*, probably from the man's name Glúmr.
Out Skerries	from the Norse *Austrskeri*, eastern skerries, or *Út-skeri*, outer skerries. Most scholars tend to choose the latter.
Housay	from the Norse *Húsey*, island with a house or farm.
Bruray	from the Norse *Bruarey*, island with a bridge or forming a bridge between two islands.
Whalsay	from the Norse *Hvalsey*. This may be a typical

comparison name, suggesting that the island has the shape of a whale, or it may refer to whales being stranded there.

Bressay —the origin of this name is obscure. It is written *Brúsey* in a document from 1490. It has often been spelled Brassay. Edmondston therefore suggests that it derives from *bard*, meaning edge or border.

Noss from the Norse Nos, *meaning a high, rocky promontory, here seen from the island of Bressay.*

Noss — from the Norse *Nos*, meaning a high, rocky promontory.

Mousa — from the Norse *Mósey*, island of heath or moor. Probably from *mós*, the genitive form of the Norse *mór*.

Egilsay — from the Norse *Egilsey*, probably derived from the man's name Egill.

Muckle Roe — from the Norse *Rauðey Mikla*, the big red island.

Papa Littla — from the Norse *Papey Litla*, little priest island.

Vementry — from the Norse *Vemundarey*, from the man's name Vémundr. Munch first suggested this, and later scholars have agreed with him.

Papa Stour — from the Norse *Papey Stora*, big priest island.

Ve Skerries — —Munch thought this name derived from the Norse *Vestrskeri*, the western skerries, whereas Edmondston suggested that its root was the Norse *va*, meaning danger.

Vaila — from the Norse *Valey*. The island was called Valøy in a document from 1490. Valr has several meanings in Norse: as a noun it meant a falcon, but it could also mean a horse, as well as a field of battle. As an adjective it meant round.

Hildasay	from the Norse *Hildisey*, probably from the man's name Hildir.
Oxna	—Munch suggests that the Norse name may have been *Yxney*, from the Norse yxn, an ox.
St Ninian's Isle	—earlier this was known as Rinansey and St Ringan's Isle. Rinan and Ringan are other names for the same saint.
North and South Havra	—probably like Oxna this is a comparison name, from the Norse *hafr*, a ewe. Munch suggested Hafrey as the original form.
Trondra	—the probable Norse form is *Prondarey*. Both Munch and Jakobsen suggested that the root might be the man's name Prondr. If so, it has definitely no connection with Trondheim, as suggested by Jakobsen. That name refers to the hardy people called the Prændir who settled in that geographical area. Of course, there is no reason why they should not have settled in Trondra as well! However, as pointed out by Dr Hovda, when used of islands this name often meant a boar; the name may therefore also be a comparison name.
West and East Burra	—on the evidence of the sagas Munch suggested that the Norse form was Barrey. Both Jakobsen and Edmondston disagree and suggest the same original name as for Burra in Orkney: *Borgarey*, from borg— castle.

West Burra. From the evidence of the sagas, Munch suggested that the Norse form was Barrey. Both Jakobsen and Edmondston disagree and suggest that it has the same origin as Burra in Orkney: Borgarey, *from borg-castle.*

Foula	from the Norse *Fugley*, island of birds. It has also been called Uttrie, the outer island.
Fair Isle	from the Norse *Friðarey*. Friðr was an adjective with many meanings, including lovely, kind, living and peaceful. In Thorfinnsdrápa the Orkney skald Arnor Thordarson writes 'at Eyjum friðri'—in those fair islands; friðarland was a refuge, a sanctuary; and friðr was also a kenning used in skaldic poetry for a woman. The island was called *Insula Bella* by the Scottish historian Buchanan. Probably the name today reflects the original meaning, but it is also possible that the name is a noa-word related to the sea-language—as the island is a dangerous place for seafarers.

Shetland farm names have long been in the focus of scholarly interest because, correctly interpreted, they may give us the history of the Norse settlement. Some 3400 farms have names of Norse origin; more have been recorded but have disappeared. Not all the farms were settled at the same time and much division of land has taken place. The first settlements were probably named simply from some striking natural feature: Sand, Klett, Vik. A man-made feature like a broch or a fort would inspire such names as Borg or Virki. Such a settlement is Brough, from the Norse *borg* in Eswick, which remained an important farm up through the centuries under changing owners.

Among the earliest farm name elements are *-setr*, *-bolstaðr*, and *-staðir*. They mean roughly the same, a farm. The evidence of these names is interesting, but somewhat confusing. The -setr names are found especially in northwestern Norway where they are mostly marginal farms. However, this was not true of the original -setr farms in Shetland where their average size was 12 merks, but the name remained productive for some time for divided farms. It is a puzzling fact that there are no -setr names in Faroe and Iceland. As these countries were settled in the late ninth century, the inference to be drawn is that the -setr names, which are also found in Orkney and the Hebrides, must be considerably older. Today the element appears as -setter or -ster, as in Dalsetter, Gunnister and Voxter.

In western Norway the -bolstaðr element was used of a special kind of settlement consisting of several farms clustered around a tun. The land was not split up but run as one property. This seems to have been followed up in Shetland as the -bolstaðr farms are usually found in groups of two or three, often with an early chapel. Names are mostly formed with adjectives or words for compass directions, and end today in -busta or -bister, as in Muklebusta, from the Norse mikli—large, and Isbister from the Norse austr—east. This farm name element seems to have been in use for a long time and is the most typical indication of Norse settlement in the west; in fact all other Norse place-names fall within the -bolstaðr area.

With the -staðir names we seem to get closer to the Viking Age. There is only one such name in Faroe, but it is by far the most common farm name in Iceland. All the -staðir farms in Shetland were important. Their average size was 33 merks, which was twice the size of the -bolstaðr farms. The use of the -staðir names seems to point to a change in social organization, with the emphasis on the individual. Pagan beliefs no longer prevailed, and the names are not made from the names of the gods, but with a man's personal name as the first element: Ulsta, Colsta, Gunnista. This points towards the new time that was coming, the Viking Age, whose creed was so aptly summed up in what one Viking told King Olaf the Saint before the battle of Stiklestad in 1030—he believed in his own might and means and said 'so far that belief has served me well'.

Later elements also tell their own story. As the land grew scarce it was divided again and again. The commonest element of all, *hus*, is found in 550 names. Thus Esthus, Northus, Wasthus and Soothus would at one time have been one farm, until division became necessary.

Place-name research in Shetland has been centred on the Norse names, to some extent also on finding pre-Norse elements. Perhaps this is so because of the aura of romance surrounding the Norse names, evoking the dashing Viking or the free odaller, whereas the Scottish period has never been seen as contributing anything, always as taking something away. The Gaelic element *pund*, for animal enclosure, as in Pundin Gamla, had been adopted even in the late Norse period. Over the years after 1469 Lowland Scottish influence left its mark on the place-names. Anything else would have been strange; Norn and Scots were, after all, closely related languages. Thus borg became broch in the sixteenth century.

The most common Scots elements found in Shetland are *knowe, dek, brae, fauld*, and *quarry*. Yet it is the patterns imposed on the existing Norse names that have caused more of an impact than anything else in the Scottish period: Loch of Spiggie, Burn of Aith, Holm of Skaw, Wick of Collaster. The naming system is consistent and mirrors the pattern in mainland Scotland. There has also been a certain sound-substitution in the spelling, which again as time goes on leads to a change in the name itself. This is especially true of v into w, as in Lerwick from leir-vik, and the pronunciation Waas for Walls from Vágar.

Today there are also English place-name elements coming in: *side, field, view, park*, and *hill*. The influence from English is strong and is about to break up many of the old pronunciation patterns. It has not mattered so much that the ou in Baltasound had no business being there, as everyone in Shetland pronounced it Baltasund anyway, but the newcomers today do not. The printed word has a way of winning through with time.

The Ordnance Survey maps are intended for the English speaker and are often misleading, at best inconsistent: the Norse word *varða*, a name historically important because it described a beacon or lookout-place, appears as -vird, -vord, -firt and wart. The story goes that the reason why the map has Walls when the name was locally pronounced Vaas or Waas, is that the cartographer did not like 'the Scotch habit of dropping the l'. The list of such changes is endless. No attempt seems to have been made to listen to the local pronunciation or look into the etymology of the name. In fact the cartographer seems to have felt a strong urge to introduce a meaning of his own sometimes! Thus Sudheim in Whalsay, pronounced Sudam and meaning simply the southern part of the original farm, became Sodom! It can only be hoped that this name appealed to the Scottish writer Hugh MacDiarmid's sense of humour when he spent nine years of his life there in the 1930s.

In defence of the cartographers it may be said that they had a difficult task, as English lacks many of the sounds that are common in Shetland, such as the modified vowel sounds. Therefore, it is really up to the Shetland people themselves to do something about preserving and recording the place-names. A systematic evaluation of the research done so far and a collection of more material are essential, as time is running out. Owing to a changing economy the loss of names is great, and with them will be lost an invaluable part of Shetland's cultural heritage, as well as important historical source material.

12 THE CULTURAL HERITAGE

Dem at loves da Shetlan culture—
　　Dem at loves da Shetlan tongue—
Hing you in ta whit belangs here,
　　In parteeclar taech da young.
Why sood we no pride wirsells in
　　Whit wir faeders passed ta wis?
Why dan sood hit be abandoned?
　　Why sood we skjimp whit is wirs?
The Shetland Tongue, George P. S. Peterson.

Apart from fragments, the Norse literature that once was a living tradition in Shetland survives today only in *The Ballad of Hildina*, or *The Earl of Orkney, and the King of Norway's Daughter, a Ballad,* as it was called by George Low when he wrote it down in Foula in 1774. The first part of this ballad tells of how the Earl of Orkney abducts the Norwegian princess Hildina while her father is away. The King goes to Orkney to challenge him. Illugi, one of the King's men, thwarts an attempt at peace. The Earl is killed in the ensuing battle, and Illugi throws his severed head in Hildina's lap. In the second part of the ballad Hildina is forced to marry Illugi, whose name literally means 'of evil mind'. She takes her revenge by having him burned alive on their wedding day.

This ballad is unique and so is its history. It is known only from the garbled version taken down by a man who did not understand anything of what he was writing. The ballad is not historical in the sense that it describes a real event, but it is a poetic version of a theme that was known and used even in the Viking Age. Both the form and many of the expressions used throughout the ballad are part of a common Nordic tradition. It may not have been made in Shetland, as the ballads wandered, but the casting of the Earl of Orkney as the romantic lover does suggest a Shetland or Orkney origin.

In the original legend Hild is the daughter of King Hogne. She is abducted by Hedin, the King's foster brother. Her father finds them, and in the battle that follows both Hogne and Hedin are killed. The battle is without end because every night Hild wakes the dead. This legend appears first in the Anglo-Saxon poem 'Widsid' from the fifth century, and is also used in the German poem 'Kudrun'. It is mentioned by Earl Rognvald Kali Kolsson, the Orkney poet, in his Háttalykill, and by Snorri Sturluson in his Edda. In the older versions Hild incites strife and is merely a personification of battle—the Norse word for battle was *hildr*, and a frequently used kenning for battle was Hild's play. For later writers her motivation in waking the dead is the romantic desire to see her lover again. In the Hildina ballad the pagan, supernatural element has been removed altogether, and the character of Hildina has become fashioned to the ideals of the age of chivalry, when the ballad was probably made.

This tale of love and violence was part of a rich ballad tradition that has now been lost:

The great delight, however, of the ancient udaller's convivial hours was the recitation of Norwegian ballads. Shetland was ... from time immemorial, celebrated for its native poets ... Not longer ago than seventy years a number of popular historic ballads existed in Shetland ... (Samuel Hibbert, *A Description of the Shetland Islands*, 1822)

At one time Telemark, Agder and the western counties of Norway, together with Orkney, Shetland, Faroe and Iceland, formed one cultural area that had Bergen as a natural centre. For the study of Norse ballads it is sad that practically all of the Shetland tradition is gone, as the answers to many intriguing questions disappeared with it. The Shetland ballads and stories seem to have been closely related to Norwegian and Faroese tradition:

Most or all of their tales are relative to the history of Norway; they seem to know little of the rest of Europe but by names; Norwegian transactions they have at their fingers' ends. (George Low, *A Tour through Orkney and Schetland*, 1774)

About a century after George Low took down the Ballad of Hildina from William Henry in Guttorn, Dr Jakobsen was given a fragment of old verse at Lerabakk in Foula. This is the version taken down phonetically by Dr Jakobsen as well as the way it probably read in its original Norse form:

I have malt mældra min
Ek hef malit meldra minn
                      I have ground my morning-meal

I have supet usen
ek hef sópat húsin;
                      I have swept the floor;

ende seve de sede lin
enn á sefr at sæta lín,
                      still the old wife sleeps,

and dene komene lusa
ok dagrinn er kominn i ljós.
                      and the daylight is in the lum.

This is the story of the harassed husband who has to look after himself and the house while his wife sleeps on till late in the morning. In another fragment from the same song, also found by Jakobsen, the husband tries to force the hens to lay, and when he does not succeed, he starts swearing at the black hen: 'Idla jálsa swarta tap—be damned, black hen'. This is classical comic verse found in all Scandinavian countries. The oldest written version is included in a collection of Danish verse from the sixteenth century. The kenning *lín*, linen, for a woman is often used in Icelandic poetry, but otherwise this fragment is closest to the Faroese version.

For a long time Norn tradition existed as a subculture. The first school in Shetland was started at Walls in 1713 by the Society for the Propagation of Christian Knowledge. In 1872 the passing of the Education Act made school attendance compulsory. Education then became the way to success for everyone who wanted to get on in life. For the Shetland dialect and for local culture it was a two-edged sword, as school teachers tried to teach their pupils 'to speak proper' and avoid 'vulgar expressions'. Over the years Shetlanders became great readers, and according to library statistics more books are read per head of population in Shetland and Orkney than elsewhere.

The German writer Goethe said 'Every district loves its dialect; for it is, properly speaking, the element in which the soul draws its breath'. In the second half of the nineteenth century there was all over Europe a marked literary interest in the local region, its characteristics, traditions and language. Out of this interest grew a desire for a region to protect its culture from the influence of a growing urbanization and a centralized state. Any writer with this in mind will be faced with the dilemma of what medium to use, the dialect or the national language. While the dialect may be ideally suited to the subject and the mood, it does not reach beyond the region in question and thus defeats its own purpose. Very often it has no written standard form. This also describes the situation of the Shetland writers. Too often and too easily work by dialect writers is dismissed as local or regional writing and not taken seriously by the literary establishment.

The first Shetland writer of any note is George Stewart (1825–1911) of Levenwick, who started out as a teacher in Dunrossness and ended up as an immigrant farmer in British Columbia. In 1877 he published his collection of stories, ballads and lore as *Shetland Fireside Tales* in Edinburgh. In his ballads he takes up the old tradition of using song as a record of local events:

Every event seeming to have any significance in the eyes of the people—as a shipwreck, storm, haaf incident, peculiar custom, noted people, heavy snowfall, appearance of big schools of whales, a house on fire, and the rest— was made the subject of a 'rhyme' or 'ballant', the 'makkar' or rhymester usually wandering from house to house reciting his 'story'. As most folk had retentive memories, the ballads and tales were 'minded upon' and recited around the firesides during the long evenings, or outside at some work where a lot of folk were gathered, as on a fish beach, in a haaf lodge, at a sheep-kru. (P. A. Jamieson, *Letters on Shetland*, 1949)

As often as not the stories would change in the telling, when something was added or taken away. Today most of the ballads and tales are forgotten as they were not written down. Thus Stewart was the first local rhymester to have his work presented in a literary form.

Much of the Fireside Tales is written in Stewart's own childhood dialect. His book became very popular because it seemed genuine and true to life. It helped rouse Dr Jakobsen's interest in Norn:

Thomas Edmondston's Glossary and 'Shetland Fireside Tales', which is written partly in the Shetland dialect, formed the basis of my knowledge of Shetlandic, when ... I set out in the early summer of 1893, ... for the first time to Shetland, to investigate what might be left of the old language locally known as Norn. (*An Etymological Dictionary of the Norn Language in Shetland*, London 1932)

The best known Shetland writer is probably James John Haldane Burgess (1862–1927), who wrote both in English and Shetlandic. He became blind while he was a student at Edinburgh University, but he completed his exams orally. He was a gifted linguist, who also mastered Norse, which became a lifelong interest. He impressed people in Norway by writing articles in journals there in a fluent, self-taught Norwegian. Of his numerous books, the novel *The Viking Path—A Tale of the White Christ* (1894) is the best known. The story takes place in Shetland and in Norway in the time of transition from pagan to Christian belief. Burgess knew his subject well, and the novel was well received and even translated into German as *Der Vikinger Pfad*. It is written in a heroic style in a high-flowing English rather far from the terse style of the sagas, and its characters do not come alive. Yet it appealed to the literary taste of his time; in 1908 a German scholar even used Burgess and his work for a doctoral thesis called, *J. J. Haldane Burgess, ein Schetlanddichter*.

Today Burgess is remembered mainly for the work he did in the Shetland dialect. The most popular of his books is *Rasmie's Büddie*, a collection of dialect poems about an island character called Rasmie. The poem *Scranna* describes Rasmie's conflict with the Devil—a conflict where Rasmie is the winner. He is sitting quietly in front of his fire when the Devil appears, dressed as a clergyman, and tries to tempt him with friendliness, drink and the prospect of worldly success, but Rasmie is not taken in by him, he remains the dour, down-to-earth Shetlander. It is possible to see this poem as an allegory of Shetland life and history:

Rasmie is the old Shetlander of perpetual possession, the udaller of Norse heritage, poor and now also 'old and careworn', after the centuries of oppression. And the Devil, being a clear case of 'a wolf in sheep's clothing' is exactly what he is depicted as: the gentleman oppressor from the south, who cannot coerce or trick the native Shetlander to sell his soul for anything he has to offer, and so is bound to lose the fight. (Lauritz Rendboe, *The Shetland Literary Tradition*, Odense University 1985)

There is such an amazing number of dialect writers belonging to this golden age of Shetland literature. Although they are not all equally readable or interesting today, the overall quality is impressive. One whose work is still read is Basil Ramsay Anderson (1861–88). His poetry is made poignant by the story of his life, as in *Nicht-fa'* :

> The nicht is gatherin' dark, mither,
> I'm gaun—they ca' it 'hame';
> But dinna, dinna greet, mither,
> Lest I should Heaven blame.

Anderson was born in Unst. His father drowned at the haf when he was 5, leaving Basil's mother to cope with a family of small children. Finding it difficult to express his ideas in English, Anderson wrote his best poetry in Shetlandic. Though he could write humorously, his work was also influenced by his interest in politics and his deep religious conviction. But he was only 26 when he died and had not had the chance to develop his talent fully. Both Anderson and his brother got the kind of tuberculosis that used to be known as 'decline' and died within three months of each other.

Anderson uses imagery taken from crofting life to express his faith:

> Da Lord len me His Heevenly staff
> Till Christ sall lift my kishie aff.

His great dialect poem *Auld Maunsie's Crö* also takes its subject from crofting, and is widely considered to be the finest poem yet written in Shetlandic. As well as being free of sentimentality and moralizing it is very well structured. It tells the story of the crofter Maunsie who builds himself a crö to grow kail in. Through this work we learn about the life in the surrounding community: the fishermen in the sixern who use Maunsie's crö as a 'meed' and the people working the fields. Anderson sees his subject in widening circles, and from a day in a crofting community he goes on to describe the cycle of the year and the new generations, who had 'mair ta dö/Dan mind Auld Maunsie or his crö.'

Anderson's poems and reminiscences appeared after his death in a small volume called *Broken Lights*. It was edited by another Shetland writer, Jessie Saxby (1842–1940). She belonged to the gifted Edmondston family of Unst, and throughout her long life she remained passionately interested in everything connected with her native islands.

She is a prolific writer who over the years produced some 30 volumes of stories and poems written in English. But she also collected rhymes, folklore and described old customs, and today she is remembered for her facts and not for her fiction.

The glossary of Anderson's poems was prepared by Gilbert Goudie, another well-known Shetlander of the time. A banker by profession, he took a keen interest in all aspects of early Shetland history. His book *The Celtic and Scandinavian Antiquities of Shetland* was published in 1904 and has become a reference work. With the Icelander Jón A. Hjaltalin he translated the first English version of the *Orkneyinga Saga*.

Still another legendary historian and folklorist is Lawrence Williamson of Gardie in Mid-Yell. All his life he took an interest in the place-names, dialects, history, genealogy and general culture of Shetland. He generously gave the language material he had collected to Dr Jakobsen, who considered his help outstanding.

L. Williamson, who regards his native isles, their memories, and old traditions with deep affection, is a man of a strongly marked, scientific cast of mind, ... and had, long before I made his acquaintance, constructed for himself a phonetic alphabet for use in connection with his linguistic notes. (*An Etymological Dictionary of the Norn Language in Shetland*)

Williamson knew more than anybody else about Shetland's old culture, and his home at Gardie was sought by all those who shared his interests and wanted to learn more.

The first Shetland newspaper was called *The Shetland Journal* and appeared in June 1836. It was started by Arthur Anderson, who became wealthy through his shipping activities. He intended to have the paper printed in Shetland, but this proved impractical, and the paper was published in Fleet Street and sent back to Shetland. At first 500 copies were printed but the circulation soon increased to 2000, as it sold very well. The paper took a Liberal view and discussed the social issues of the period. It also contained much practical information and advice: the fishermen, for instance, had a regular feature called 'Fishermen's Neuk' where they were told of new fishing trends. Yet the paper's continual problem was one of communication; it became increasingly difficult to comment on current events in Shetland for a staff working in London. In 1838 the scope of the paper was enlarged when it was changed into *The Orkney and Shetland Journal*. However, just when it showed promise of becoming an important medium for the Northern Isles, the paper folded through extraneous difficulties.

The first paper to be printed in Shetland was *Shetland Advertiser*, which was started by Charles D. Jamieson in 1862 and lasted only 18 months, having developed a reputation for its outspokenness. In 1872 came *The Shetland Times*, which voiced Liberal views. This weekly paper has survived changing fortunes and today has the market to

Thursday 4 pm, checking the first copy off the press, editor Jonathan Wills, with printers Hamish Cutt and Donnie Johnson. The Shetland Times has a circulation of more than 10,000.

itself, with a circulation of more than 10,000 copies. According to the Orkney writer Eric Linklater there is no local newspaper in Britain that shows 'a more realistic, intelligent, and comprehensive awareness of the problems of its own environment'. It has lately brightened its editorial image, and remains an important factor in Shetland life. For some time there was a rival newspaper known as *Shetland News*; this appeared in 1885, at first championing the Conservative cause but later switching to the Liberal Unionists, and was published until 1963.

The Shetland News was run by the Manson family, who have for a long time been prominent in Shetland's cultural life. An annual publication eagerly looked forward to was *Manson's Shetland Almanac*, which was a record of events as well as lore and is now an important historical source. It was also a local directory. Some large projects were undertaken by Thomas Manson while he was editor of *The Shetland News: Shetland's Roll of Honour and Roll of Service* was a presentation of the 3600 men who fought in the First World War and survived and especially of the 600 who had died. This was followed by *Lerwick During the Last Half Century* and *Humours of a Peat Commission*, which were both written by Thomas Manson. These works were first serialized in the paper and later published in book form. Today these works fetch fantastic prices at auctions.

In the 1920s a group of men with left-wing views, calling themselves the Economics Club, tried to publish a magazine called *The Shetlander*; this only had a short-lived career of a year. After the Second World War the writer Peter A. Jamieson (1898–1976) took up the idea from the earlier magazine and started publishing *The New Shetlander* on a shoestring in 1947. His aim was to create a forum for the Shetland cultural heritage. The magazine was strongly political, but was open to all views. Of course, making it pay was always a problem: it started out as a monthly magazine, then became bi-monthly and now has four issues a year. During the oil construction period it sold some 3000 copies a year. In 1956 John and Laurence Graham took over as joint editors. The magazine remains an interesting commentary on political and cultural issues, and it is also a stronghold of Shetlandic. Over the years numerous dialect writers have found an outlet in the pages of *The New Shetlander*.

In 1980 a monthly magazine called *Shetland Life* was launched by The Shetland Times, with James R. Nicolson, a well-known non-fiction writer as editor. Its declared purpose is to discuss in detail the more important issues in the islands, and also to record tradition and lore that is in danger of being lost. Still another important publication is the *Shetland Folk-Book*, which is issued by the Shetland Folk Society. Although preserving the old culture has been the main object of the seven volumes published till now, modern verse and stories are also included.

One of the most committed members of the Folk Society ever since it was formed in 1945 was T. A. Robertson (1909–73). He signed all his poems as Vagaland, and it is by this name that he has become perhaps the best loved of all modern poets in Shetland. He was born in Westerwick near Skeld, but lived in other parts of the west side as well. He identified with Walls and therefore used the name Vagaland for that district. His poetry is simple and direct and often has some of the quality of the historical ballad. Although he had an MA degree from the University of Edinburgh and wrote poetry in English too, he considered Shetlandic his mother tongue. His poem *Tuslag* was included in *The Oxford Book of Scottish Verse*. He had a natural gift for expressing himself in a lyrical poetry that also reveals his attitude to life and people:

> ... naethin sall staand at Ragnarök,
> Whin da seevent whirlwind blaas,
> Bit da kindness an love in human herts ...

Among the poets popular today are Stella Sutherland and Rhoda Bulter, who both write in Shetlandic. Stella Sutherland, who lives in

Bressay, published *Aa My Selves* in 1980. She is able to write with feeling without becoming sentimental. Rhoda Bulter has published a number of books. She makes a strong impact by giving words a new and unexpected meaning, but simultaneously her verse seems as natural as breathing.

Spontaneity is the essence of all her writing. It bubbles and effervesces whether in personal recollection, both grave and gay, in vivid description, or in sheer fantasy. She uses the dialect in all its colloquia! richness and with a vigour and exuberance ... (John J. Graham in *Link-Stanes*, 1980)

The young poet and novelist Robert Alan Jamieson has published two novels in as many years: *Soor Hearts* in 1985 and *Thin Wealth* in 1986. He breaks new ground both by writing Shetland novels, the first to appear for a long time, and using the impact of oil on the people

The young Shetland poet and novelist Robert Alan Jamieson.

as a theme. He solves the question of language by using English with the odd dialect word. A modified Shetlandic which is understandable also for readers with no previous knowledge of it, is used in the dialogue—a realistic method for a writer who wants to reach further than the local readership.

Thin Wealth reflects the many different attitudes to the coming of oil, and is in many ways a social documentary on a decade in Shetland history, with the question 'Tinks du it will ever be da same again?' as its main theme. There are shrewd observations sometimes presented with low-key irony. Jamieson uses vivid modern images, occasionally bordering on the obvious but nevertheless always meaningful; for example, he sees the oil rig off the coast as 'that giant wading bird, boring and sucking with its beak beneath the ocean, a modern day sea monster ducking and hiding, out of slingshot on the edge of the visible ocean'. Although marred by a melodramatic ending, this is an exciting novel, difficult to put down for one who wants to learn more about the mystery that is Shetland.

In the same way that Chris in Lewis Grassic Gibbon's *Sunset Song* can be seen as a personification of her native Scotland, Linda, the main character in *Thin Wealth*, is perhaps symbolic of Shetland. 'She carries with her the buried memories of a troubled past, is caught up and loses her way in the turmoil of the oil boom, strikes back and eventually ... finds her true self through a new insight into her traditional past.' (John J. Graham in *The New Shetlander*, Voar 1986)

Literary life in Shetland today has an amazingly broad base. There are many good writers and much debate. Some excellent poetry has been written by dialect writers who have avoided the pitfalls of false sentiment better than earlier writers. Perhaps there has at times been an unfortunate tendency to use the dialect for a rather primitive situation comedy. And so far there has not been a Lewis Grassic Gibbon or a J. M. Synge to portray the Shetland psyche—the definitive Shetland novel or play has not yet appeared. But who knows, it may come any time! This is the advice given by the poet William J. Tait to his fellow writers:

> Oh Shetlan poets, *fin* your tred! Poo ower your een
> Nae mair ooey blankets ...
> An write.
> Write wis up; write wis doon; write wis aff; bit for Goad's
>   sake write
> As if you meant it. Mean it. An good luck!

Local radio

Since it first went on the air in May 1977, Radio Shetland has been an important cultural factor. Its programme 'Good Evening Shetland' has become very popular and has a high listener frequence. It can also be heard quite clearly in Faroe. Broadcasts go out every winter evening between 5.30 and 7.30 pm, with a short break for news from Radio Scotland at 6 o'clock. Broadcasts are shorter in the summer. With a staff of four to do everything it is pretty hectic at times, and all lend a hand. Among the most popular programmes are the conversations in broad dialect between the two women characters Tamar and Beenie, as enacted by Mary Blance and Rhoda Bulter. Much of their talk is improvised as they go along, and this makes it spontaneous and often very funny. Rhoda Bulter is sometimes responsible for the useful calendar of events known as 'What's On'. In her own special way she parodies herself in this role:

Dill be a disco held in Shuknaskoard fae 10 a'clock da night,
Wi music by da Whitterits an dir guest star Sheena Bright,
An da WRI in Havera meets da night at half past eight,
Da competition is a bag a neeps, an you hae ta guess da weight.
An dir a Sale o Wark in Hascosay in aid o moorit rams,
Bit you'll no win in wi high-heeled shön or if you're takkin drams;

Poet Rhoda Bulter, as Beenie, one of the characters in a very funny and popular programme on Radio Shetland.

The lovely old Kergord Mill in Weisdale has been purchased by the Shetland Arts Trust to provide an arts and crafts centre and exhibition area.

It oppens at seeven a'clock da night or mebbe a start afore,
Admission is onnly 50 pence an payable at da door.
(From *Whit's on' an 'Da Wadder*, Shetland Life 1982)

It was felt for a long time that with all the archaeological and historical finds made in Shetland, a museum was sorely needed to house them. Things came to a head when The St Ninian's Isle Treasure and the Gunnister Man also went 'oot da sooth mooth' to Edinburgh. Somehow the funds were found to build Shetland Museum. Within three years the museum was out of space and items offered have had to be refused. Although it is small, Shetland Museum has had to function as a regional museum. It therefore cannot specialize but must cope with archaeology, local history, maritime artefacts, local crafts like knitting and natural history combined.

Shetland Museum is also responsible for running the very popular Croft House Museum at Boddam in Dunrossness. This shows what a Shetland croft would have been like about a century ago. More of the old farming life can be seen at the privately owned Tingwall Agricultural Museum, which was opened in 1975. Its main collection of old crofting implements is housed in the old granary of the eighteenth-century Veensgarth Farm. There is also a replica of an old-style bedroom installed in the bothy.

To take care of a variety of cultural tasks, Shetland Amenity Trust was set up in 1983. Since then it has been involved in a great number of different projects in several parts of Shetland. The two main objectives of the Trust are to help preserve anything of historical interest in Shetland and to improve the countryside. They have made a 'Bruck an Muck' squad clear away rubbish from roadsides and beaches, remove eyesores and derelict cars. They have made the Old Haa in Burravoe in Yell into a lovely little museum, appointed a fulltime archaeologist for Shetland, carried out a feasibility study for a new museum and restored the Bød o Gremista, to mention only a few of their projects.

The Shetland Arts Trust was established in 1985 to assist and encourage artistic and creative talent. With this in mind, the Trust has purchased the old Kergord Mill in Weisdale to provide an arts and crafts centre and exhibition area. This will give Shetland artists and craftsmen a welcome opportunity to show their work.

13 MUSIC

Shetlanders are much addicted to fiddling. Formerly there were large numbers of fiddlers in every parish. . . . No wonder that tunes are so abundant. Several of them are fairy tunes, and are likely very old; many are of Norse origin and many Scotch. (L. G. Johnson, *Lawrence Williamson of Mid-Yell*, 1971)

Shetland has an old distinctive culture in music, and is a centre as rich as any in Europe for traditional music. To some it may seem surprising that such a rich music tradition and interest should be found in a remote place like Shetland. Yet cultural impulses wander, and Shetland was never remote in this sense; indeed the islands were placed at a musical crossroads of the world. No living music is isolated. In our century the radio has brought all kinds of music to Shetland and made American music especially popular. The construction period in the oil boom brought in not only workers but also the artists to entertain them, and lately the Russian trawler crews have added to the cosmopolitan character of the islands. The Shetland music is gay and vital, and it goes from strength to strength as it assimilates further strains, the way any living tradition does.

Few traditional songs have survived. A fragment in Norn known as *The Unst Boat Song* goes a long way back and was once part of a long song. The following text offers a tantalizing glimpse of a period when the old epic ballads were still known and sung:

There is one species of dance which seems peculiar to themselves, in which they do not proceed from one end of the floor to the other in a figure, nor is it after the manner of a Scotch reel; but a dozen or so form themselves into a circle, and taking each other by the hand, perform a sort of circular dance, one of the company all the while singing a Norn Visick. This was formerly their only dance, but has now almost given entire way to the reel. (George Low, *A Tour Through the Islands of Orkney and Schetland in 1774*, p163)

Once the dancing style described here by George Low was common throughout Europe. Woodcuts and drawings of the late medieval period show dancers moving round in a circle with their arms linked. The ring of dancers would sing ballads of love and war set in a distant, heroic age. Sometimes a male singer would present the ballad, with the dancers singing a refrain. This ring-dancing still survives in Faroe.

In the old days what appears to be an ancient ceremonial dance was performed by male dancers at local weddings. It survived longer in Papa Stour than anywhere else, and was taken down in writing in 1788. Samuel Hibbert saw it performed there in the early nineteenth century:

The fiddle strikes up a Norn melody, and at the sound of it a warrior enters in the character of St. George, or the master of the Seven Champions of Christendom, a white hempen shirt being thrown over his clothes, intended to represent the ancient shirt of mail that the Northmen wore, and a formidable sword girt to his side, constructed from the iron hoop of a barrel. St. George then stalks forward and makes his bow, the music ceasing while he delivers his epilogue. (*Description of the Shetland Islands*, 1822, p556)

The seven dancers represent the 'Champions of Christendom': St George of England, St James of Spain, St Denis of France, St David of Wales, St Patrick of Ireland, St Anthony of Italy and St Andrew of Scotland. They wear coloured sashes in their national colours; St

The Papa Stour Sword Dance.

George as their leader also wears a blue ribbon. They are accompanied by a fiddler who plays the old Shetland tune 'The Day-Dawn' as the first dancer enters. Each dancer performs in turn while St George sings his praise in verse. Then they all join in a circle and the real dance begins, where the swords are used to make up star- or rose-shaped figures.

The Papa Stour Sword Dance must surely be quite unique in the way it has grafted the characters of a Pre-Reformation romance by the English writer Richard Johnson onto a ceremonial dance whose original theme was death in battle. The sword dance seems to have been very popular in the Middle Ages and it was known all over Europe in different variations. In order to make room for all the saints the Papa Stour version has added a seventh dancer to the original six. The sword dance was first described in Brugge in Belgium in 1389 and then again by the historian Olaus Magnus in Sweden in 1555.

Dancing remained popular, especially at Yule when the young people would meet in the roomiest house in the neighbourhood and dance till midnight. Not even the religious revival of the 1840s could quite quell this love of dancing, and it is still the custom for both young and old guests at weddings to dance until morning, sometimes for three nights running.

The instrument mostly used at weddings and dances has traditionally been the fiddle. Early sources also mention another instrument called a gjü or gue:

... among the peasantry almost one in ten can play on the violin. There are still a few native airs to be met with in some parts of the country, which may be considered as peculiar, and very much resemble the wild and plaintive strains of the Norwegian music. Before violins were introduced, the musicians performed on an instrument called a *gue*, which appears to have had some similarity to a violin, but had only two strings of horse hair, and was played upon in the same manner as a violoncello. (Edmondston, *A View of the Zetland Islands*, Vol II, pp59–60)

This instrument was probably the same as the Norse *gígja*. In the Didrik Saga from the thirteenth century one of the characters boasts that besides reciting poetry he can play the harp, the fiddle, the gígja and all kinds of string instruments. It is interesting to note that in modern German the fiddle is still known as *Geige*.

Traditional music still alive in Shetland largely consists of fiddle tunes. Some of these go a long way back, and were handed down by ear directly from father to son, for many generations. Fiddle playing seems to have been a male interest; the men would play while the women knitted. The talent naturally ran in families, and many of the old springs and reels were made up in these musical families. Their tunes soon became known all over Shetland and were integrated into the social life of the community.

Each district had its own distinguished families or individual fiddlers to entertain at social gatherings. There was 'Da Fiddler o' Flamister' in South Nesting with his seven fiddle-playing sons. Fredamann Stickle, known as 'Freddie da Fiddler', was a German sailor who was stranded in Unst with only his fiddle and the clothes he stood up in. He became legendary for his music and is still known for his 'Stumpie's reel'. There was Laurence Peterson of Vidlin, known as Lowrie o' da Lee. The island of Whalsay in particular has long been famous for its fiddlers.

Still the names of the men who made the music are often forgotten while the pieces they created have become community property. As the music has depended upon memory it has probably been reshaped through the years as generations of fiddlers added their own variations. Despite these changes it is true to say that Shetland fiddle music has a basic style which is molded by tradition. To the untrained ear Shetland fiddle music sounds very 'busy'. This effect is explained by the way it is played:

The technique of playing Shetland fiddle music is quite distinctive, and follows more the style of the Hardanger fiddle than either Scottish or Irish, although there are some similarities with the latter. The playing of two or more strings at one time with open strings ringing, and 1 down and 3 up bowing, accented notes and 'lang draws' on the back strings, and grace notes and turns as ornamentation give the music a special sound. In some melodies the tuning is altered to AEAE or ADAE. (Anderson/Swing, *Haand me doon da Fiddle*, 1979)

An old saying has it that it takes two wizards to produce fiddle music: the fiddle-maker and the fiddler. This may be ideally true, but the simple variant of the fiddle was within everybody's means, and there was a fiddle hanging on the wall in most crofts. The ministers obviously felt threatened by this interest in music and tried to suppress it—one minister was even known to have smashed all the fiddles he could lay his hand on. To the serious-minded this love of music often seemed like fecklessness. As one story goes a very upright teacher in Out Skerries was going to propose to a young woman. He called one evening after school at her father's croft and found the whole family busy unloading a boat load of peats from Whalsay. But the young woman was not helping, she was inside the house dancing to fiddle music. He never even went inside the house as he realized then and there that she was not suitable for a poor man's wife, and gave up the idea of marrying her.

One of the reasons why the Church frowned on the fiddle music may be that it was so closely linked to Shetland folklore, which to incomers would be known as 'superstitions'. Many of the old springs were said to be trow-inspired. In Norwegian folklore the music played by the njuggle would throw a dangerous spell on those listening to it.

The trolls, on the other hand, gave no sign of being interested in music, and therefore differed from their Shetland cousins the trows, who were passionate music lovers. They would go to great lengths to entice a fiddler into their hill to have him play to them. In return for this he would learn new and striking tunes. In fact most of the earliest Shetland fiddle tunes were said to be inspired by the trows.

Among the best-known trow tunes are *Hyltadance* and *Winyadepla* from Fetlar. Of these the Hyltadance is the oldest. It is some 350 years old and one of the oldest tunes in Shetland. The farmer of Colbinstoft heard the trows singing and dancing while he was trying to fish from the craigs below Busta Hill. Much later, in 1803, Gibbie Laurenson from the croft of Norderhus in Gruting set out with his mare and a load of corn that he wanted to grind at the water mill in Virva. While he was at the mill the trows came in and danced the night away. When Gibbie came home, he whistled a tune he had heard them play. His son called it 'Fader's Tøn' and often played it on the fiddle. Later it was named after the lovely Loch of Winyadepla.

Unfortunately people do not seem to see or hear the trows any more, so this source of inspiration has quite dried out. This has not stopped the Shetland fiddle music in going from strength to strength. So much of what the Shetlanders heard abroad was adapted and given a Shetland twist. They would take their fiddles with them even on the whalers, and there is said to be a strain of Eskimo music as well, as Shetlanders would meet 'da Yakks', as they called them, in Greenland or the Davis Straits. The whaling is still remembered in a well-known reel called 'Da Merry Boys o' Greenland':

Da news is spreadin trowe da toon:
A ship is lyin in Bressa Soond.
Tell da boys sho's nortward boond
Ta hunt da whale in Greenland.
(Lyrics by B. Tulloch of Mid Yell)

Up aloft an set da sail,
Hingin on wi teeth an nail;
We're goin nort ta hunt da whale
Da Merry Boys o' Greenland.

The strong position of musical traditions in Shetland today may be due to their many outstanding musicians. Among these are Tom Anderson, Aly Bain, Willie Hunter and Debbie Scott who are all fiddlers, and Willie Johnson, a guitarist. Tom Anderson from Eshaness is the grand old man of Shetland music. He was awarded the M.B.E. in 1977 and has also been given an honorary doctorate at the University of Stirling in acknowledgement of his work for traditional fiddle music.

As part of the Hamefarin festivities in 1960 Tom Anderson gathered together some fiddlers to play traditional music. This group became The Shetland Fiddlers Society. Some time afterwards they played to the Queen on her visit to Shetland, and were described in the national press by Magnus Magnusson, who was then a reporter, as 'the forty frenzied fiddlers'. They have popularly been known as 'Da Forty

Fiddlers' since. The Shetland Fiddlers Society is now a celebrated group dedicated to performing Shetland music. Their weekly practice sessions at Isleburgh Community Centre in Lerwick are a tourist attraction, and in order to promote Shetland knitwear they often perform wearing pullovers in a Fair Isle type of pattern. At least three members of the society descend from Fredamann Stickle, the Unst fiddler.

The two young musicians Kenny Johnson and Debbie Scott, of Papa Stour, also make and repair string instruments. They have started their own business called Shetland Luthiers. In 1986 their firm won a prize in the Scottish final of the Livewire competition which was set up to encourage young business ideas.

A musical event that seems to have come to stay is the folk music festival which is held every year in May. There were those who had long felt that with the enthusiasm of the local people for so many kinds of music and because of their long traditions and rich heritage, Shetland should have its own folk festival. The idea was well received, and the first festival was staged in 1981. The idea was to make it as much as possible a festival by the people and for the people of Shetland. Therefore the events were spread to community halls all over the islands, and local organisers were brought into the work. It quickly became clear that the festival had to be an annual event, and some 400 people are now involved every year in trying to make it a success.

Visitors to the festival have come from far and near, and all kinds of music have been played: traditional, folk-rock, bluegrass, music for Irish, Scottish, Norwegian and Morris dancing, as well as contemporary and neo-classical music, so as to suit many different kinds of tastes. Folk music groups and artists are brought in, but they are outnumbered by the local performers. They play to audiences of both young and old where the majority are local people with a great capacity for enjoyment, willing to stay up all night if need be to listen to the music.

Debbie Scott, one of Shetland's outstanding young fiddlers, in her workshop, 'Shetland Luthiers'.

14 FISHING

No life is, in my opinion, more arduous than that of a fisherman, and particularly of a fisherman in Shetland. (*Journal of Edward Charlton*, M.D., 1832)

The North Sea is one of the most important fishing waters in the world. Shetland is strategically placed where this sea joins the Atlantic ocean, and the islands lie on a shallow shelf where the feeding conditions are exceptionally good for many species, including cod, haddock, whiting, ling, mackerel, and herring, as well as shellfish. Shetland,

The Bød at Symbister, Whalsay. Commercial fishing in Shetland began with the Hanseatic merchants. They would arrive in the spring and open their 'bøds', or booths.

therefore, has long been a centre of the European fishing world, with many nations competing for the fish around her coasts.

With nautical skill handed down through the centuries, Shetlanders are natural sailors and fishermen. Their prowess was perhaps acquired as much through necessity as from inclination, as fishing in Shetland waters was not always plain sailing or fair dealing; too many saw its possibilities for exploitation. Only recently have the social and economic conditions in the islands allowed the Shetlanders some initiative in their own fishing, although politically the going is still rough at times.

Commercial fishing in Shetland began with the Hanseatic merchants, whose period of power and prosperity stretched through the fourteenth and fifteenth centuries. The sale of fish was initially channelled through the Hanseatic 'kontor' in Bergen. Later, merchants went to Shetland to deal direct with the fishermen, who received fishing tools as well as luxury goods like tobacco and alcohol in exchange for their fish. Although most of the trade was done by barter, money was then brought into the islands, enabling the people to pay their rents in cash. The merchants, who evidently were not all German, would arrive in the spring and open their 'bøds', or booths:

... the merchandis of Holland, Zeland and Almanic cumis yierlie to Schetland to interchange uither merchandyis with the peple thairof ... (H. Boece, *The History and Chronicles of Scotland*, Vol. I, p81, Glasgow 1827)

The merchants grew in number and importance; thus Sandwick Bay was called Hambourgh Haven or Bremerhaven on contemporary maps. In the old Lund churchyard in Unst two slabs, from 1573 and 1585, commemorate Bremen merchants who died while in Shetland for the summer. When translated from Low German one inscription reads as follows:

In the year 1585 on the 25th July, being St. James's day, the worthy and well-born Hinrick Segelcken the elder, from Germany and a burgess of the town of Bremen, fell asleep here in God the Lord. May God be gracious to him.

The fish sold to the Hanseatic merchants came from inshore fishing, as can be seen from the location of the old trading places. The trade was important to the islanders who with luck might rise above the subsistence living they could otherwise scrape from their crofts. However, the salt tax of 1712 and, more especially, the customs duties imposed after the Union of Parliaments between England and Scotland in 1707 made foreign trading impossible. Attempts had been made before to curtail the activity of the foreign merchants, but the islanders' pleas on their behalf made the authorities relent 'seeing traffecting with forraners is the only meane of their lyvelyhood'. (Reg. Privy Co., Scotland, Vol. I, p182)

Since the Shetland economy had come to depend on the trade in fish, the foreign merchants left a vacuum that had to be filled. It was mainly the local landowners who stepped into the breach, in order to protect their interests and get cash rents from their tenants. As the traditional outlets were closed to them, the landowners and their agents had to break into new markets, and this was difficult with no experience. However, by the 1730s an important market was found for dried salt fish in the Mediterranean area, especially Spain, and as this market grew so too did the Shetland fishery. Later much of the trade went to London.

Climatic changes seem at the same time to have made the fish move further out to sea than before. In the fishing grounds at the edge of the continental shelf good catches of cod as well as ling could be had. This is why the deep sea fisheries, which dominated life in the islands for more than 150 years, came to be known as the háf fishing, háf being the Norn word for ocean. Háf fishing has become legendary, viewed today in a heroic light. The men rowed to the fishing grounds in six-man open boats called sixerns. Until the 1840s these boats were brought from Norway in pieces ready to be put together. They were clinker built, of $5\frac{1}{2}$ m (18 ft) keel and $2\frac{1}{2}$ m (8 ft) beam, about 9 m (30 ft) in overall length, and had square sails that could be used only for certain wind conditions. They were little fitted to weather a severe storm.

Buoyant as corks in a seaway, they are very tender at first, though stiff enough when down to their bearings. The sail used is a dipping lug, hoisted on a mast stepped nearly amidships, and occasionally you may see a small jib or foresail set as well. They pull six oars double banked, and use one thole-pin, called a *kabe*, and a *humlabund*.... The names of every article of a boat's equipment, and most of the terms used in the navigation or management of it, are of pure Norse derivation. (John R. Tudor, *The Orkneys and Shetland*, London, 1883, p132)

So as to be near the fishing grounds, háf fishing stations were built at outlying points, such as Norwick in Unst, Funzie in Fetlar, Gloup in North Yell, Out Skerries, Grif Skerry, and Fethaland in Northmaven. Every station was close to a stony beach where the boats could be pulled up at the onset of bad weather. Primitive huts amid the fish offal were the men's quarters. The fishing season lasted from the middle of May till the middle of August, and for that period the men were bound by contract to their landlord.

Each boat had from 7 to 8 miles (11–13 km) of line with some 1000 baited hooks. The lines would be set in the evening but sometimes set again if the first haul was unsuccessful. The men usually made two trips a week, sometimes staying out two nights at a time, if the weather was fine. They then had to go practically without sleep on a diet of oat-cakes and water. It was a hard life. Anxious not to lose their fishing lines, which sometimes were all they owned, they often took foolhardy chances in bad weather rather than cut their lines and head back. Many a crew, thus leaving it too late to return when the gale increased, were drowned near land. The men often came from one family and this made the loss even harder to bear for those who were left behind.

The new merchant-lairds might have the fish trade thrust at them but they soon learned how to make the best of it. At the peak of the háf fishing in the early nineteenth century, around 2500 tons of white fish were caught each year. The lairds realized that the sea was more valuable than the land. In order to make room for more people, the crofts were divided into smaller and smaller units, so that fishing for a living became the only way of making ends meet. The fishermen sold the fish to the lairds at prices stipulated by the latter, and were then free to spend the money thus earned in shops run by the same lairds. This came to be known as the truck system, and it was an economic dependence approaching slavery. There was no escape from it: if a fisherman's son went whaling in the summer, his family had to pay a fine to the landlord. Most families were hopelessly in debt. This state of affairs was strongly criticized by Christian Pløyen, the Danish government representative in Faroe, when he visited Shetland in 1839:

From this wretched state of dependence, from which the Shetlanders are unable to extricate themselves, it follows that as a body they are poor, often miserably so; whilst the landlords live in luxury, and the whole profit of the skill and industry with which the fishing is carried on falls to the rich, the toil and danger to the poor. (*Reminiscences of a Voyage to Shetland, Orkney & Scotland in the Summer of 1839*. Transl. Catherine Spence, Lerwick 1894)

The fishing ground off Fethaland lay about 30 to 35 miles (48 to 56 km) north-west of the station. On the east side they often had to go even further than that to reach the 'háf'. The sixerns were vulnerable so far out at sea, as was proved in 'da grit gale' of July 1832, when 17 boats and 105 men were lost. More were at first missing, but the Dutch herring 'busses' fishing off the east coast saved several crews. One crew was saved by a boat bound for America and did not come home till the following January; another sixern was driven to Norway. In 1881, once again in July, a short but severe storm struck the northern fishing grounds. The men cut their lines and ran for the coast, but ten boats with 58 men did not make it back to their stations. It was called the Gloup Disaster because most of them came from there. The háf fishing was never the same afterwards—the days of the open boats were over. The Crofters' Act of 1886 also broke the sway of the lairds.

Advent of the smacks

The more resourceful of the lairds as well as a small group of merchants with capital made during the Napoleonic Wars, realized the limitations of the háf fishing as early as at the beginning of the nineteenth century. They invested in decked sloops in sizes up to 35 tons. Some of the boats were also owned by the fishermen who manned them. There were those who had escaped the crushing poverty by whaling near Greenland or by serving in the Royal Navy and getting prize money in the war. In the 1820s the government encouraged the use of larger boats by giving a tonnage bounty for vessels over 20 tons. The fleet of sail-powered fishing vessels, known as smacks, grew.

The crews of the sixerns set their lines on the bottom of the sea and thereby failed to catch the shoals of cod that sometimes swam between the sea bed and the surface; by using hand-lines that could be regulated to any depth the smack fishermen therefore had a different range. By chance, a rich cod-bank was discovered south-west of Shetland, off Foula. For most of the nineteenth century this was the main fishing bank for the smacks; it was spoken of as the Home Cod Grounds. But the main advantage of the smacks was that they could go so much further out than the sixerns; indeed as time went on they ventured further and further, as far as Faroe and Iceland, even to the Davis Straits and North Cape of Norway. When the trips became longer it was necessary to clean and salt the fish on board so that it would be ready for drying on coming back to Shetland.

As time went on a pattern became established for the cod fisheries. Little or no fishing was done in the winter months apart from the occasional trip in good weather to the home grounds. At the beginning of April most of the large smacks would set out for the Faroe bank south-west of Suðuroy, where they nearly always found fish at that time of year. A second trip to Faroe was made in the summer, but if the fishing failed there, they went to Rockall instead. The largest boats would do their autumn fishing off the north coast of Iceland.

Large companies grew up in the wake of the cod fisheries; among them Hay & Co. in Lerwick and Nicolson & Co. in Scalloway were perhaps the best known. The smacks needed deeper harbours in the lee of the wind, preferably on the west side to be closer to the banks. Places like Scalloway and Voe therefore prospered in the nineteenth century. This was also because the cod fishermen worked at the fishing all year round and were not bound by a croft, but could settle where they found it convenient. Thus the old Shetland pattern of a combined crofting and fishing was broken.

On his visit to Shetland in 1839 Christian Pløyen was greatly impressed by the intense activity connected with the fishing he witnessed everywhere. But he was not pleased to see boats come in loaded with fish from the Faroe banks 'while we sit by with our hands in our laps and complain that we do not fish'. Later Shetlanders would instruct the Faroese in fish-catching and curing, and before long they were coming to Shetland to buy up the smacks. But the decline which came in the Shetland cod fisheries from 1880 onwards had other causes besides the growing Faroese competition. Life at the cod banks was hard and the expanding British merchant fleet gave better working conditions. It became difficult to recruit a crew; the last Shetland smacks in operation were manned by Faroese. But the most important reason for the decline in the once prosperous cod fisheries was the boom in herring fishing.

Herring fishing

Herring had been fished in Shetland waters for centuries, mainly by the Dutch, who had carried on a highly specialized bulk fishery for herring from the sixteenth century onwards. They followed the herring every year from Shetland to the English Channel. They would congregate in Bressay Sound around the middle of June every year, and as many as 2500 busses, as their boats were called, were reported at one time to be fishing on the Shetland coast. The Dutch were long considered the experts in the catching and processing of herring, and were also the first to develop the more productive technique of catching herring by using drift-nets from bigger boats on the open sea. However, in the nineteenth century the Scottish, English, and Norwegian fishermen quite took over as the main catchers and exporters of herring.

The rich herring catches affected Shetland only indirectly, through the trade they brought in. The herring fishing required bigger boats and more equipment than were available in the islands. In 1808 the British government tried to encourage local participation by offering a bounty of £3 per ton to vessels over 60 tons, but this was followed up by only one local owner. The capital simply was not there at the time.

In the 1830s, however, there came a sudden boom in the Shetland herring fishing. The peak year was 1834 with a production of 41,000 barrels of salt herring. Boats were often bought second-hand from Scotland; they were known as half-deckers and were a great improvement on the sixerns. Out Skerries, Whalsay, Burravoe and Uyeasound were the main herring bases. But the herring failed from 1839 onwards, as did the markets, and in 1840 the fleet was caught in a great gale at sea with a heavy loss of boats and nets. This led to the failure of Shetland Bank and the leading supplier of fishing gear, Hay and Ogilvie. With no capital the herring industry in Shetland collapsed, and most of the half-deckers were simply beached and never used again.

Then the tide turned once again. In the late nineteenth century there was renewed fishing activity all around the North Sea, with herring accounting for some 70 per cent of the overall catches. It was all done from bigger boats than before. The first big fishing boat arrived in Shetland in 1876, and within ten years there were 350 of them. This fleet enabled the men to follow the herring after the Shetland season was over, and to carry on deep sea fishing away at the banks on a much larger scale than before. The expansion in the herring fishing was therefore closely related to the structural changes in the fishing fleet.

The large-decked boats drew the men away from the smacks and the sixerns which were now finally discarded. Curing stations grew up everywhere. There were 180 sail boat stations all over Shetland taking part in the herring fishery, but most of the fish was landed at Baltasound and in Lerwick, where all the available ground near the harbour was used for curing. Scalloway and Sandwick were also important centres. 'The rapid development of the herring fishing industry in Shetland is without a parallel in the whole of the industry in Scotland.' An official report from the Fishing Board for Scotland states this in the peak herring year of 1905, a year when everything succeeded: weather, market and prices. Boats from all over Britain took part, curers came for the season, and there was bustle and activity everywhere. Roughly a seventh of the catch was taken by the home fleet of 300 boats. At the same time the local landings of white fish fell to 351 tons. The question is, of course, how much Shetland benefited in the final analysis from becoming committed to herring.

The effect of the wars and new technology
The introduction of steam drifters meant a serious setback to the Shetland herring fishing. Often, sail boats were becalmed as they were returning to base with a large catch and would have to dump the fish overboard; the steam drifter, on the other hand, could return quickly in spite of unfavourable winds and tides. The Shetland fishermen did not have the available capital for such boats and were ousted from herring fishing. It was a familiar story.

The First World War meant the loss of the important markets in Russia and Germany. The fishing did pick up again after the war, but high coal prices and low herring prices haunted the fishing in the interwar years. Just after the First World War quite good catches could be had of demersal fish like halibut and haddock on the grounds around Shetland. Many of the fishermen who fished for herring in the summertime, went for haddock during the winter. The vessels used for the herring fishing were laid up in winter, and for the haddock line fishing they would use smaller boats with oil engines installed. The boats would leave in the afternoons so that the men could set and haul their lines by midnight. In good weather they would come back for another set of lines. This kind of line fishing was hard work for the whole family. The women were left with the croft work and still had regularly to get up at three in the morning to bait lines. Children would have to untangle the lines and prepare the bait.

After the Second World War a completely new fishing industry developed. The coal-run steam drifters were few. Instead had come the so-called dual-purpose vessels that could be used for fishing both herring and whitefish, as they were equipped for both trawling and seining. Government loans and grants helped finance the buying of these boats. The switch to motors caused a change in the population pattern with a concentration of activity in places like Burra, Scalloway, Whalsay, Out Skerries and Lerwick. Still the herring often proved elusive, especially in a cold summer.

In 1965 came an abrupt change in the pace of fishing when the Norwegians applied modern technology to the herring fishing, using purse seiners equipped with power blocks and sonar. In that year a fleet of 200 Norwegian vessels fished as much herring alone as the other North Sea nations together. The Shetlanders and others soon followed suit, with the predictable result that herring stocks dwindled because of overfishing. In 1977 the North Sea was closed to herring fishing altogether. There was a cautious lifting of the ban in 1983, and two years later the landings in Lerwick were the best for nearly 50 years. As from 1986 the stocks of spawning herring seem to be back to normal, but even so The International Council for the Exploration of the Sea (I.C.E.S.) suggest that the herring fishing in the North Sea should be reduced by some 20 per cent in the next few years.

Fishing today

In the last few years Eastern European factory trawlers, known as klondykers, have been a familiar sight at anchor in Bressay Sound every summer. They buy up the catches of herring as well as some mackerel direct from the purse seiners and process the fish on board.

In the last few years, Eastern European factory trawlers, known as klondykers, have been a familiar sight at anchor in Bressay Sound.

As many as 17 boats have been there at a time, and Shetlanders are getting used to seeing Russians in the streets, though the notices in Russian in some shop windows may prove puzzling to other visitors! The klondykers buy up to 80 per cent of the herring catches. This creates very little employment ashore, but it is good for trade. A factory for the processing of herring is called for, but many consider this too much of a gamble because of the 'here today, gone tomorrow'–nature of the herring as well as the volatile state of the international herring trade. Still, plans will go ahead for a pelagic-fish-processing factory at the Dales Voe oil rig repair base, which turned out to be redundant as soon as it was completed.

In the whitefish trade the traditional curing methods have given way to other forms of processing, with the emphasis on fresh fish of high quality. The fish can be sent from Shetland as refrigerated cargo, but the bulk of the catch landed in Shetland is filleted locally and frozen for the home and export market. The first locally owned fish processing plant, Iceatlantic Sea Foods Ltd, opened in Scalloway in 1960, and since then the fish processing industry has expanded to the point where it now employs as many people as the fishing itself. In 1986 Whalsay Fish Processors Ltd won the Queen's Award for export achievement. Most of their production goes to Australia and the United States of America.

Another export industry is fish farming, mostly of salmon, which has had an explosive development in Shetland. Salmon farming on a commercial scale first began in Garderhouse Voe, near Sand, in 1982. Today there seem to be salmon cages in every voe. The Shetland Islands Council, as well as The Highlands and Islands Development Board, have backed local people who wanted to set up in this business, with loans and grants. Applicants have had to put up only ten per cent of the total cost themselves, but fish farming is a high risk business.

Shetland is well suited for this new industry because of its indented coast with clean water of the right temperatures. From the time the smolt comes to the fish farm it spends its life in its cage; when it has reached a weight of 5–6 kg (11–13 lb) it is ready to be slaughtered. By then it will have eaten about twice its weight in feedstuff. Fish farming is thus a highly effective use of resources. Although the feed is expensive, fish farming has so far been a very profitable business, with market prices much higher than production costs. This has naturally led to increased production in many countries with a keen competition in world markets.

Fish farming also provides some of the raw material for a new industry that has recently been established. The Shetland Smokehouse at Skeld has a range of smoked products, made mostly from salmon and herring, but also mackerel and whitefish are much in demand. But not all their products are smoked; they also offer such specialities as gravlax.

Mary Fraser from Culswick removes a tray of freshly-smoked herring, one of the many products from the Shetland Smokehouse in Skeld.

One of the latest additions to the Shetland fleet, the million pound Andromeda II, *owned and operated by the fishermen themselves.*

Today the Shetland fishing fleet consists of 110 vessels of varying sizes, employing some 600 men. The larger boats are equipped with all kinds of technological fishing aids: echometer, radio telephone, the Decca navigator to find their position at sea. There are refrigerated holds to make the catch stay fresh. The industry has become very capital-intensive—a purser seiner costs about two million pounds. It has also become highly efficient, with fewer fishermen earning more money than before. An unusual feature of the Shetland fleet is the fact that it is owned and operated by the fishermen themselves.

Yet the North Sea countries can now catch more fish than nature can replace which means that fewer boats will fight for the fish that are left; in addition, there has been a continuous decline in the stocks of mackerel, which have reached dangerously low levels. This fishing should now perhaps be closed altogether. Most species of whitefish are also overfished—the stocks of spawning cod and saithe are lower than ever before. The time has come for further restrictions to be imposed if the industry is to survive at all.

Conservation is therefore a word much used by the nations around the North Sea, for fish is an important resource to all of them. The British fishing policy now depends on the other EEC members, to whom North Sea fishing often seems to be merely a political pawn. The view has been commonly held in Shetland that the fishing in British waters was given away for entry into the EEC, with Britain eventually keeping roughly one third of the fish in what were once sovereign waters. It took ten years of difficult negotiations before the Common Fisheries Policy was signed in 1983, designed to end wrangling between states over the size of their fish catches.

'Total allowable catches' (TAC) for the North Sea are set by the EEC and Norway—determining the maximum amount of fish that can be fished of any species. These catches are then divided into quotas for each country. This is a hot topic among fishermen who are often incensed at seeing foreign vessels fishing in their waters when they have used up their own quotas. Thus almost a quarter of the Norwegian North Sea herring quota of 200,000 tonnes is fished from waters around Shetland, while the quota for local boats in the same area is only 11,500 tonnes. There has also been blatant cheating on the quotas by member countries; obviously there are diverging interests.

The Shetland fishermen insist on 'regional preference': Shetland-based vessels should have first preference for fishing in Shetland waters—as coastal communities with no other resources depend on the sea for their survival. Today Shetland vessels only catch about 10 per cent of all the fish taken from their own waters. It would not be unreasonable to suggest that the Shetland fishing industry should double in size and be allowed to catch some 20 per cent in local waters.

Fishing is of vital importance to the present day Shetland economy.

Rather more than 20 per cent of all Shetlanders are today employed in the fishing industry either as fishermen, fish-processing plant workers or in the ancillary service industries. More than 60 per cent of all Shetland exports consists of fish and fish products. As oil-related activities decline, the importance of the Shetland fishing industry will become even more marked. The island location, so far from the main European markets, obviously makes many kinds of industrial development impossible. It should therefore be a natural conclusion that fishing and fishing-related industries are the best prospect for future economic development within Shetland. It is to be hoped that this fact will be taken into account by the British government and the EEC when further decisions on fisheries policy are taken.

Fishing is a chancy business and planning ahead is difficult. To prophecy about future perspectives is not possible in an industry with such a complicated structure. It may be said that its very unpredictability is its most time-honoured characteristic. However, Shetland meets the challenge of the future with a high quality of seamanship, and in no other industry is personal skill so important as in fishing.

15 KNITTING

All the folk of the north isles are great artificers of knitting. . .
(*Random Memories-The Coast of Fife*, Robert Louis Stevenson)

It has been said that there are but two industries in Shetland—that from time immemorial the men have been fishermen and the women have knitted. How this came about is still uncertain for surprisingly little is known about the coming of knitting to the north of Europe. Not much research has been done to discover how long the various techniques have been known or where they first came from. Knitting has long been one of the chief exports of not only Shetland, but of Iceland and, of course, mainland Scotland.

There is no evidence that the early Norsemen knew how to knit, but both the sagas and artefacts found in Norse areas show that spinning and weaving were common work; the Oseberg finds show that it could also be a fine art. So also in Shetland: at Jarlshof soapstone loom weights going back to the ninth and tenth centuries were found inside a house and on a midden. In the thirteenth century house at Jarlshof 52 loom weights were found in one place—probably where the loom once stood.

The craft of knitting seems to appear in northern Europe in the sixteenth century, spreading along the waterways to the Baltic and North Sea areas–greatly helped by Hanseatic trade. As early as 1582 the bishop of Hólar in Iceland received part of his rents in knitted stockings. And the first Icelandic Bible translation, from 1584, describes Christ's coat in John 19:23, as knitted. The casual, but also very clever, use of this word to explain the complicated nature of the coat, shows that knitting must have been an everyday occupation in Iceland at the time. In an official list of the belongings of a man executed in Bergen in 1567 one item is thus described: '1 pair of old worn knitted Faroese stockings, 4 shilling". In Shetland the court book for October 1615 shows that Mans and Olav Jeillisones of Heiesetter were accused of having stolen a black sheep from Marioun in Stove and 'made ane pair of sockis of the woll thairof'.

Thus knitting seems to have reached the northern regions at more or less the same time, and this may partly explain the many similarities in tradition. Common to these areas is the fact that wool was always easily available from native sheep. Knitting was also infinitely more practical than weaving—no heavy work on a cumbersome space-consuming loom was necessary. It was also more sociable as knitting combined easily with story-telling around a peat fire in the evenings. Inside or outside, both hands could be usefully employed. The knitting could be done while minding the farm animals or while carrying the kishie with peats home on your back—the length of your 'makkin' was as good a way of measuring the distance as any.

The texture of the wool from Shetland sheep would make knitting a far more practical process than the weaving of wadmel—the thick woollen cloth that used to be made on most crofts. The original Shetland sheep are small and slight with extremely soft, light and fine wool which is ideal for knitting. Originally this wool was never shorn but pulled off when it was about to fall off naturally—a process known as 'rooing' in Shetlandic. In Romsdal in Norway this soft wool was known as 'rui'. The method of rooing enabled the whole length of the old wool to be removed without disturbing the new wool growing up for the next fleece. The thickening of the wool from clipping was also avoided. The wool from Shetland sheep came in a wide range of natural colours besides white and black, and the old names for them are in use even today: emskit (bluish-grey), mooskit (mouse grey), moorit (dark fawn or sandy), and shaela (between grey and brown). The naturally black wool is known as Shetland black.

Knitting elsewhere in Britain and in continental Europe was mostly done by craftsmen who were often organized in guilds, but this was never the case in Shetland—it was definitely a home handicraft, with knitting, carding and spinning all done there. For a long time the spinning was done almost solely by distaff as the spinning wheel was not generally adopted until rather late. Dying of the wool was not common as natural wool was considered warmer and already came in such a variety of shades. The soft wool lent itself easily to shrinking, which gave it a felt-like quality. At first this was done to imitate the wadmel, later because it was warmer and gave better protection in clothing such as mittens and caps. The process from sheep to product was a long one, as noted by a visitor to Shetland:

. . .the wool is very rough, yet of it they make the finest stuffs and stockings that you will readily find of wool, but it costs them a great deal of pains to fine it. (Sibbald, *Description of the Islands of Orkney and Shetland*, Edinburgh, 1711, p 21)

In 1951 the fully-clothed body of a man was found in a peat-bank on the south side of the road to Gunnister in Northmaven. All the woollen clothing was well preserved. There were two knitted caps—one of them with a turned-up brim—as well as knitted stockings, gloves and a purse containing three late seventeenth century coins.

The body may be that of a traveller who was buried by the roadside where he had died; but the knitted items, especially the purse in a pattern of red and white on a grey background, do suggest that he was a native Shetlander. Both caps had been shrunk from a larger size to make them weatherproof. The garments were extremely well knitted in quite sophisticated techniques.

For a long time, however, it was quantity rather than quality that would best describe Shetland hosiery. During the seventeenth century Shetland was visited by a steady stream of foreign traders and fishermen. Although they came because of the fishing, a brisk trade in hosiery, mostly stockings and gloves, resulted. Another visitor to Shetland tells of how the Dutch fishermen, gathered in Bressay Sound every summer, would buy stockings from the local people:

Stockings are also brought by the Country People from all quarters to Lerwick and sold to these Fishers, for sometimes many thousands of them will be ashore at one time, and ordinary it is with them to buy Stockings to themselves, and some likewise do to their Wives and Children; which is very beneficial to the Inhabitants. . . (Rev. John Brand, *A Brief Description of Orkney, Zetland, Pightland Firth and Caithness*, 1701, pp 198-9)

In 1951, the fully-clothed body of a man was found in the peat-bank on the south side of the road to Gunnister in Northmaven. All his woollen clothing was well-preserved. (National Museums of Scotland)

When a tax was levied on foreign salt in 1712 in a British attempt to take over the profitable salt herring trade, it had a disastrous effect on the Shetland economy, as the market for knitted goods virtually disappeared:

These Dutchmen used formerly to buy a considerable quantity of coarse stockings, for ready money, at tolerable good prices, by which means a good deal of foreign money was annually imported which enabled the poor inhabitants to pay the land rent and purchase the necessaries of life; but for several years past that trade has failed, few or none of these busses coming in, and those that come, if they buy a few stockings is at a very low price, whereby the country people are become exceeding poor. (Thomas Gifford of Busta, *An Historical Description of the Zetland Isles*, 1733, pp 5-6)

The income from knitting was urgently needed as the population growth put pressure on the other meagre resources. Hose would be sent to markets abroad along with a cargo of fish to make up weight, and gradually this trade built up, from £1500 in 1767 to £17,000 in 1797. But then the Napoleonic Wars brought another setback. On the whole the exported goods were of poor quality, referred to in the records as 'coarse woollen hose'. It took 50,000 pairs of stockings to make up the sum of £1500 in 1767, as they sold at sixpence or less a pair. Indeed, it is questionable whether the work involved actually brought in any money at all, as pointed out by the minister of Delting when reporting on his parish:

. . . after all their toil they often do not receive the original value of the raw materials employed . . . it would be preferable for them to sell the wool rather than take up their time manufacturing it in so unprofitable a manner. (Sir J. Sinclair, *The (Old) Statistical Account of Scotland*, Edinburgh, 1791-99)

Shetland Lace
Obviously the fine Shetland wool was worthy of being used for things other than the heavy articles of the early days. Thus from early in the nineteenth century the type of knitting known as Shetland lace developed, used for making shawls fine enough to be pulled through a wedding ring, and of exquisite workmanship. There are many stories of how the technique came to be used but common to them all is the belief that it began with the copying of some beautiful imported lace. As an industry Shetland lace knitting developed under the patronage of people like Edward Standen of Oxford, who was engaged in the hosiery trade and happened to see a lace shawl while travelling in Shetland in 1839. Standen helped introduce the Shetland fine knitting into the London market and he also lectured on and held exhibitions of the work.

This growing industry was helped by having a ready market. Not only shawls, but also lace mittens, veils and baby clothes, mostly in white, were in fashion, and these garments sold very well in the 1840s.

There was also a great demand for woollen underclothing which was believed to be good for the health. Shetland House, the retail shop and mail order business established in Edinburgh in 1830 by John White & Co., supplied a special quality of Shetland underwear to sanatoriums all over Europe.

By and by there was a certain specialization: Northmaven was noted for soft underclothing; Walls and Sandsting for socks and 'haps' as the smaller shawls are called; Cunningsburgh, Whiteness and Weisdale for gloves; Nesting for stockings; and Lerwick for shawls and veils. Unst was famous for the high quality of the knitting. It was said about the knitters that they carried the patterns in their heads and the technique in their hands, and indeed they had to—nothing was written down. Most of them would learn by looking, and the really skilled ones could invent new patterns, but it is interesting to speculate on how much was owing to outside influence and what was individual skill.

Shetland knitted goods were becoming increasingly recognized. At the great Exhibition of 1851 an entry of Shetland knitting won a medal. Shetland knitted garments were popularized by Queen Victoria shortly after her succession, and a beautiful collection of knitted goods was brought together by the women of Shetland and presented to Princess Alexandra when she married the Prince of Wales in 1863. Shetland knitwear has remained more or less fashionable ever since.

Fair Isle knitting

It is a question of conjecture as to when the craft of stranded knitting, where two or more colours are used to form patterns, appeared in Shetland. It must surely have been known in the seventeenth century if the Gunnister find is anything to go by. As early as 1776 the first known Icelandic book of patterns for stranded knitting appeared, evidently drawing heavily on the rich pattern traditions of weaving and embroidery. Thus stranded knitting was not new to northern Europe, and it is likely that such a skill would have been quickly adopted by the Shetlanders who depended on knitting for a livelihood.

The technique of using many bright colours became known as Fair Isle knitting because that is where it seemed to have developed. When Sir Walter Scott in 1814 writes of the women of Fair Isle trying to sell their knitting to passing merchant vessels, he dismisses it as 'trifles'. In 1822 Hibbert describes the fishermen he sees off the coast of Dunrossness:

The boat-dress of the fishermen is in many respects striking. A worsted covering for the head . . . is dyed with so many colours, that its bold tints are recognised at a considerable distance, like the stripes of a signal flag. (*Description of the Shetland Islands*, p 96).

Apparently, the first to record the tradition of the Armada and its connection with the Fair Isle patterns was Christian Pløyen, the Danish government representative in Faroe, who says that the people of Fair Isle

> . . . knit night-caps and gloves of curious, variegated patterns, which according to tradition, they learned from the Spaniards, when the Duke de Medina Sidonia, in the year 1588, was wrecked there in the Admiral's ship of the Invincible Armada. I have related the tradition as it was told to me . . .
> (*Reminiscences of a Voyage to Shetland, Orkney & Scotland in the Summer of 1839*, p 168)

In her popular book *Sketches and Tales of the Shetland Islands* from 1856 Eliza Edmondston of Unst described the Fair Isle knitting with its many bright colours—so different from the naturally muted colours of traditional Shetland goods. She suggested a connection between Fair Isle patterns and the extraordinary historical event of the wrecking of *Gran Griffon*, a flagship of the Spanish Armada, on Fair Isle. The idea fired the romantic imagination, and the story has been told to the present day in spite of being improbable and far too simplistic.

According to the Fair Isle inhabitants themselves the distinct style of their knitting has evolved over the centuries, and takes its patterns from many different sources. The Armada Cross is only one of a variety of designs and there are many Norwegian stars as well as designs inspired by crofting life. The gift of a kaleidoscope to the island around the turn of the century also gave the knitters many new ideas. The coloured-pattern knitting sold well enough to bring in a fair annual income to Fair Isle, although for some time it did not seem to attract much attention or have any fashion impact. But by 1910 the trade in lace knitting had declined in Shetland, and stranded knitting became common instead. Fair Isle patterns were tried and experimented with.

Then in the 1920s Fair Isle knitwear suddenly became the rage. The front covers of Vogue and other fashion magazines showed golfing outfits, winter sports' sets, pullovers, cardigans and dresses where the Fair Isle knitting was imaginatively used in an infinite variety of design and colour. And when the Prince of Wales let himself be photographed in a Fair Isle style pullover holding his favourite dog or driving off from the first tee as captain of St Andrews Golf Club, the trend was definitely set. For some years there was an unprecedented boom, with orders coming in for thousands of garments, and most knitters therefore had to adopt the Fair Isle style of knitting. In 1930 the hand-knitting industry gave an estimated turnover of £60,000 to Shetland.

Twentieth century knitting progress

At the same time the industry was changing character. What had been wholly a cottage industry was becoming more organized. Even in 1900 it proved difficult to spin enough yarn at home, and fleeces were sent to Scotland where they were blended with coarser wools. At most this yarn contained 60 per cent of Shetland wool; then the distinctive softness of the wool was lost. There was a steady decline in hand-spinning and by the 1930s it had become the exception rather than the rule. A few manufacturers, among them T. M. Adie and Sons in Voe, went on making sweaters from genuine Shetland-spun wool. Sir Edmund Hillary wore an Adie sweater when he conquered Mount Everest in 1953; 'the Everest sweater' has remained popular ever since.

It was only a question of time before machines were put to work in the knitting itself. The first machine seems to have been adopted by the firm of Pole Hoseason in 1925, and others soon followed their example. It also became usual for knitters to buy their own to use at home, and gradually, the frame-made garment became the more common. Obviously, the wholly hand-made sweater is more expensive but does not necessarily look better.

In 1921 the Shetland Woollen Industries Association was formed. One objective was to encourage the use of real Shetland wool, but the trade, worried by the number of imitations appearing everywhere, wanted a 'Made in Shetland' trade-mark. However, it proved impossible to protect it as manufacturers would claim they were using a yarn containing Shetland wool. After the Second World War the situation grew even worse, as the word 'Shetland' became used as a generic term to describe any lightweight warm sweater, whether made in Israel or Taiwan. It was even used to advertize yarn that was 80 per cent acrylic, as 'Shetland style with wool'.

The knitting industry did very well in the first decades after the Second World War, but the oil business of the 1970s proved a strong rival, as many women found oil-related work more profitable. Thus the knitting industry fell into decline for a while. However, nowadays much has improved, and knitting is once again an important industry. In 1985 half a million garments were produced worth some £6 million; nearly every home derived some income from knitting.

In 1983 The Shetland Knitwear Trades Association was set up, with the aim of winning back for Shetland knitwear the high reputation it once held in world markets. Its 50 members are seriously committed to the knitting industry as a living and they have registered their own distinctive trade-mark 'The Shetland Lady', which hopefully will be easier to protect from imitations than the old one. Meanwhile the Shetland Islands Council allocated an annual grant of over £200,000 to The Shetland Knitwear Trades Association for the first four-year period to boost the industry. The Council helps new businesses get started and old ones expand. It also supports the various projects to promote and market real Shetland knitwear in the United Kingdom and abroad.

The result is a highly exclusive business promoted by a sophisticated

Nearly every home derives some income from knitting. Mrs Joan Coutts, Fetlar, shows an unusual jumper which she knitted 45 years ago and which has won many prizes. Mrs Coutts has knitted since she was 5 years old.

marketing campaign. In 1985 two beautiful brochures were produced and distributed to retailers. Resultingly, there has been a brisk demand from both Britain and overseas, and people are beginning to look for The Shetland Lady symbol. A shop has been opened in London, selling only Shetland knitwear, and a mail order business, Real Shetland Knitwear Ltd, has been set up. Again the industry depends to a great extent on home knitters, whose number has been growing again, so that some 1800 work in their own homes. Thus the industry is ideal for maintaining a scattered country population.

Designers have been called in to help analyze fashion trends and advise the knitters on how to adapt their traditional patterns to the changing whims of fashion. Not all knitters are equally willing to do so and it is indeed a crucial question common to all crafts—should the market adapt to the traditional or must the craftsman bend to the law of the market-place? There is no easy answer. But surely in the crafts imagination always had to be curbed by the functional, and a tradition that is being kept alive is of little value. A craft needs innovation and can never be static; each generation must be allowed to contribute according to current taste.

Spinning

The need for a Shetland spinning industry has long been evident. A small wool mill was in operation in Baltasound for a few years in the late 1940s. In 1980 Peter Jamieson set up a small experimental spinning mill in Sandness in West Mainland, Jamieson's Spinning Shetland Ltd, using the natural colours, but producing a wide range of coloured yarn as well. This is an important step forward for the Shetland wool industry. So far this wool is not much cheaper, but it has the market to itself, and orders for undyed yarn have come in from as far away as Japan. It is most in demand within the industry itself.

The real Shetland wool will also be welcomed by the hand knitters, who knit mostly traditional garments. They are poorly paid for their work as few customers are prepared to pay a realistic price. Although new designs are valued higher, many knitters are reluctant to take on this kind of work.

There is also a manufacturer of fully-fashioned knitwear in Shetland. They employ some 50 people and export mainly to the United States of America. Just as the hand-frame machines were opposed when they were introduced there is some resistance to machine knits. In actual fact, all the producers complement each other and produce high quality knitwear for different sectors of the market. The machine knits are bought by the large department stores, the hand-frame knits go to small shops who order just a few of each design, and the handknits sell to the exclusive shops in the upper end of the price bracket.

The name Fair Isle became used all over the world to describe stranded knitting, and just as Shetlanders reacted to seeing the island name used as a general term for knitwear, the Fair Isle people disliked the many imitations of their designs, even those made in other parts of Shetland. However, there are subtle differences so that the discerning eye cannot mistake the genuine article. Fair Isle has more geometrical patterns where Shetland patterns tend to be more flowery. It is also typical of Fair Isle that each band of pattern begins and ends with two rows of solid colour.

To protect the genuine article and help market it, Fair Isle Crafts was set up in 1980. It has its own trade mark, and the articles are hand-framed by the knitters in their own homes. The firm is a co-operative run by the knitters themselves, without any middlemen, and they have long waiting lists for their products.

The knitting industry is an exciting and colourful part of Shetland life. It has overcome hardship and changing fortunes over the years to the point where it now exports its goods all over the world. Yet it remains basically a craft with scope for the individual imagination.

Jamieson's Spinning Shetland Ltd, in Sandness. Started by Peter Jamieson in 1980, this is an important step forward for the Shetland wool industry.

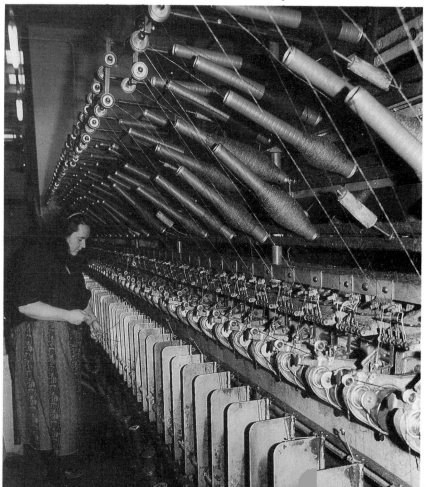

16 CROFTING

Eence Dale ta Brouster mustered
A thoosand folk an mair
Ta dell, an draa da boats doon,
An cast, an maa, an shair;
Bit noo da laand is bare.
Kwarna farna? Vagaland

In most Shetland districts the soil is more suitable for grazing than for growing corn or vegetables. The climate is not propitious either, and winds have often wrecked the crop just when it was about to be harvested. Still, not so many decades ago crops of oats and bere were quite common to meet the needs of the local people rather than for export. The islands were never self-sufficient in grain; in earlier times they would get meal from Orkney and send wool in return. Later they would trade fish for corn from foreign merchants, and therefore the Corn Laws, which forbade this import until they were repealed in 1846, were bitterly resented in Shetland.

The enclosed land would be divided into *merks* and *ures*. According to the old rentals, a merk should contain 1600 square fathoms, and an ure would be the eighth part of a merk. However, the size of the merk seems also to have partly depended on the quality of the land, and this made the system confusing. As a result of this difficulty in estimating the value of their land, the Shetland landowners were not accepted as voters in the parliamentary elections during the eighteenth century.

The enclosed land would make up a *tún* or township, which would vary between 4 and 70 merks in size. Most townships had access to the sea, and the cultivated land would be separated from the hills and moors by a township dyke. Most of these dykes were pre-Norse, but they were not necessarily made at the same time. Usually they were turf dykes, with a core of stone. While some of them have been in use to this day because they follow natural township boundaries, the purpose of other dykes, like the Finnigord of Fetlar, seems more obscure. They puzzled the Norse settlers too, who made them part of their lore.

The uncultivated land beyond the township dyke has been known as *skattald*. This word is found only in Shetland and derives from *skattr*, the Norse word for tax or tribute. Tax was only paid on cultivated land, but skattald seems at first to have been used about the whole inhabited township as a taxable unit and only later acquired its present meaning of hill land. According to udal or ódal law everybody also had a right to take peat, turf for thatching and mould for byre litter from the skattald. In earlier times grazing in the skattald was in many places quite unrestricted, and this right did not depend on the size of the farm. The skattald, therefore, has been the home of the farm animals that are native to Shetland. Common to these are their hardiness and their ability to fend for themselves in all kinds of weather on meagre hill pastures.

Shetland ponies

The Shetland pony or 'the Sheltie' is one of the smallest breeds of pony in the world. Generally these ponies measure less than 1 m (40 in.) at the shoulders. They are rather stockily built and very strong in relation to their size: Shetland ponies have been known to haul loads or carry back-weights that would be considered heavy for much larger horses. Their coat is rather coarse and becomes quite shaggy in winter.

Their origin can only be guessed at. Most probably they are of Celtic origin, but there may also be later strains of the Norwegian fjord horse or the Nordland horse. The Pictish stone found on Bressay had a drawing of a horse on it and bones from a small pony were found buried in the kitchen midden of the Pictish settlement at Jarlshof. 'Their horses are very small and tiny in stature, not bigger than asses,

The Shetland pony or 'Sheltie' is probably the smallest breed in the world.

nevertheless they are very strong in endurance', said an Italian visitor to Shetland in 1568.

The crofters' first priority would be food and shelter for their cows, and to get these through the winter somehow was as much as they could hope for. The ponies would mostly run wild in the skattald or the open fields all the year round. They seem to thrive in the wild and lose condition when confined. When pasture was scarce they could eat rack on the shore, but were often weak as a result by the time they were needed for the voar work on the croft. The ponies only did light work on the croft, like carting peats or seaweed on their backs, not being used for draft work, as there were no roads, until the middle of the eighteenth century. But as saddle animals they were a necessary means of transport, even though long-legged riders probably would have to hold up their feet:

Winter is the season of general mirth and festivity in Zetland, although the wish to visit each other is greatly interrupted by the difficulties which are attendant on travelling. As there are no regular roads, a journey over land is a serious undertaking, for the ground is wet and unequal and the ponies are low. (Arthur Edmondston, *A View of the Ancient and Present State of the Zetland Islands*, Edinburgh 1809)

It was earlier believed that the Shetland pony remained so small because it lived under severe conditions. The opposite proved true, as the breed tended rather to grow smaller when reared in a warmer climate and better fed. On account of its size, but also because it is an intelligent and faithful animal, it has been very popular as a mount for children, and today this is its main market.

In the late nineteenth century selective breeding was carried out to produce a smaller pony for work in coal-mines. Their size and their hardiness qualified them for this service, so that many of them had to exchange the freedom of the Shetland hills for the dark depths of the mine.

Cattle

Like the pony the native Shetland cattle probably evolved from a mingling of Celtic and Norse breeds. Even a hundred years ago pure specimens were few and far between, and most cows were more or less of mixed stock. But they were recognized as a distinct breed, and in 1910 a group of Shetlanders formed a Herd Book Society and made a number of registrations. Still, the breed almost died out.

The Shetland cow has a very thick and strong body. It is noted for its resistance to disease, and its good milk yield. Though light, the beef is tender and of good quality. However, from the 1930s onwards their place was increasingly taken by crossbred cattle and Aberdeen Angus, as these gave a higher yield of milk and beef. Unfortunately, these species proved more costly—nearly two Shetland cows could be kept for the same cost as one of the others. Today there are about one hundred purebred Shetland cattle, of which only a few are kept in Shetland. The Shetland Islands Council now gives a subsidy towards the keeping of the Shetland cows and bulls, and this may encourage more people to keep herds of them.

Sheep

The pony shares the exposed hills of the skattald with another hardy breed—the Shetland sheep. The origin of this breed is not certain, although tradition has it that it was brought across to Shetland by the Norse settlers. They may have interbred with the primitive Soay type of sheep believed to have existed there already. In Foula there are horned short-wooled ewes with grey bellies, but most Shetland sheep show few of the characteristics of the Soay breed today.

The Shetland sheep are small and fine-boned. The rams have short horns which will spiral as they grow older. But it is mainly the tail which will show us whether a sheep is an old Shetland purebred or not, as this breed has a short tail of only 13 vertebrae where most others have 20 or more.

The most striking characteristic of the Shetland sheep is the fineness of their wool, indeed it is considered the finest wool known, and has a soft, silky touch. Colours range from black to white: the really black sheep have now become quite rare, while white and moorit sheep are quite common. Traditionally, the wool was plucked or 'rooed' in June, and this was often the only time they were rounded up. The owners would drive or 'caa' the sheep before them across the hills and into the crö, and then they would identify their own sheep by their lugmarks—the characteristic holes or slits in the ears. Apart from rooing and lambing time the hill sheep would get no herding, nor were they ever housed, but would be left to fend for themselves in the skattald.

The Shetland sheep look rather like goats, and have a similar agility. Thus they can often be seen grazing at the very edge of the cliff where the best grass grows. Wandering in search of food, they eat seaweed during frost and snow; even when they are some distance away from the sea they seem to sense when the sea is on the ebb and will flock to the shore. A hardy lot, they sometimes have two or three lambs at a time and are also long-lived. As hill sheep they will reach an average weight of only 22 kg (48 lb), but the meat has a special flavour which makes it much sought after. In fact there is a very great demand for Shetland lamb on the Continent, but this trade is hampered by the lack of an EEC slaughterhouse in Shetland.

As they were isolated the Shetland sheep were not crossed with other breeds until the end of the eighteenth century when several new breeds were brought to Shetland: Merino, Dutch, Scottish Blackface and Cheviot. During the nineteenth century the old Shetland sheep were ousted by the Cheviot and Blackface, and seem to have survived mostly in the hills of Papa Stour and Foula. The end result was a marked deterioration in the general quality of Shetland wool. This caused concern, and in 1927 the Shetland Flock Book Society was founded. Although everybody realized the need to maintain the purebred Shetland sheep, it was considered uneconomic by modern standards. It therefore took a long time for the tide to turn, and even in the 1970s the sheep were classified by the Rare Breeds Survival Trust as an endangered species. Yet according to plan, the main product of the new spinning mill in Sandness will be high quality wool from purebred sheep.

In the last few years thousands of acres of hill land have been reclaimed. When the standard of the pasture improves heavier cross breeds are used, a result of Shetland ewes being crossed with Cheviot or Suffolk rams. These are increasingly in demand in southern markets. The total number of sheep and lambs of all breeds in Shetland is some 300,000. More than a third of these are lambs. Of these the best of the flock will be kept for breeding, but the rest goes to market. Some

Tommy Jamieson from Lochside, Walls, with his Shetland collie, Raskel.

are slaughtered in Shetland, but some 65,000 lambs are shipped out to Aberdeen every year, mostly as stores—lambs to be fattened in richer pastures.

Over the centuries the small hardy shepherd dogs known as Shetland sheepdogs or collies have been used to guard all these sheep. As the cultivated fields were not usually fenced in the old days, one of the tasks for the sheepdog was to keep the farm animals from straying on to the crops. It was therefore known in Shetland as the 'Toonie' dog–the tún or township dog. As with the other animals native to Shetland its origin is uncertain, and it is probably a mixed breed, although it is similar to small Icelandic dogs. It was recognized as an independent breed in 1909.

Land ownership

Over the last few centuries the question of land ownership has perhaps been the most crucial issue in Shetland. There is tradition in the islands of the ódallers of old who owned their land absolutely:

The udal or allodial tenure . . . is the most ancient mode of holding lands in Zetland, and appears to have been the principal one, while the islands remained under the sovereignty of the kings of Norway and Denmark. It is said to have been founded on an old Norwegian law of St Olave, or Olla, by which a man was obliged to divide his property, heritable as well as moveable, among all his children equally. (Arthur Edmondston. *A View of the Ancient and Present State of the Zetland Islands,* 1809)

This system of inheriting property often led to the splitting up of land into small uneconomic strips, and this was one of the reasons why farms were sold or lost through debt. But there has also been such a persistent tribal memory in Shetland of trickery and double-dealing by incomers that it seems quite likely that many of the large estates were amassed through very rough methods indeed.

In the nineteenth century the ódallers were becoming rare enough to cause interest and comment among visitors. In 1832 a young English doctor visited Jerome Johnston at the farm of Crosbister in Fetlar, and wrote down this description of him in his diary:

. . . I was surprised to find that Jerome Johnston had been long in Egypt with the British army, and that he could, moreover, give a most excellent description of the countries he had visited. His narratives were interspersed with various godly sayings, which carried one back to the days of the old Scottish covenanters; the Shetlanders are particularly prone to such phrases as 'wi' God's hjalp, 'He abjuv will guide wis.' Jerome was certainly, however, no covenanter, but he had more interest in my eyes as being one of the old udallers of Shetland, a class of men likely, in a few years, to become totally extinct. (From the *Journal of Edward Charlton, M.D.*)

The majority of people working the land in Shetland became tenants,

Ruined croft on Unst. Holdings were very often small, and the crofts did little more than sustain the people who lived there.

or crofters. Their tenure was often insecure, and most of the time the landlord could dictate the terms—this was especially true during the peak population years of the nineteenth century. Sometimes crofts were vacant in some areas because tenants had emigrated or died from one of the many epidemics; when this occurred it gave a young man the opportunity to have his own croft.

However, as the holdings were very small, the crofts did little more than sustain the people who lived there and brought insufficient rent to satisfy the landowners. Some kind of additional income was necessary, and in Shetland it was natural to look to the sea. Fishing tenures therefore became common, and as the men were working 'da haf' from May till August, the land consequently suffered. Throughout the nineteenth century visitors would often point out how bad conditions were:

The greater part of the Shetland tenants appeared to me to be sunk into a state of the most abject poverty and misery. I found them even without bread; without any kind of food, in short, but fish and cabbage; . . . their little agricultural concerns entirely neglected, owing to the men being obliged to be absent during the summer at the ling and tusk fishery. (Patrick Neill, *A Tour through Orkney and Shetland*, p vi, Edinburgh 1806)

It also occurred to some lairds that it might be more economical to get rid of the people altogether and fill up the land with sheep. Such clearances began in the Lambhoga district of Fetlar in 1822 and went on for the next 50 years. Some districts, like the North Isles, were especially hard hit. The island of Fetlar lost about one third of its population and still shows the scars of a brutal land policy. In November 1874, 27 families from the four crofting and fishing communities of Corston, Garth, Quam and Neeflans on the Quendale estate in Dunrossness were thrown out on the world, to find themselves new homes as best they could. The stone from their houses was used to build new fences.

Some lairds also took the ancient right to the skattald away from their tenants. In 1867 the tenants of the large Garth estate, with holdings in Bressay, Delting, Yell and Unst, were told by their laird that 'All privileges of grazing upon scattalds, removing 'truck', etc., are reserved by the proprietor. No tenant is allowed any privilege outside the boundry of his farm, with the single exception of the boats noust as presently enjoyed.'

Conditions became so bad in all the crofting districts that the government was forced to act. The Napier Commission was set up in 1883 to enquire into the plight of the crofters in the highlands and islands of Scotland. Among the grievances they noted were that there were often no written leases, that rents were too high and often summarily raised, and that improvements to their land or farm buildings only led to an increased rent, as the croft then became more valuable. The loss of the skattald was the most serious matter of all. The report of the Napier Commission led to the passing in 1886 of the Crofters' Holding Act, which gave security of tenure and fair rent to the crofters. But it did not give back the skattald to those who had lost it.

The old townships were worked on a share-all principle. The buildings were often grouped together on the less fertile land. The farming land was held in what was known as 'rigga-rendal' or 'run-rig'; the rigs being strips of land. To drain the land there were ditches, known as 'stanks', between the rigs, and the rigs would change hands every summer, to make sure that everybody had a chance to work the good land. Both during the voar and hairst crofters would help each other get the work done, and this community spirit applied in most of the daily work.

By the end of the nineteenth century the system of land rotation had largely come to an end, the land was divided up into permanent holdings, and any new houses were built on the individual croft. However, in some townships the meadow land was still worked as scattered hay plots which changed hands every year, as late as the 1950s.

The Crofters' Act gave the crofters security of tenure and the right to heir the croft to their successors. Rents and rates were low, so that as tenants they had everything in their favour. Thus few seemed anxious to buy, even when the opportunity offered itself. But the economical situation of the crofters had not really improved. It was becoming impossible to live on the income from the croft alone. Emigration was the answer for many; others gave up the old crofting ways and chose to specialize in sheep or looked to herring fishing for extra income. With the upheaval of the First World War many crofts became vacant and were taken over by crofters who wanted more grazing land to make their holding economical. As it became more and more common to run two or more crofts the deserted croft houses fell into disuse and dereliction.

In the years following the Second World War the government found it necessary to assess the plight of the crofters anew, and concluded:

We have thought it right . . . to record our unanimous conviction . . . that in the national interest the maintenance of these (crofting) communities is desirable because they embody a free and independent way of life which in a civilisation predominantly urban and industrial in character, is worth preserving for its own intrinsic value. (*The Taylor Commission on Crofting*)

A Crofting Commission was set up to look after the interests of the crofters, deal out the crofts that became vacant and generally see that rules were followed. Many crofters applied for and got a share of the skattald, and grants were given for reclamation of the hill land.

These changes brought new vigour to agriculture, and in the 1960s the crofters began to receive sheep subsidies and prosper. But with the coming of oil many crofters took full-time jobs in the oil business, and had little time for the land; resultingly, there was a marked change from cattle to sheep, which need less tending. This has caused an imbalance, and much land would improve with the keeping of cattle. With the passing of the construction phase the number of oil-related jobs declined. Young people wanted to come back to the land, and The Shetland Islands Council found it necessary to work out a ten year plan for agriculture. The plan advocated that the land should be reseeded and improved upon and the keeping of the native breeds encouraged. Funds are made available for this work both as grants and low interest loans to the crofters.

Today there are 2267 holdings in Shetland, but only some 1500 persons make their living from them. This is because families often run more than one croft or because their main source of income is obtained elsewhere. According to official figures 53 per cent of the crofters belong to the latter category, and are sometimes referred to as 'hobby' crofters. If so, they have chosen a strenuous hobby, where they have to turn their hand to most jobs and be a kind of jack-of-all-trades. But it is still a fact that there are many absentee crofters today, and they are as much of a problem as absentee landlords represented in the old days. In theory their crofts can be taken from them and given to somebody else, but this rarely seems to happen in practice.

There are those who believe the crofting system to be an anachronism in this day and age. The rules of land tenure in Shetland are now so complex that only specialists can disentangle them. The landowner has the privilege of owning the land but has no say over it. His income from it is negligible. The crofter does not own the land but has complete control over it. He also has the right to buy the land, should he so wish, but he might then lose some of his grants. As a crofter he is eligible for a wide range of grants and subsidies not open to owner-occupiers, and to remain a crofter may therefore be advantageous. Such a checkmate system as this may have spared Shetland from undesirable property developments and land speculators and also partly served to maintain a scattered population. Still, the present system seems outmoded and unfair. One solution would be for the crofters or the authorities to buy the land from the landowners and turn it into agricultural co-operatives, as this might give to crofting the flexibility it needs. Shetland crofters might not take kindly to such ideas, but surely there is a strong case now for a simpler and fairer system.

17 OIL

'Tinks du it will ever be da same again?'
Robert Alan Jamieson, *Thin Wealth* 1986

'The greasiness of the North Sea is next to saltiness its most remarkable quality', wrote the Bishop of Bergen in 1752. He went on to say that if a ship caught fire, then North Sea water would not put this out but rather make it worse. Even so the discovery of oil came as a great surprise to most people. The Norwegian geologist who had stated he would personally undertake to drink any oil that might come out of the North Sea would probably have preferred to swallow his words instead.

During the last few years Shetland and oil have become linked in the popular mind. But Shetland had the oil industry thrust upon her in the early seventies when the local industries of fishing and fish processing, crofting and knitwear were doing quite well, and people were optimistic about the future. At a time when recession was beginning to bite elsewhere, Shetland had almost full employment and a stable population. There was no development plan, as none was considered necessary.

Change began in 1971 when exploration for oil and gas reserves in the North Sea off Shetland was intensified, and onshore supply and helicopter bases had to be established. Most Shetlanders were positive towards this development, thinking it would bring in more work and probably improve harbours and communications. Then in August 1972 Esso and Shell announced that they had found oil and gas in The East Shetland Basin, a geological area north-east of Shetland. This find was named the Brent field; later other important fields were discovered as well. By law all oil and gas taken out of the British sector of the North Sea must be landed somewhere in Britain. The nearest possible landing point for the Brent field was Shetland. A major crude oil loading terminal in Shetland was already being quietly planned by the oil companies, as the find had actually been made in June 1971, more than a year before it was announced.

Within a year the positive attitude to the oil industry was replaced by scepticism, even hostility, to further development. One reason for this was reaction to the lack of openness shown by the oil industry itself. There was also a wide-spread fear of what such a huge operation could do to such a small, close-knit community as Shetland. An oil-rush could swamp the local industries as well as the traditional culture and leave a waste land when it was all over. It was clear to most Shetlanders that it was the oil industry that needed Shetland, and not the other way around. The first intimations of what could happen came when land speculators who sensed what was going on, descended upon the islands like locusts.

In the course of 1972 it became evident that major oil developments in Shetland were inevitable. Without warning the Shetland Islands Council, or Zetland County Council as it was then, was thrown in at the deep end of what looked like very stormy waters. But the Council rallied with amazing speed to make several moves with respect to planning and legislation. Their main concern was to contain the oil activity as much as possible in one place of their own choosing, and to secure the largest possible revenues from this to be spent on developing the traditional Shetland industries. The Council realized that as long as central government did not start worrying about national interests, they were at that stage in a unique bargaining position as far as the oil companies were concerned.

The Sullom Voe area in Delting seemed the natural place for an oil terminal. The voe itself was deep enough to take large tankers and the land was mostly sheep runs or empty moorland. Originally, there had been an old settlement of 11 crofts on Calback Ness, but most of them were cleared in the 1860s to make room for sheep and the last crofter had left in 1950. The nearest community was Graven which had been overrun once already, when the R.A.F. used the area as a base during the Second World War and left it without clearing up. The derelict site was an eyesore that nobody would miss, but the building of an oil terminal, which might become the largest in Europe, would be even more of an irreversible process.

As soon as it became known that Sullom Voe (whose probable derivation is ironically 'a place in the sun') was the area intended for development, a group of Scottish businessmen reached an agreement with the local landowners, and bought or took options to buy some 40,000 acres of land. They established a subsidiary company which they called Nordport, for the supervised building of an oil base. This made the people of Shetland extremely angry as Nordport was the name that the Zetland County Council had given to their own plans for the area.

It became obvious that wider political powers were needed, and the Council therefore took the necessary steps to get a Private Bill passed through Parliament to safeguard Shetland interests. Its passage was not without delays and obstacles, and it was not until April 1974 that the Bill became law as the Zetland County Council Act, which gave the Council practically all the power they had originally asked for— in fact more wide-ranging powers than any other local authority in Britain. This enabled the Council to exercise complete jurisdiction as a harbour authority over Sullom Voe, to acquire by compulsory purchase the land to be used for oil-related development, to issue licences to dredge or to construct works within the three mile territorial limit, to take shares in business ventures, and finally to use the income from oil to establish a reserve fund. In other words, the Act gave the Council, as a local authority, unique powers not only to obtain income from oil but to control oil development. If it so wished it could also become an active partner in the oil industry.

There was political scepticism in Parliament over granting such unprecedented power to a local authority. However, various events had led to the granting of the Act. The Bill coincided with the Arab threat to stop oil deliveries to the West and therefore Britain was particularly keen not to hamper the progress of their own oil production. In addition, the issue of Scottish devolution was involved: one of the most important arguments for devolution was based on the Scots' claim to the oil. However, if the North Sea oil was brought ashore in Shetland, it could equally be considered the property of the islanders, who had little enthusiasm for being ruled from Edinburgh. Thus the Act took some of the wind out of the sails of the Scottish National Party and placated determined Shetlanders simultaneously.

People in Shetland were perhaps prepared for disruption in the construction period, but it was difficult to imagine beforehand what form the pressure would take. In some respects it turned out to be like living through a war once again. The airstrip at Sumburgh Airport was extended by the Civil Aviation Authority in a hurry to cater for the heavy traffic of choppers and planes. In one of the peak construction years 700,000 passengers used this airport. Its waiting hall would be packed with men in anoraks or weatherproofs, with helmets and strange-looking gear, waiting for arrival or departure of planes and helicopters. In addition, an endless stream of earnest-looking planners and bureaucrats were arriving, and there was a lively shipping traffic with boats going back and forth to the oil rigs. Shetland thus became a beehive of activity where the old crofting life existed side by side with the ultimate in modern technology. An old dialect word like 'rig', used for a field, acquired a new and different meaning. A popular cartoon by F.S. Walterson showed a croft dwarfed by an oil rig in the voe, with a crofting wife by the peat stack 'calling him in fae da rig'.

At Sullom Voe work went ahead with the laying of two huge pipelines from the Brent and Ninian oilfield complexes halfway over to Norway, each of 90 cm (36 in.) diameter and about 100 miles (160 km) long, at a price of close to a million pounds a mile. Onshore,

Tugs swinging a 270,000 ton DW tanker at jetty 4, Sullom Voe.

Europe's largest crude oil terminal prepared for action, with an impressive cluster of tanks and pipes and separation plants, and a certain strange, futuristic beauty of its own. The terminal has its own 120-megawatt power station, its own port authority and its own jetties which can take tankers over 300,000 tons. With its enormous facilities, the terminal was built to receive 70 million tons of oil a year, which represents half of the estimated production in the British sector, and will meet some 70 per cent of Britain's total energy needs. The first offshore oil was piped into Sullom Voe in November 1978.

During the peak construction period there were some 7000 people working at Sullom Voe. Only about a thousand of these were Shetlanders; the rest came mainly from Scotland and Ireland. They were housed in temporary but comfortable camps at Firth and Toft near the construction site and, in an attempt to avoid friction, kept as far from the ordinary Shetlanders as possible. The camps had their own recreation facilities, and artists were brought in to entertain the oil workers.

'Brave little Shetland' might have won the first round with the passing of the Zetland County Council Act, popularly known as the Shetland Bill, but all was not plain sailing for the Shetland Islands Council in their dealings with the multinational companies. The oil companies seemed to have adopted a policy of non-confrontation with the Council and accordingly played down any problems they met. This did not work with the Shetland Fishermen's Association, who felt deliberately deceived and aggrieved by the lack of discussion about the oil companies' future activities. Thus the Council were first told that 1200 construction workers would be needed, and a camp to house them was built at Firth. Later another camp was built at Toft to house another 1800 men. Commenting on this, the *Shetland Times* wrote that 'there has still been no explanation as to why the original estimate for the peak number of workmen needed on the terminal should turn out to be less than half the actual figure.' Later this figure was, of course, doubled once again. The oil companies continued their clever manoeuvrings, always understating their plans and avoiding frank discussions in a way that seemed, in retrospect, deliberate policy.

But too much secrecy and a lack of consultation with the people of Shetland was a criticism often levelled against the Council, too. People felt that they were told only of finalized decisions rather than proposals. Negotiations between the Council and the oil companies made slow progress, and the crucial ports and harbour agreement had not yet been signed by the time the first oil came on stream in 1978. This delay was to prove problematic for the Council, who by that time were deeply involved in the building and operation of the oil terminal. The land was owned by the Council, but an agreement on rating valuation still had to be reached, and the Council also had sole responsibility for the building of jetties and the upkeep of the harbour. The terminal, however, was controlled by a company called Sullom Voe Association Limited, jointly owned by the Council and the oil companies.

The Council had other responsibilities as well: houses had to be built for families coming in, schools would be needed for their children, and the roads had to be widened and improved. Extending amenities beyond those required by a small rural community necessitated the borrowing of money and, although much of their debt has been rapidly paid off, the SIC have faced heavy interest charges on their initial debts of some 140 million pounds. Among the items on the credit side were the payments from the oil companies under the disturbance agreement, the harbour dues and the rents from the lease of land. In the decade from 1975 until 1985 Shetland made a total amount of 174.753 million pounds on oil, of which 110 million pounds came from taxes. But by the year 2000 it is thought that Shetland will make some 200 million pounds less than originally estimated.

By the time the construction phase was completed at the end of 1982 most of the oil workers had left, a new rhythm of everyday life, with oil, had to be found, and other changes accepted. As there was virtually no unemployment in Shetland when oil came, it meant that existing industries came under a strong wage pressure if they wanted to keep up with what the oil industry was paying. Knitting was probably the industry to be hardest hit, as women who had been employed as outworkers by the knitwear manufacturers, took jobs at the terminal rather than sitting at home and knitting. The impact on fish processing was also considerable. Many small businesses gave up the unequal fight and closed down; building costs soared; and housing has remained very expensive in Shetland. The general price level of consumer goods and services also seems high as it is common for an economy to boom and inflation to rise in the wake of oil, and it may take time for the effects to wear off.

The oil industry inevitably affects the environment. Within a month of the berths at Sullom Voe opening to tankers there was a spillage of bunker oil from the *Esso Bernicia*, and about 4000 seabirds were killed and the eastern shores of Northmaven were polluted from Fedaland to Mavis Grind. The equipment for cleaning up proved quite inadequate, and many miles of fences had to be erected to keep livestock away from the oily foreshore. This was an unfortunate accident, but there were also cases of ships deliberately dumping oil. To counteract this menace, aerial surveillance of tankers was introduced, which also proved useful for catching tankers that took dangerous short-cuts close to the Ve Skerries instead of following the regular route west of Foula.

Within the terminal area the long narrow Orka Voe was filled in and shortened with some 11 million cubic metres of peat and rock. New roads were built and old ones were widened; the scenery of Shetland itself was changed. With an amazing lack of care and foresight, much of the material needed to provide aggregate for roads or concrete was taken out of the hillside in Mavis Grind. Over the centuries this narrow entrance to Northmaven was a romantic landmark to visitors—in some ways it *was* Shetland. Today the ugly blasted hillside has taken the romance of Mavis Grind away, and most people pass without giving it a thought.

Another controversial issue is the question of housing. In an effort to achieve integration of incomers and avoid the building of a kind of boom town, new houses were scattered among villages that were reasonably close to the terminal. Perhaps there were too many houses grafted on to the old crofting pattern for integration to succeed—a certain 'them' and 'us' division could not always be avoided. Many felt that it would have been better to build a New Town, perhaps at Brae, but the Council's argument against it was that all the investment in infrastructure would then have been centred on the new population only, whereas they wanted as many as possible to benefit.

It would be difficult to find a community where more has been done to secure local control over the oil development than Shetland. Opinions about their degree of success are divided. Today the mood of the Council is resigned, even bitter. Long term planning has turned out to be difficult, if not impossible, and there is little hope that the government changes to be made in the rating system will be to Shetland's advantage. The Shetlanders even feel that they have been deceived by the oil companies, who once upon a time assured them that they would be no worse off as a result of the coming of oil. The oil revenues turned out to be much lower than expected, as the forecasts of expected tanker traffic given to the Council were inaccurate. In spite of having obtained over £100 million in grants from central government towards cost of construction under regional policy criteria, the oil companies have persistently tried every conceivable dodge to get their rates bill and their harbour charges reduced.

The oil companies, on the other hand, have accused the Council of having been overly optimistic and in consequence spending too much money. Since the Council get 75 per cent of their income from the oil terminal, they say they should be satisfied. Rent problems are also unresolved: the companies have made no payment to the Council as owner of the terminal for their occupation of the site since 1974; the Council's professional valuers estimate the rental valuation for a fully operational terminal to be in the region of £100 million a year, whereas the oil industry base their argument on 'bare unimproved land value' and offer about £1 million a year. With little hope for an amicable solution, the case was taken to court in 1986 and is still unsettled.

1. Margaret Stuart with her collection of old Fair Isle knitwear with her son Ashton; the collection was begun by her mother, Margaret Stout, a Shetlander.

2. The spectacular coast scenery at Brae Wick, Eshaness.

3. In late and early summer, the islands are carpeted with wild flowers.

4. Wick of Breakon, Yell. The coast, north of Cullivoe, is as beautiful to visit in winter as in summer.

5. Crofter Bertie Moar brings down sheep from the hills to Murrister, Bridge of Walls.

6. Everyday, twice a day, the endless feeding of salmon goes on. When the fish reach a weight of 5-6kg they are ready.

7. Mid-Yell churchyard and village. Every 17 May, the Norwegian National Day, Shetlanders put flags and flowers on the grave of the men from the *Kantonella*, wrecked off Mid-Yell, in 1941.

8. The beautiful and dramatic west side of Papa Stour.

9. The impressive east side of Noss, one of the most popular islands to visit with its thousands of seabirds.

10. Dunrossness. Underneath the massive bastion of Fitful Head the green and fertile fields are among the best land in Shetland.

11. From Bressay, the fog is seen rolling in over Lerwick at the end of a hot summer day.

12. Watching over the Roost at Sumburgh Head, is Shetland's first lighthouse, built in 1821.

13. Midnight cow, midsummer. This is the time of 'the simmer dim' when day and night seem to merge imperceptibly in a muted light.

14. The beautiful island of Vaila has an interesting history and part of Vaila Hall dates back to 1696.

15. Skaw, on the north-east side of Unst, is the most northerly dwelling in Britain.

16. Jarlshof. Two trough querns for grinding corn together with their rubbing stones.

18 LOCAL GOVERNMENT

Með lögum skal land byggja–with law shall the land be built

This motto for the County of Shetland is an old proverb belonging to the common legal heritage of the Nordic countries. It may originally have been quoted to the tingmen when the assembly opened as it is the pithy first line of the Law of Jutland and can be found in Swedish as well as Finnish laws. The oldest written source for the proverb is the Law of the Frostating—also known as 'the law that St. Olaf gave'. Frosta is a peninsula north-east of Trondheim, and in the Middle Ages it had the tingstead of one the four legal districts of Norway.

In a slightly different form this proverb was later included in the Icelandic law-book Járnsida: *með lögum skal land byggja, en eigi með ulögum eyða*, (with law shall our land be built and not be laid waste through lawlessness) and this seems to be the original of the Shetland motto. The writer of *Njál's Saga* lets Njál himself use these words in one of his speeches to the Allthing, just before AD 1000 . However, in *c*. AD 150 a Roman lawyer, Sextus Pomponius, writes 'Civitas fundaretur legibus'—society should be built by law. Perhaps what this motto shows foremost is the continuity of European history.

The old Shetland Law Book is traditionally said to have disappeared around 1611. Probably this law code was adapted from the Law of the Gulating. This Ting was held in Gulen, at the mouth of the Sognefjord, and it was the main assembly for Western Norway. The Law applied in Shetland and Faroe too, but representation from these areas is not specifically mentioned. It has rules for everything from fishing to burial, and many of them can be recognized in later Shetland customs. The Law of the Gulating is so old that its origin is unknown, but the oldest Icelandic law, from just before 930, was patterned on it. Probably the first Norse settlers brought the law with them, so that it was not in any way alien or imposed on Shetland from above. It was spoken of later as 'the old law of St Olla'.

In the Middle Ages the islands were divided into 12 parishes as now. There were also many local tings. The tingstead of Delting– was probably at Dale, and the ting for Nesting met at Neap. In addition there were Aithsting, Lunnasting and Sandsting as well as two lost names that have no present-day equivalent: Rauðarþing and þveitaþing. The main ting seems to have been held on a holm in Loch of Tingwall; early in the thirteenth century it is referred to in Diplomatarium Norvegicum as the *loghting*. This Lawting was the main assembly of all odallers or freeholders and would meet for a week every summer. We are told that in 1577 as many as 760 odallers met at Tingwall to inquire into the illegal actions of Laurence Bruce of Cultmalindie, the man who built Muness Castle in Unst.

To call the men together in a time of crisis or to a ting meeting a summons known as the *tingbod* would be sent out. The law laid down very strict rules regarding its delivery: if the people were out three notches must be cut in the door-frame and the symbol left above the door. In Orkney, Shetland and Faroe a cross was used as the tingbod— a custom perhaps borrowed from Celtic Scotland. The custom seems to have survived for a long time, because as late as in the middle of the last century the cross was carried in Shetland to give warning that caaing-whales were in the voes.

Administration of the islands was carried on by the Foud and the Lawman, with one underfoud and one lawrightman in each parish. The foud summoned the courts and carried out their decisions. He also collected the taxes, which were paid in wadmel, butter and fish oil. The office of foud was given in tack by the King, but the Lawman was elected by the people themselves. He was a paid official who presided at the courts and interpreted the Law Book.

As late as 1583 an appeal was made to Bergen on a point of law, and the court there upheld the interpretation already made in Shetland. The Court Book of Shetland for 1602–4, which was edited for the Scottish Record Society shows that Norse legal practice was still followed at that time. The last Shetland lawman was Niels Thomasson of Aith. The Stewart earls appointed four sheriff-deputies to share the lawman's duties. The worst of the lot was said to be Harry Colville who was thrown over the cliffs at Neap in Nesting in 1596.

Since the Union of Parliaments in 1707 Shetland and Orkney have returned one representative to the British Parliament at Westminster. Before the Reform Bill of 1832 gave franchise to the middle classes there were no qualified voters in Shetland, as only the owners of freehold land worth £400 or more were allowed to vote. Land in Shetland was still measured in the old merks and ures and thus did not qualify. Landowners insisted on a new valuation, but it was to no avail. In Orkney there were all of seven on the roll of voters, and they seem to have accepted that only the relatives of the Earl of Morton, who held the Earldom estates in Orkney, had a natural right to be elected. When in 1766 Sir Lawrence Dundas bought the Earldom of Orkney and Lordship of Shetland for £60,000, the right to hold the

Orkney and Shetland seat in Parliament was tacitly made part of the bargain.

In the election of 1833 Shetlanders voted for the first time, with dramatic results. The two contestants were both Orkneymen: George Traill, seeking re-election, and the very popular Samuel Laing of Papdale, who for many years afterwards served as Provost of Kirkwall. The poll in Orkney showed a considerable majority for Laing. Because of bad weather the boat bringing the result from Shetland was delayed, and the tension in Orkney grew. When the Shetland votes were at last counted, they tipped the scales in Traill's favour. The Orkney people were furious.

There were . . . several serious cases of assault. Captain Baikie turned out to help his party; but in coming down his steps, he was met in the face by the fist of Skipper John Dearness. Mr. Traill Urquhart was doubled up by a blow under the ribs and died soon afterwards as a result of it. (*Orkney Miscellany*, Vol.I, p 78, Kirkwall 1953)

The first Shetlander to be returned to Parliament was Arthur Anderson, one of the most remarkable men that Shetland has fostered. He had started out as a beach boy for the Bolts of Cruister in Bressay, and when he left in 1808 to join the Navy, he was told by his employer to 'Dø weel and persevere.' After a life of adventure he became involved in shipping and was one of the founders of the Peninsular and Oriental Company, today known as the P.&O. Company. When Anderson decided to contest the 1847 election, he campaigned in the islands in a chartered steam-yacht—the first of its kind to be seen in the North Isles. His opponent was a member of the Dundas family, and Anderson made the most of this fact. He maintained that Shetland had never been properly represented in Parliament, as their member had always been first and foremost the representative of some private family, with cousins wanting to be made parsons, captains, admirals or generals. Their votes in Parliament had been bartered for personal privilege instead of local improvements. Why had no grants of public money to build piers, harbours and roads ever been given to Shetland? Why was nothing done to facilitate local trade and industry? Anderson was duly elected, but he served only one term because his health deteriorated.

The Liberal Party has long had a strong standing in Shetland for a variety of reasons. The fact that the passing of the Crofters' Act in 1886, which changed the life of so many people in the islands, was due to Gladstone and the Liberal Party, has never been forgotten. The party has been willing to listen besides being less dogmatic and less centralized than the two major political parties, Conservatives and Labour. It is only recently that the Scottish Labour party has become positive to local democracy—perhaps because it has had to see Bills affecting Scotland only and solidly opposed there, go through in

Parliament on the votes of English members. For all of 33 years, from 1950 to 1983, Orkney and Shetland were represented in Westminster by Jo Grimond. For many years he was also the leader of the Liberal Party and thus gave political status to his remote constituency.

Politically the last 20 years have been intense in Shetland. Although the Shetland people see themselves as British, they have never felt Scottish; they think of themselves as Shetlanders primarily. Although their ties with the rest of Britain are strong, they are still very much conscious of their separate identity. To some extent this may be based on awareness of their own history, but the romantic Nordic revival came at the turn of the century and belongs to the past. The lovely stained glass windows of Lerwick's Town Hall depicting Norse Kings, as well as the choice of an Icelandic motto, belong to this period.

Although the Shetlanders still feel a strong kinship with Scandinavians their independent political stance of the last two decades is perhaps based more on a realistic assessment of their present geographical position: a small remote group of islands far from the corridors of power in Edinburgh, London and Brussels. They have come to realize that English members dominate the House of Commons, and many of them know little and care less about Shetland interests. Often these interests even clash with those of central government. At the same time they have seen the Faroese people prosper and become self-reliant in their move towards self-determination, and they ask 'Is aa we hear aboot yun place true?' And if it works for Faroe, why not for Shetland?

The old Zetland County Council had been set up in 1889. As they had long felt a need for increased power, they sent a delegation to Faroe in 1962 to see how their system worked. They decided that the reason for its success was 'the right and power of the Faroese to manage their own affairs, and the application of special measures to special problems'. The Zetland County Council then suggested to the Secretary of State for Scotland that a certain measure of autonomy should be granted to the islands, as it would benefit all concerned. Instead they learned to their horror that central government had plans for further centralization which would effectively put an end to a separate Shetland administration.

As part of the radical reform of local government in Britain in 1973 the Scottish counties were replaced by nine regions. According to the original plans Shetland, Orkney, Western Isles, and the northern counties of Scotland, including Argyllshire, would constitute one vast but thinly-populated Highland Region, to be run from Inverness. But people in Shetland felt that because of the distance involved it would spell disaster for them to be tied in with such a region. They protested so loudly that the then Secretary of State for Scotland thought he had better go north and see what it was all about. The story goes that when he passed through Cunningsburgh he was stopped by students with a sign telling him that he was entering the Republic of Shetland, and could they please see his passport? They then handed him a visa for his stay in the islands.

It may have been these political demonstrations, so unusual for Shetland, which did the trick, so that they were granted full regional powers, apart from the fire service and the police which are directed from Inverness. Then through the Zetland County Council Act of 1974 the powers of the single, all-purpose local authority were further extended to the point where it became a virtual partner of the oil industry. On 15 May 1975 the new Shetland Islands Council took over.

The Council has 25 members who choose their leader, the convener, from their own number, and is assisted by a chief executive. There is also a Lord Lieutenant in the islands, as the Queen's representative, but it is an added complication for the islands that for matters outside their own authority they must variously refer to Inverness, Edinburgh, London or Brussels. It can be trying at times for the councillors having to rush cap in hand to one of the centres of power to explain how their blanket legislation will cause havoc in Shetland.

The Scottish Office is responsible for agriculture and fishing, development and planning, as well as for law, education and health. In the late 1970s Scotland's own need for devolution led to a Government Bill for a Scottish Assembly being discussed in Parliament. Had the bill been passed it would have given the Assembly the right to change the form of local government in Scotland. The aim of the Scotland Bill was to decentralize power, but in Shetland it was feared that for them it would mean the opposite. In an attempt to safeguard island interests Jo Grimond rushed through an amendment one minute before time was up in one of the shortest and most effective speeches in parliamentary history.

The amendment, which was carried by a large majority, said that in any referendum on Scottish devolution the votes from Orkney and Shetland must be separately counted. If the vote in either island group went against devolution, then a commission should be set up to review any changes necessary in government. The 'Grimond amendment' caused a glow of pride in the islands.

It has been said that the Council represents the population of a sizeable village, but has to deal with the problems of a nation. The framework within which they have to work often appears to be unnecessarily rigid. And whenever the councillors feel they are gaining insight into the many complex subjects, the rules are bound to change! Central government can at times be so insensitive to island needs that it is felt to be irrelevant. It is understandable that Shetland looks to Faroe, as well as the Isle of Man and the Channel Islands, with their varying degrees of self-government.

As udal or ódal ownership of land has never been abolished in Shetland, there have also been clashes between Scots and Norse concepts of law. Much of the conflict has been over the right to the foreshore and the ownership of any treasure and artefact that may be found. By udal law property rights extend from the highest stone in the hill to the lowest stone in the ebb. If a treasure is found it should be split equally among the owner of the land, the finder and the ting.

When the St Ninian's Isle treasure was found in 1958, the question of ownership became important. Professor Knut Robberstad from the University of Oslo maintained that the matter ought to be solved according to udal law, so that the treasure would be split three ways among University of Aberdeen as the finder, the owner of the land and the crown. But the Court of Session in Edinburgh declared the crown to be the sole owner. This decision was based on the tenet that the crown shall have that which belongs to nobody else, but such a tenet has never been valid in Norse law.

There is a local proverb that says 'Da riven sleeve haads da haand back', but in recent years Shetland has not been held back by poverty from following up her opportunities. The islands began to want more say in their constitutional status, and in 1978 the Nevis Institute produced a study in depth of the various options that might be open to Shetland. These ranged from the status quo, through various forms of devolution, condominium and federation, to complete independence. The study had been commissioned by the Shetland Islands Council at a cost of about £40,000. The report concluded that a special status could give the Shetlanders the right to manage their economy for their own interests, and like Faroe they might make their own settlement for a 200-mile (320 km) limit with the EEC. Such a status would also allow them to maintain their cultural identity, but it would all be at a price: it could cause bitterness and division in the rest of Britain.

The lively political debate led to the launching of the cross-party organization, the Shetland Movement in September 1978. It was born out of a desire among a small group of intellectuals known as the Shetland Group to see the islands take more responsibility for their own government to stimulate growth. Their chief aim was the granting of wider powers to Shetland Islands Council and a special status to Shetland, involving limited law-making and tax-raising powers.

The Movement asked the islanders to back a six-point programme of pragmatic aims on issues affecting Shetland. The first point was to call for a regional fishing policy which would involve Shetlanders in the licensing of boats fishing in the area, as well as in determining the size of the quotas to be allowed. They would also conclude reciprocal agreements with other regions or countries on behalf of Shetland fishermen. The Movement called for more freedom in the spending of Government aid and oil revenues, especially in assisting local firms suffering from the construction of the Sullom Voe terminal. They also wanted the Government to accept full responsibility for any pollution caused by the oil industry.

The Shetland Movement has been variously described as consisting of intellectuals, petit bourgeois, red-necked fascists or chauvinists. The Movement itself has maintained that it is not inspired by an inward-looking Little Shetlandism but sees itself as part of a much bigger and more general movement away from over-centralization of government. It immediately recruited enough members to make it the largest political group in Shetland.

Whereas Shetlanders had once been considered indifferent, even apathetic, to political issues, they were now waking up with a vengeance. In a referendum held in the islands by the Council in March 1978 a majority of nine to one voted in support of a commission being set up to consider Shetland's position. After requests from Shetland for an examination of the governing of the islands, the Montgomery Committee, named after its chairman Sir David Montgomery, was set up four years later. Its mandate was to review the powers of the islands' councils of Orkney, Shetland and the Western Isles.

The results were disappointing. The Montgomery report, published in 1985, advocated a greater say for the islands councils in their own affairs. To achieve this the committee made 49 recommendations, but the government accepted only 37 of them and turned down everything that was really important to the islanders, including the suggestion that the islands' councils should be given a single block allocation for capital expenditure which they could manage at their own discretion. Nor did the government accept recommendations for widening the scope for Shetland's use of oil-related income.

One of the most interesting political events of the eighties was the decision of the Orkney and Shetland Movements to field a candidate for the first time in the general election of June 1987. They were already actively involved locally, as in the 1986 election for the Shetland Islands Council five of the candidates standing as Movement members were elected and two narrowly defeated. The Movement are the first group to contend for parliamentary power primarily on local issues, although they do have national policies, too! Not surprisingly their choice of candidate was John Goodlad from Hamnavoe in Burra Isle. He has for some time been employed by the Shetland fishing industry as secretary of the Shetland Fishermen's Association and chief executive of the Shetland Fish Producers' Organisation Ltd. He did well in the election, but the Liberal candidate Jim Wallace retained his Orkney and Shetland seat, although with a reduced majority.

The Movement fears that the oil-related prosperity cannot last, and that the islands must therefore secure their post-oil economy, centred

One of the most interesting political events of the eighties was the decision of the Orkney and Shetland Movement to field a candidate for the first time in the General Election. Their choice was John Goodlad from Hamnavoe, here seen canvassing with his wife Wilma.

on fishing. This industry is very largely controlled without the islands, with quotas and restrictions mostly being decided in Westminster or Brussels. The British have never used their veto in the EEC fishing because in national terms fishing is a minor industry. According to the Movement, the British Government and the EEC are not really concerned about what happens in Shetland, and they believe that their only hope for the future is to acquire greater control over the exploitation of their own resources.

It seems natural to ask whether Shetland can handle more power than they already have? In all fairness it must be said that some expensive mistakes have been made, such as the Dales Voe Base built by Lerwick Harbour Trust. From the time it was officially opened in 1985 till it closed down around a year later it had no business. The council also lives in fear of a drastic fall in the rateable value of the Sullom Voe Terminal before Shetland has cleared her main capital debt.

But if the Shetlanders have made mistakes there is at least a satisfaction in knowing they are their own mistakes. They have also brought about many successes: the Shetland Islands Council took prompt and decisive action against oil tankers polluting Shetland waters on their way to and from Sullom Voe, in spite of hardly any support from central government. They have fought an untiring campaign for Shetland fishing interests at the EEC negotiations in Brussels, and they have formulated a Shetland Fishing Plan. They have promoted a ten year plan to develop farming and crofting resources, and built schools and community halls and homes for the elderly. They have improved communications between the isles by running heavily subsidized car ferries. This list is long.

The oil era made Shetlanders politically aware, and council decisions are now often contended, but mostly people grudgingly admit that 'dey're laekly døin der best'. But a former chief executive to the council put it this way: 'Shetlanders, because of physical separation, do not see how their local authority out-performs almost all others . . . 'Shetland councillors do not think of themselves as politicians. And yet that is what they are, and their task is often a thankless one. Like all politicians they must expect to be continually challenged on the efficiency of their administration and their policy-making.

19 LERWICK

> While there are tales of Lerwick
> Recalled and handed down.
> Lives on the Northern Venice
> The little, old, grey town.
> *Northern Venice* by Vagaland.

Lerwick is a town dominated by the sea. This is apparent in the way it faces and opens up to Bressay Sound, and a visitor should always see it for the first time from a ship. The older houses along the seafront are built partly in the water, and beyond them the slate-roofed houses of grey stone rise, gable over gable, to the top of the hill where the Town Hall towers above it all, like a cathedral. Every quarter of an hour the mellow chimes of its clock mark the hour.

This is a town of many faces: its look of age is illusory, and yet it is not really a modern town. To people in the rural areas who come there to shop it is 'da toon', and for nearly a thousand youngsters it is a centre of secondary education. It is also a cosmopolitan town, and there would be nothing unusual in hearing Russian and Faroese spoken at the same time along the narrow, twisting main street of Lerwick. Although the town has grown in size over the last few years, it is not big enough to get lost in. The town is also the home of Shetland

To British visitors, Lerwick is excitingly alien, but butchers Smith & Co make sure that there will be no language problems in their shop!

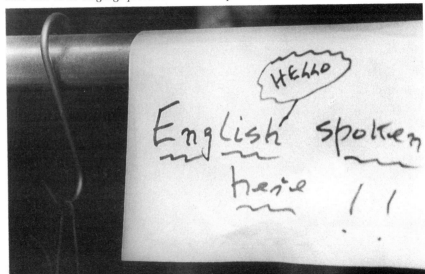

administration, with the air and the atmosphere of a capital, and a very charming one at that.

Lerwick is the most northerly town in Britain. To British visitors it is excitingly alien, and many believe this is due to Scandinavian influence; to Norwegians too, it is strange, even though they will feel wonderfully at home. So many different factors went into the making of it, and the result is really quite unique. The only place that in any way resembles Lerwick is the Orkney town of Stromness, which also shares some of the general history.

Dutch fishermen first discovered the vast shoals of herring that would appear annually in Shetland waters. By the end of the sixteenth century they were fishing there regularly, and the town grew up to trade with and cater to these Dutch fishermen. They used to gather in their squat ships, known as 'busses', in Bressay Sound, because there they found a large and protected natural harbour. Their fishing season in Shetland stretched from Johnsmas on 24 June until St James's Day on 25 July. The busses would come in the fortnight before the fishing began, and also return from the fishing ground every Saturday evening to lie at anchor in Bressay Sound until Monday morning.

Trading booths sprang up along the Lerwick shore, and knitted stockings, gloves and garters, as well as birds' feathers, were bartered for luxury goods like tobacco and brandy, but also sold for foreign coin. Not everyone was pleased with this:

There they frolic it on land, until that they have sucked out all the marrow of the malt and good Scotch ale, which is the best liquor that the island doth afford.' (From an MS in the Advocates' Library, *c.* 1618)

Apparently the goings-on shocked the rest of Shetland too, as in 1625 the Court in Scalloway ordered that the booths should be 'utterlie demolished'.

As the Dutch herring fishing continued to grow, Lerwick grew with it. At one time the incredible number of 22,000 Dutchmen fished from 2200 ships. The herring was said to bring them an annual income of some three million pounds. But their good fortune also gave them jealous enemies: in 1703 a French fleet attacked the Dutch vessels while at anchor in Bressay Sound and set fire to a great number of their ships. Still the Dutch returned, bringing with them traditions and festivities. At the close of the summer's fishing the Dutchmen would have a grand raceday on Shetland ponies. They would gather in a field south of the town and gallop out for half a mile or so and back again. This event was known as the Fishermen's Gallop.

By the end of the seventeenth century there were about 700 people living in Lerwick. The town had its own church and was trying to become separated from Tingwall parish. After a century of steady growth, the population suddenly exploded in the early nineteenth

century—from 1400 inhabitants in 1801 to 3000 in 1833. Houses were
built as the need arose, without the benefit of planning. There were
many people living under the most primitive conditions in overcrowded
houses. In Sooth Kirk Closs, one of the narrow lanes running up the
steep hill above the shore, 250 people inhabitated 16 houses, with 38
people in one house alone.

However, through the activity caused by the cod fishing and even
more by the herring fishing a well-to-do middle class arose, of merchants
and professional people, who could afford to build pleasant houses.
Christian Pløyen, the commissioner of Faroe, was quite impressed by
Lerwick when he visited Shetland in 1839:

The neat houses, the handsome apartments, the floors all carpeted, even to
the staircases of the inn where I was lodging, the elegant grates ornamented
with bright polished brass. Everything made me feel that I had come to the
land of opulence. (*Reminiscences of a Voyage to Shetland, Orkney and Scotland*,
trans. by Catherine Spence, Lerwick 1894)

Squalor, sophistication and style existed side by side in Lerwick
throughout the nineteenth century. Even then it was described as a
queer, old-fashioned town, in spite of being in a continual state of
change. In the heyday of the whaling and herring fishing the streets
and the waterfront would be teeming with people of many nations.
For the country people, perhaps walking into town to sell their knitting,
it was a place of adventure and a thousand marvels. To the fishermen
and sailors who used it as a port of call it was an exciting place, a
rowdy place, that must be talked about in low tones if there were
women present. To the owners of the many ships that used to call at
Lerwick to refit and get crews, it was a place where hardy and hungry
islanders would sign on for less than the going wage.

Lerwick in those days was spoken of as a northern Venice; all along
the Lerwick shore house doors would open on the sea and there would
be rings at the door-posts for tying up the boats. Thus people could
step from the living-room into the boat as easily as into the street and
goods could be easily loaded and unloaded. Each courtyard in the sea
was known as a lodberry, the word deriving from the Norse *hlaðberg*
and referring originally only to a flat rock by the shore where boats
could be moored for taking on board goods. In old pictures of Lerwick
this sea front of lodberries is perhaps the most striking feature.

In smuggling days the lodberries were extremely convenient; according to tradition there were even tunnels going underneath Commercial
Street to houses on the other side. When the foreshore was reclaimed
in 1886, only the lodberries to the south of the pier survived. They are
still largely intact and give us an idea of what the town must have
looked like before the great changes came, towards the end of the
nineteenth century.

When the foreshore was reclaimed in 1886, only the lodberries to the south of the pier survived, and this one must be the most photographed house in Shetland!

It had become increasingly evident that a development of the harbour was needed to cope with the growing traffic. Many visitors give vivid descriptions of the ordeal they had to go through to get ashore with their luggage:

. . .on steaming up in front of the town we were assailed and boarded by a score or more of small craft, who swarmed and pushed, and strove and jostled each other at the boat's side, till one of the boarders had his hand severely crushed against the paddle-box. If we had been in Indian and not in British waters, we might have supposed it to have been an attack of Malay pirates. My companion and I were advised by a gentlemen who had been there often before to capitulate to 'Peter', who took possession of his prey, and kept possession of us till we finally left the place. For it is to the honour of the Lerwick boatmen that, once they have fought their battle, each is allowed to carry off his captive and make the most of him, without further strife. James Brown Gillies, (*Benjie's Tour in Shetland*, Edinburgh 1870)

These boatmen were soon to lose their livelihood, and the sea front would change its character. The Lerwick Harbour Trust was set up in 1877 for the purpose of building a pier of some size. In June 1886 the Victoria Pier and the Esplanade were formally opened. The sea front between Queen's Hotel and Fort Charlotte changed its character completely; gone were the lodberries and the little private piers. Traces of them can, however, still be seen. Thule Bar used to be Tait's lodberry. An otherwise puzzling iron ring in a house wall shows us where boats were once moored.

But development did not stop there, as commercial needs grew and demanded further changes. Today the Esplanade is cut off from the sea. Most of the harbour activity has moved northwards; the fishing fleet migrated to the Morrison dock and the ferry traffic to the new terminal at Holmsgarth. The oil-related developments were concentrated in the north end of the harbour. The changing scene and life of the harbour was a colourful part of the old Lerwick. 'Hanging around harbour-sides' wrote Robert L. Stevenson, 'is the richest form of idling'. In the summertime the old harbour is packed with sailing-boats from the maritime nations of Europe and is even today an exciting place to be 'hanging around' in.

Walking along the long winding Commercial Street, popularly known as 'the Street', and trying to dodge the cars also has its exciting moments. The street is so narrow in places that it is necessary to hop into lanes or doorways when meeting up with a lorry. Strangely there seems to be no local lobby for making it into a pedestrian precinct, but this will surely come. The whole street is paved with flagstones, although some of them have been replaced by concrete slabs. Fortunately most of the old houses, which as often as not present their gable ends to the street, still remain. The following description is more than a century old, but might just as well have been written today:

> On taking a walk through the town, you find that your first impression as to its irregularity was pretty correct. If one could fancy all the houses in a town of upwards of 3000 inhabitants engaged in dancing a Scotch reel, and that just as they were going *through the reel* the music had ceased and the houses had suddenly taken root, he would form a pretty accurate impression of the plan of Lerwick. (*Half-Hours in the Far North*, Wm. Isbister Ltd, London)

There is still a working blacksmith right in the town centre—the only one left in Shetland. The same business has been there since 1890.

During its long history Commercial Street has been the scene of strange encounters. In 1880 Conan Doyle, the man who later created Sherlock Holmes, signed on as surgeon on the whaler *Hope* of Peterhead. While the ship lay in Lerwick harbour, Conan Doyle and the cook-mate got into an argument with a Cunningsburgh man, which ended in a fist fight. Although Conan Doyle liked to think of himself as a boxer, the local man was big and powerful, and before the two soothmoothers knew what was happening, they were flat on their backs and out cold.

This incident took place in the square outside the post office, but it pales into insignificance compared with the happenings some decades later. On 1 November 1914, people in Lerwick watched in horror and incredulity as the 40 employees of the general post office were marched to the County Jail between two lines of marines with fixed bayonets. There they were kept locked up in cells for six days without having any idea of the charge against them. Then they were just as suddenly released, without being given any official explanation. As Shetland had become important as a naval base where all shipping coming from America was stopped and checked, it was generally assumed that the post office staff were suspected of tampering with official war mail going to or from the naval base at Swarbacks Minn. *The Shetland News* printed an indignant leader:

Not even the outbreak of war created such a profound sensation in Lerwick as did the arrest of the entire staff of the Lerwick post office who were thrown into prison like a band of common felons. The most ugly feature of this infamous act has been that in the south the loyalty of the Shetlanders has been called into question... Nothing less than a full inquiry will satisfy the whole outraged community of Shetland.

But no inquiry was ever made, perhaps because in wartime there would be other priorities as well as worse inequities.

Fort Charlotte at the north end of Commercial Street adds to the interesting picture that Lerwick presents from the sea. Although it was never much of a fort, it was supposedly built by Cromwell to protect Bressay Sound against the enemy in the first war between the English

Blacksmith Willie Farquhar (left) *with friend Laurie Bruce, at the door of the Smithy in Lerwick, founded in 1890.*

and the Dutch in 1652–54. It was sacked by the Dutch in 1673 during the third Dutch war, but was rebuilt within a few years. In the nineteenth century there was no garrison in the fort, which was run by one sergeant. The comfortable men's quarters were let as private apartments and were quite sought after. The ramparts were then still furnished with 12 cannons, which proved too much of a temptation to Lerwick youths, who once had great fun firing them and waking up the citizens of Lerwick in the middle of the night. The Board of Ordnance told the Lerwick authorities that if they wanted to keep the guns on the battlements, they would have to see to it that such episodes did not occur again. Not to be daunted the Lerwegians replied that if the fort could not even protect their own guns, what was then the use of it? After that the fort was turned into a prison and a depot for the naval reserve. Today it is used by the Shetland Islands Council.

Running up the steep hill from Commercial Street are a number of narrow-stepped lanes. In the old days they were known as 'closses', but at some point all the names were unfortunately changed into compounds with the non-descript word 'lane'. This area used to be the slums of Lerwick. There was little or no drainage so that when it rained water would stream down the lanes. Nor would there have been any sanitation. But today the lanes have taken a second lease of life; most of the houses have been done up and are now sought after dwellings, being both distinctive and traditional.

The lanes end in the ridge known as Hillhead. Towards the end of the nineteenth century a new town was built in the area beyond Hillhead. Straight new streets were named after Norse kings, for this was a period of romantic Nordic revival, when Shetlanders gloried in their Viking past. This is a striking characteristic of the large upstairs hall of the Town Hall as well, where the magnificent stained glass windows are a pageant of Shetland's history. The foundation stone of this building, which by many is considered the finest in Shetland, was laid on 24 January 1882 by HRH Prince Alfred. The Town Hall is built on a commanding site in the new town, and for those intrepid enough to venture out on the tower roof, it has a fine view of the old town and the surrounding countryside. The exterior of the building is made in local freestone from Bressay, with stone dressings from Eday in Orkney.

The whole Town Hall building shows the civic pride the citizens of Lerwick took in their town. It dominated the town not only in a physical sense, but socially as well. Weddings, dances, private receptions, as well as concerts and plays and political meetings would take place there. Public affairs were also run from there, as it housed both the Sheriff Court and the town administration. Lerwick became a royal burgh in 1818, and was run by a town council.

In 1975 Shetland Islands Council replaced both the old Zetland

County Council and the Lerwick Town Council, which was sadly missed by many Lerwegians. At the same time people in the rural areas have often resented the centralization of services and amenities in 'da toon'. But the Town Hall has become the property of the Shetland Islands Council and is used by them for meetings of the full council as well as by committees. Today only the hall upstairs is still used by the town people.

The Bød of Gremista in the northern part of Lerwick is another interesting old building. It is a plain two-storied house which has been restored mainly because of its historical importance. Arthur Anderson was born in this house and lived there until he had to go out and earn his living at quite an early age. The house used to belong to the Nicholson estate where his father worked as a fish factor. It may date back to the seventeenth century. Anderson became one of the principal shareholders of the P. & O. Company when it was founded in 1837, and by a strange turn of events their ships dock not far away from the place where he was born.

Anderson never forgot his native islands, and with some of his great wealth he founded the two institutions known as Anderson Educational Institute and Anderson Homes. They were both built during the 1860s in a Tudor-Gothic style. The lovely old school taught about a hundred students. Above its main entrance there is a panel with an inscription reminding the students to do well and persevere, as this was advice to which Anderson himself attributed his success. The school prepared them mainly for university studies and had a high reputation for scholastic excellence. Today the Anderson High School has around one thousand students, and new buildings have mushroomed to meet the pressure of modern education. Arthur Anderson wanted the homes to be a refuge for widows, in memory of his wife.

The modern Lerwick is moving away from the harbour as the town spreads towards the south-west. By the shore of the Loch of Clickhimin lies one of the best preserved and interesting brochs in Shetland. Around a century ago the water level in the freshwater loch was higher, so that the broch was connected to the shore by a causeway, which can still be seen. Across the loch lies the new and popular Clickhimin Leisure Centre. There were those who doubted the need for such a place when it was being planned, but they have been proved wrong. The level of usage is high, as it has some 120,000 visitors a year, and the enterprise has also won national prizes.

Around the turn of the century the district of Upper Sound was still a grouped township where the land was held in 'run-rig' and life went on much the same as it did before the houses of Lerwick had begun to edge closer. Sound seems to have been one of the earliest settlements in Shetland, and its inhabitants viewed the growth of Lerwick without pleasure. Indeed, there was an old saying about it:

Modern Lerwick is spreading towards the south-west, and by the shore of the Loch of Clickhimin lies one of the best preserved and interesting brochs in Shetland.

> Sound was Sound when Lerwick was none
> And Sound will be Sound when Lerwick is gone.

But it did not work out that way. The housing developments reached Breiwick in the 1920s and Lochside and Sandveien after the Second World War. Since then Upper Sound has changed character as well, although it is still possible to trace the outline of the old township.

The three tiers of Lerwick mirror its three phases of development— from the rather dull modern housing estates to the quiet elegance of Hillhead and then down to the bustle of Commercial Street and the harbour. Thus much of modern Lerwick no longer has the same intimate connection with the sea. Still the sea plays as all-important a role in the lives of its people as it ever did.

20 SCALLOWAY AND ITS ISLANDS

—They lie before us—
Gem-stones set in a sun-gilt sea—
Oxna, Papa, Burra, Havra,
Linga, Langa, and Hildasey.
The West Isles, Vagaland

These lovely islands protect the ancient Shetland capital of Scalloway from the Atlantic and make it a haven for ships. The Norsemen would also have appreciated the position of such a good harbour close to fertile land, so that this area became a natural administrative centre. Later, Earl Patrick Stuart acknowledged this tradition when he built his castle there.

There are several possible explanations of the name. To anyone seeing Scalloway for the first time from the sea, however, the visual impression is so striking that it is hard to see how the name could be

A modern wind-mill profiled against the sky.

anything but nature-descriptive. The wide bay is round, almost saucer-shaped, and the hills behind it give to the area the look of an amphi-theatre. Probably the original name was therefore Skálavágr, from *skál* meaning saucer or scale. This type of descriptive name is common, thus there is a Skålevik in Norway and a Skálavík in Iceland. The historian, P. A. Munch, however, linked the name of Scalloway to the word *skáli*, meaning house. Both derivations are linguistically possible.

Today the ridge framing the town is brutally broken by the large quarry near the Scord, so that the best view of Scalloway is from above. A modern windmill is profiled against the sky, but the most striking feature, even after four centuries, is the sombre ruin of Earl Patrick's Castle. It was built in 1600 by Andrew Crawford who also designed the Earl's Palace in Kirkwall, and it must have been a fine building when it was finished. The Rev. John Brand visited the place in 1700 when the building was already falling into disrepair:

This House or Castle is 3 Stories high beside Kitchines, and Wardrobe, and hath in it many excellent Chambers, and other Apartments with their several Conveniences; Also there hath been much good painting, some of which is yet to be seen, tho much defaced; the Chambers are high between floors, but especially the Gallery or Dining Room: in the Kitchin there is a Well in the side of the wall, the water whereof is very good tho little used: The Sclaits have for the most part fallen from the Roof, and are daily falling with every Storm, so that the Timber, much of which is yet very good and fresh is beginning to rot and consume, by the rain falling through the house from floor to floor. (*A Brief Description of Orkney, Zetland, Pightland-Firth & Caithness,* Edinburgh 1701, pp139–40)

According to tradition Earl Patrick forced the islanders to build this castle, and he gave them neither food nor pay for their labours. Those who did not show up for work were fined. There is a case recorded in 1606 where Andrew Umphray when charged by the Earl to pay 2000 merks according to the contract he had signed, absolutely refused to do so. He maintained that the contract was null and void as it had been 'extorted by fear and dead-dome', the Earl having threatened to stab him through the head with his knife. This must be the 'Andro Vmphra' of Berry who carried the survivors of the *Gran Grifon* to Dunkirk in September 1589. For this service the Spanish admiral gave him 3000 merks, and Earl Patrick seems to have considered himself entitled to two-thirds of this amount.

Another man to stand up to Earl Patrick was the minister of Northmaven, the Rev. Pitcairn. When he did not succeed in showing the Earl the error of his ways, he is said to have suggested the inscription that is still visible above the doorway on the ground floor of the tower:

Cujus fundamen saxum est, domus illa manebit;
Labilis e contra, si sit arena, perit.

'The house whose foundation is rock will stand; but it will perish if built on sand.' The essence of this text is taken from Luke 6, and the rock referred to is analogous with the teaching of Christ. Earl Patrick must have been ignorant of the context, otherwise he would surely have realized the subtle irony, the typical Shetland skyimp, hidden in this inscription. The sand his house was built on was oppression.

The story goes that Earl Patrick was so ignorant of Christian ways that when he was sentenced to death in Edinburgh in 1615, they had to stay the execution till he had learned the Lord's Prayer. Given his time and age this seems incredible. Of course, there are points of similarity between this story and the Norwegian folk tale called 'Death and The Boy'. Death agreed to let him say the Lord's Prayer before he died, and after that the boy took great care not to say it!

During the time of the Commonwealth in the 1650s some of Cromwell's soldiers were garrisoned in the Castle. Almost three centuries later it was used to store equipment for the Shetland Bus people.

But Scalloway has other historical buildings. After the fall of the Stewart earls the importance of the Scottish landowning families grew unchecked. Dominating the harbour is the Old Haa', built when James Scott, a merchant in Scalloway, married Catherine Sinclair, heiress to the large estates of Scalloway and Houss in Burra. Later Gibblestone House replaced the Old Haa' as the home of the Scotts. They became financially embarrassed in the 1850s, and the estates were broken up.

Also associated with Scalloway is the titled Mitchell family of Westshore. The remains of their house are still to be seen in the large walled garden they left behind. In 1752 Sir Andrew Mitchell, who was then Sheriff Depute of Orkney and Zetland, was permitted by the Earl of Morton to take building materials from the Stewart Castle to be used for building his manor house at Sand.

Still, until the second half of the nineteenth century it would be wrong to call Scalloway a prosperous place. In 1703 it had only 90 inhabitants. The change came when Scalloway became the centre of the Faroe fishing industry. Smacks went to the fishing grounds off Faroe and Iceland, and their catches of cod and ling were salted and laid out on the beaches to dry. Vessels from Spain and Portugal came to Scalloway to buy the fish; and sometimes up to 15 large boats called in the course of the season. A local joke had it that perhaps the circulating of gospel tracts among the Spanish crews was not such a good idea after all, as it would not really be good for trade if Spain should become Protestant!

Around the turn of the century this industry came to an end and the herring fishing took its place. Although today Lerwick is the main landing place for herring caught by purse seiners, herring are still landed at Scalloway too, as the local fish-processing plant, Iceatlantic, can take up to fifty tons a week for freezing and kippering. The main species landed at Scalloway are cod, haddock and whiting.

Boys from the local fish-processing plant, Iceatlantic, enjoy a tea-break in the sun. Scalloway Castle in the background.

A century ago the islands so lovingly mentioned by Vagaland were all inhabited. Linga and Langa had only one croft each; but Hildasay and Papa had three or four. Oxna had 36 people living there in 1901. As long as people depended on fishing and subsistence crofting the small islands could maintain a settlement. The First World War meant the turn of the tide for such small communities; with the men away and perhaps never returning life was not viable for those left behind. Gradually the modern world caught hold of them in other ways too, but it was not an existence suitable for compromise—as soon as transport became necessary the fate of the small islands was sealed. People emigrated, if no further perhaps than to Scalloway or Burra.

It was just before the turn of the century that children playing in Oxna found a gold armlet of the Viking time beside a skarf's nest on the island. The spot was rather bare because the turf had been scalped away to make better soil in the arable areas. The armlet was partly exposed and lay glittering in the sunlight, and this attracted the attention of a young boy. He had some difficulty in pulling it out from the roots around it. Later a teacher from Burra saw it in his Oxna home and told an Edinburgh museum about it. The armlet is of solid gold, about 7 cm (3 in) in diameter, and is plaited from four gold wires. It is a massive and lovely specimen of early Norse jewellery and has been frequently used to illustrate history books. It is similar in style to some of the objects that were part of a hidden hoard found in 1858 in Skaill in Orkney.

Hildasay once had a curing station for herring and also a granite quarry. The stone was brought down to the landing-place along a small railway-track, the only one in Shetland. The story goes that this granite was even exported to Australia. But the quarry could no longer compete when concrete came into use. When the herring industry declined about the same time, there was only sheep-rearing left, and the island was abandoned by 1901. The owner of Hildasay allowed people from Burra and Trondra, where peat always had to be brought in from outside, to cut peat there, and especially the Trondra people liked to go there because the peat was of good quality, and the old pier of the curing station made a good landing-place. They all used to go peat-cutting together and it was a great social occasion. In 1897 the island was bought by an American with Shetland connections.

In the sixteenth century the island of South Havra was the home of Olaf Sinclair, the Foud of all Shetland. He was also the laird of the estate of Brew—the last great odal estate in Shetland. According to tradition the southern parts of Shetland were sometimes harassed by invading Lewis men from the Hebrides. In a battle at Sumburgh where 60 men were killed Olaf Sinclair is said to have escaped by leaping over Sumburgh Head to safety.

In 1921 there were eight families living in South Havra. They could draw on the experience of earlier generations in making a life for themselves in this fertile little island. There were drawbacks, but they had learned to master them. Children sometimes had to be tethered to keep them from going over the cliff. There was no peat on Havra, but it could be taken from the hill at Deepdale on the Mainland shore:

On fine summer evenings we would go over to the Cliff Hills for peat, which were brought down in a sledge, with several people hanging onto a rope at the back to prevent it going into the sea down the steep hillside. There was no landing place, and loading from the rocks was quite a hazardous business. (Annie Deyell, *My Shetland*, Sandwick 1975)

There was no stream to build a mill, but even in the middle of the nineteenth century they designed and built their own windmill, which became a useful landmark. It was the only corn-grinding windmill in Shetland. The small township seemed a thriving community, and a full-time school-teacher stayed there to teach the eight children of school age. Yet by May of 1923 the island was deserted.

The long narrow double islands of Burra presumably got their name from the once conspicuous broch that also gave the township of Brough its name. But historically the island is better known for the finds that have been made at the old church site at Papil. There is not much to see there today—just an old churchyard and a fairly recent church rapidly becoming a ruin. But the name suggests that its ecclesiastical connections go far back, and it was there that the Shetland scholar Gilbert Goudie in 1877 found the now-so-famous Burra stone:

As it lay, with the decorated side uppermost, at a short distance to the south of the church in the ancient churchyard at Papil, it might have been noticed at any time by any one who chose to look for it, or who, chancing to observe it, had recognised its significance as a relic of Christian art from a period of remote antiquity. But from age to age it appears to have escaped notice. (*The Celtic and Scandinavian Antiquities of Shetland*, London 1904, p44)

The Burra stone is richly sculptured, showing four priestly figures with croziers, as well as a grotesque animal. It helps throw a light on the rather obscure period of Christianity in the Northern Isles before the Norse settlement. At the bottom of the stone two rather funny-looking birdmen have been added by another stone-carver. Is this the joke of a Norseman who wanted to point out the similarity between puffins and fat priests? The original stone is kept in the National Museum of Antiquities in Edinburgh. In 1943 another sculptured stone was found in the same churchyard. It showed four walking figures carrying croziers, and one horseman. Today this stone is known as the Monks' Stone from Papil and can be seen in the Lerwick Museum.

According to tradition West Burra was known at one time as the Kirk Isle. This must have been on account of the steepled St Lawrence

The Monks' Stone from Papil which can be seen in the Lerwick Museum. (Shetland Museum)

Kirk that once stood at Papil. The church has been described by the Rev. Hugh Leigh. Apart from the two years he was suspended for beating his wife, he was for a long time minister of the parish of Bressay, Burra, and Quarff:

Here (in the Kirk Isle) is a church, within a mile of the southmost end of the island, standing near to the sound side of *Burray* called *St Lawrence* Church (built as it is reported, by the mid-most of the three *Norwegian* Sisters, the eldest having built the church of *Tingwall*, and the youngest the church of *Ireland*), the steeple whereof will be five or six stories high, though a little church, yet very fashionable, and its *Sanctum Sanctorum* (or Quire) yet remains. (*A Geographical Description of the Island of Burray*, 1654)

The old township of Symbister in East Burra is now completely derelict, but there are thriving crofting communities at Papil, Houss, Norbister and Brough. However, the land is thin, and crofting has therefore been less important than the sea. Burra was always primarily a fishing district, and the sea off the south-western part of Shetland, as far as Foula, has been known as the Burra Haf. There they fished for herring in the summer in their fourerns, the maid-of-all-work boats which served for the line fishing for the rest of the year. It was there that Christian Pløyen and his Faroese friends chose to go in 1839 when they had come to Shetland to learn fish-curing methods, as they had heard that the best fish-curer in Shetland worked there.

Hamnavoe in Burra has a better natural harbour than almost anywhere else in Shetland.

Since then, fishing has had its difficult periods and its golden times, and many types of boats have appeared, only to become obsolete and be scrapped after a few years. But Burra fishermen have always managed to keep abreast of the development, and fishing remains the most important local industry. It is full-time employment for some 90 fishermen. In relation to its population Burra probably has the most modern whitefish fleet in Britain, and an excellent modern and safe harbour at Scalloway. This was specially built for the fishing industry in 1984 at a cost of almost five million pounds. Such an all-weather dock was essential to the fishermen on the west side of Shetland. The only thing now deterring young men from committing themselves to fishing at the present time is lack of capital, as the cost of a modern fishing vessel is prohibitive.

Hamnavoe in Burra has a better natural harbour than almost anywhere else in Shetland. It is protected from the various winds by hills and headlands. Most of the Burra fishermen live in the village that has grown up there, and thus the time-honoured combination of the sea and the croft has been broken. There also used to be a renowned boat-building industry run by the Duncans of Hamnavoe. For nearly a hundred years they built boats which were keenly sought after for their excellent workmanship and seaworthiness. During the war they carried out many repair jobs for the Shetland Bus boats. Their building processes did not differ very much from the shell-built clinker methods that have been in use in Shetland over the centuries. Boats were built by 'eye'—without plans or line drawings. There are still traditional boats being built in Burra by individuals, but not commercially any more.

Hamnavoe began growing as a village towards the end of the nineteenth century, and today there are upwards of 500 people living there. When a new primary school was needed to receive the rising number of children, great care was taken with its planning. In 1983 it was given the commendation of the Royal Institute of British Architects for outstanding design.

In 1971 the three islands of Trondra, West and East Burra became connected with the Mainland by bridge. At the time Trondra was threatened by depopulation. But since the bridge came it has become so popular to live in these islands and commute to Lerwick every day that many say that Lerwick, indeed Shetland as well, is run from Burra these days!

The new primary school in Hamnavoe, which was given the commendation of the Royal Institute of British Architects for outstanding design.

21 MAINLAND

South Mainland

Together with Fair Isle the long narrow southern peninsula of Mainland makes up the parish of Dunrossness. Originally this name referred only to the southernmost part. The land is among the most fertile in Shetland, and it is not surprising that it is rich in archaeological remains and interesting features. The name derives from *Dynröst* and the Norse verb *dynja*, which meant to roar and thunder, referring to the famed Sumburgh Roost. This is the three miles of wild sea where the tides of the Atlantic and the North Sea clash ferociously, so that even in calm weather the race breaks violently.

Watching over the Roost is the lighthouse at Sumburgh Head. This was Shetland's first lighthouse, built in 1821 by Robert Stevenson, from a family of remarkable lighthouse engineers. The construction was at first delayed because the Lerwick ship that brought the building materials was wrecked off Grutness, leaving only one survivor. The lighthouse was very solidly built, with double thickness walls. Its light flashes can be seen 20 miles (32 km) away in Lerwick.

This is classical Scott country. In the summer of 1814 Sir Walter Scott was invited to join Robert Stevenson on a survey for the Northern Light-House Service. He found 'much in the wild islands of the Orkneys and Zetland which I judged might be made in the highest degree interesting, should these isles ever become the scene of a narrative of fictitious events'. The result was the novel *The Pirate*, based on the story of John Gow, the Orkney pirate, who was hanged in London. In order to use more of the folklore and the old stories he heard, Scott set his novel one century back in time. Although it appealed to the romantically-inclined of his day, the novel is hardly readable today. The characters are type-cast and do not come alive. They are set against a historical backdrop, but this is used only for local colour, and the plot and the setting never merge. Only Scott's awe of the haunting Shetland scenery seems genuine.

It was at Sumburgh Head that the pirate, who in the novel is called Cleveland, was saved after a shipwreck by Mordaunt Mertoun, the solitary inhabitant of Jarlshof. North of there lived the ódaller Magnus Troil and his two lovely daughters Minna and Brenda, and a cave in

Fitful Head was the home of Norna who was fated to live with the powers of a seer instead of knowing personal happiness.

Scott had no way of knowing that the old laird's house that he named Jarlshof was built on a site which had been occupied for three thousand years, through changing cultures. It is an incredible site; packed into three acres are successive villages representing three main historical stages: Late Bronze Age, Late Iron Age and the Norse settlement. Towards the end of the last century several strong storms exposed massive stone walls which were noticed by John Bruce, the owner of the Sumburgh estate. He lived in the nearby mansion which is now the hotel. The excavations he started were carried on by professional archaeologists, and done very carefully so as to keep the site intact as an ancient monument.

The silvery sand that covered the settlements also blew further inland and long ago buried the old estate of Brew. The old Cross Kirk of Dunrossness shared this fate. The church was too close to the sea, and at times the sand so covered everything that the spot was even called an Arabian desert in miniature. According to James Kay, who was the minister of Dunrossness in the late seventeenth century, the sand at other times blew away so that 'the coffins are discovered and sometimes naked corpses for all have not coffins'. Past the old farm and water-mill of Quendale lies the wide sunny valley of Garth. This was once a prosperous community of four small townships where settlement went a long way back. One day in November 1874 twenty-

The cliffs of Fitful Head are a well-known landmark.

seven families had to leave from there because the laird, Grierson of Quendale, wanted room for sheep.

The cliffs of Fitful Head are a well-known landmark. A possible explanation of the name is that it derives from the Norse *Fitfugl-höföi*—Swimmingbird-head. However, locally it has always been known as just Fitful. In view of that it is perhaps more likely that the name is derived from *Hvítafjall*—the white mountain, as the rest of the name then becomes superfluous. The geologist Samuel Hibbert explains why he thinks this meaning of the name is probable:

The clay-slate of which this headland is composed, has so pearly a lustre, that when the rays of the sun shine fully upon it, a whitish appearance is produced. (*Description of The Shetland Islands*, 1822, p230)

However, the Norwegian historian P. A. Munch points out that 'hvít' always becomes 'white' or 'quhyte' in Shetland place names and suggests a third possibility: *Vitafjall*—the mountain of the signal fire. A *viti* was the heap of firewood ready to be lit in a time of crisis. In Norway this way of warning was systematized since the tenth century, and it took seven nights to alert the people along the whole length of the country. Munch considers it likely that Shetland would be required by law to have the same system, being even more vulnerable to attack than Norway herself. Fitful Head would be a more likely choice than Sumburgh Head, as it is higher and can also be easily seen from Foula.

There used to be eagles nesting in the high slopes of Fitful. There were also two crofting townships, but they were marginal and were left around a hundred years ago. Today the land is used for sheep-grazing.

One of the most popular excursion sites in Shetland is the large Loch of Spiggie and the area around it. It is one of the best lochs in Shetland for trout fishing, and the long sandy beach is very popular for bathing when the weather permits it. South of the main beach is 'da peerie voe' which is the place to be to watch a setting summer sun. The Loch of Spiggie is now a Nature Reserve.

On Dunrossness beaches it is still possible at times to see the graceful and supple little boat known as the Ness yoal. Its roots go a long way back in time and place—for a long time they used to be brought across the sea from Sunnhordland until about 1860 when import duties made it too expensive. The boat would usually be crewed by three men, and was well suited to Shetland tidal conditions. Although these boats are excellent rowing boats, they can also be used with a sail.

Along the western side of the long narrow backbone of Dunrossness lie the prosperous communities of Rerwick, Bigton and Ireland. St Ninian's Isle is joined to the Bigton shore by an ayre, a long spit of sand, which can be crossed at all states of the tide. But according to tradition this was once a tidal island. It was inhabited till around 1700 when the peat ran out and people left. Today it grazes sheep for a nearby farm. In a certain light it is still possible to see traces of former cultivation near the old well named for St Ninian. The graveyard was in use until the end of the last century when people would no longer carry a coffin across the sand in a winter gale.

On 4 July 1958 the St Ninian's Isle treasure was found. Students from Aberdeen University were excavating the old church, believed to be Norse from *c.* 1150, and with a pre-Norse structure below it. A young Shetland schoolboy was a very eager helper, and as the story goes, he was told to go and dig 'over there' so as not to be in their way. Under a thin stone slab inscribed with a cross he found a box made of larch. This tree did not grow in Britain until the eighteenth century, so the box must have been brought in from somewhere else. The silver objects seemed to have been buried in a hurry.

Dunrossness has perhaps the greatest density of brochs in Shetland. At Ness of Burgi in Scatness there are also the remains of a fort which may have been an earlier stage of the broch-building. Along the east side there are interesting broch sites both at Dalsetter and the Loch of Clumlie. It is therefore a strange fact that a district with a name like Cunningsburgh, meaning King's Castle, does not seem to have any. The reason for the name is lost in the haze of history. There has been no castle or broch found so far, nor is there any oral tradition to throw a light on the name. The area is not very fertile, and the people living there have had a difficult time trying to scratch a living. They had to be stubborn and strong; according to George Low they were also the wildest in Shetland.

Because of a Norn saying he picked up there, Low has also branded the Cunningsburgh people as surly hosts—a failing indeed in Shetland where hospitality is a way of life. This was even in Low's time known as the Cunningsburgh phrase:

> Myrk in e Liora,
> Luce in e Liunga,
> Tim in e Guest in e geungna.

'Dark is the chimney, the light is in the heather, it is time for the guests to go.' This was a blunt way of telling a guest that he had outstayed his welcome. About a century later the linguist Jakobsen found that the saying was still known in Yell, although in a slightly different wording. The same saying, with small variations, has also been noted down in three widely separated districts of Norway. Indeed, Hávamál in the Elder Edda expresses exactly the same idea.

In the autumn of 1148 Earl Rognvald Kali Kolsson was returning from a visit to King Ingi in Bergen. The King had showered him with gifts of all kinds, but the most precious were two small but unusually fine-looking longships, *Hjölp* and *Fifa*—'Help' and 'Arrow'. Earl

Rognvald let his young kinsman Earl Harald Maddadarson take command of the *Fifa*. After two days they saw land, but there were breakers surrounding them on all sides and they had no choice but to run both vessels on shore, even though 'the beach before them was stony and narrow, enclosed behind by crags'.

> Crash we went, with *Hjölp* and *Fifa*
> —both were wrecked;
> The seasprays brought them sorrow,
> The waves gave grief to men.
> I see this voyage of the Earls
> —will be remembered ...
> (Dr Lucy Collings)

This happened in Gulberwick. And in spite of losing his beautiful new ships and most of his goods, Earl Rognvald was not too shaken to express himself in verse. Indeed his words proved prophetic: the voyage *was* remembered by the Shetland Viking Expedition, an international group made up of amateur divers and scientists. They spent eight weeks in the summer of 1972 investigating the historical authenticity of the Orkneyinga Saga and trying to find Norse artefacts. Oral tradition in Gulberwick connected the wreck with the mound known as King's Knowe, on the Setter side of the Bay. This area was found thoroughly compatible with the saga story, but in spite of a thorough search of the sea bed nothing of interest was found. However, one of the treasures of the Museum in Lerwick is a striking silver ornament known as 'the Gulberwick Brooch'. It was found years ago when a young boy was trying to melt it down to make himself a fishing sinker, and there is no clear account of how he came by it.

*One of the treasures of the Museum in Lerwick is a striking silver ornament known as 'the Gulberwick Brooch'. (*Shetland Museum*)*

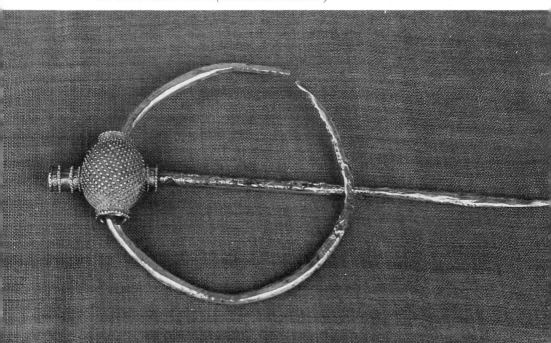

Central and West Mainland

Although place names like Nesting and Delting point to there having
been many local assemblies or Tings in Shetland, only Tingwall can
be localized with any certainty. It seems to have been held on a small
holm in Loch of Tingwall, which was approached by a stone causeway.
The loch now has a lower water level so that the holm has become
landfast. Probably regular meetings of the Ting were held here in the
early phase of the Norse settlement; before the coming of Christianity
it was perhaps also a place of pagan worship. For their main assembly
the Norsemen would choose a site with a central position which could
be easily reached from all directions.

The Ting began as a meeting-place for all free men; here laws were
made and judgments passed. Gradually, as law-making became
centralized, the Ting's main function was as a court of law. An old
tradition in Tingwall shows the common people as indirectly serving
as a court of appeal: when a man had been found guilty of a major
crime and sentenced to death, he could make a run for the sanctuary
of Tingwall church. If the people wanted him pardoned they would
let him make it.

The old St Magnus church at Tingwall had a round tower and
looked rather like the church of the same name on Egilsay in Orkney.
There were three such 'steeple-kirks' in Shetland—the other two were
at Ireland and Papil, and they were said to have been built by three
Norwegian sisters. Of the five Shetland churches dedicated to St
Magnus the Tingwall Kirk was the largest and finest. For centuries it
was the main church, so that when Shetland's archdeaconry was
founded in 1215 as one of the first in the Norwegian archdiocese, it
was based in Tingwall. Especially in pre-Reformation days the
archdeacon was a very important person, as he was the deputy of the
bishop of Orkney. For some reason the old Tingwall Kirk was pulled
down in 1790, and the stone was used to build the present church
nearby. Sir Walter Scott stayed at the manse for some days during his
visit to Shetland in 1814, and so did Christian Pløyen, the Commissioner
of Faroe, in 1839:

The manse was a very good house, the walls of sandstone, three storeys high,
spacious and comfortable, as are all the manses in Shetland which I have
seen, and only in such substantial buildings is it possible to preserve health
under such a climate as that of Shetland or Faroe. The church, on the other
hand, was bleak and in bad repair, not even clean, which it might surely
have been without expense. (*Reminiscences of a Voyage to Shetland, Orkney &
Scotland*, Lerwick 1894, p55)

The site of the old church of St Magnus was excavated at the
beginning of this century. The former church choir then formed a
burial vault. Among the tombstones found was one commemorating

In the churchyard at Tingwall, a burial vault with seventeenth- and eighteenth-century tombstones is all that remains of the earlier mediaeval church of St Magnus.

'Andrew Crawford, sometime servitor and master of work to the Earl of Orkney'. He was the architect who was responsible for the construction of the Earl's Palace in Kirkwall and probably directed the building of Scalloway Castle in 1600. A notorious contemporary of his was Thomas Boyne, the last foud of Tingwall, whose tombstone has this intriguing inscription:

Heir lyis ane honest man—Thomas Boyne—svmtym Fovd of Tingval.

Is this a man's opinion of himself or a stone mason's ironic jibe?

At one time there was a church also at the old ferry crossing at Sound in Weisdale Voe. It was wrapped in legends that appealed to the popular imagination. In his dreams a man in Weisdale was visited again and again by an angel who told him he must build a church. When the walls were up there was no wood for the roof. Then in a storm a Norwegian ship carrying a cargo of wood miraculously found a haven in Weisdale Voe. The captain gave enough wood to finish building the church, and in their joy at being saved the crew took part in the work. Although its name was Our Lady's Kirk the church became known as Da Aamos Kirk because for a long time 'olmusa' or offerings were given to it in the belief that it would bring safety to all seafarers. Men who were going away on a ship would leave a coin and say: 'Guide be wi' me and mine'. This continued even when the church had become a ruin.

Another ruin at Sound is the house that once belonged to the Clunies-Ross family; once it was a pleasant dwelling and it is still surrounded by trees that are unusually tall for Shetland. In 1786 John Clunies-Ross was born there; he left Shetland at the age of 13 for a career in the merchant navy, but settled with family and friends on the Cocos Islands in the Indian Ocean in 1826. He became the absolute ruler of the islands and a population of some 200, mostly of Malay origin, and was known as the King. When his son took over in 1857, the islands were annexed by the British government and the rule of the Clunies-Ross family acknowledged. In 1984 the islanders by their own wish became Australians, after Australia had bought the islands from the Clunies-Ross family.

From Sound the road turns west over the Scord of Tresta into West Mainland—a land of lochs and hills, voes and stacks. It is thinly populated today, but there are many traces of prehistoric settlement. Around Bridge of Walls are three settlements from the third and second millennia BC, at Pinhoulland, Scord of Brouster and Stanydale. They were agricultural villages inhabited over a long period. So far Scord of Brouster and parts of Stanydale have been excavated. Although the former perhaps gives the best picture of how life was lived in neolithic Shetland, Stanydale is the more striking because of the large structure known as 'the temple', but whose real purpose is not known.

At the entrance of Sandsound Voe was once the township of Sandsound with well-cultivated crofts to the top of the hill. Gradually the population dwindled and most people left, but now it is slowly coming back to life. Across the Voe in Sand lies the ruin of St Mary's church—only the chancel arch is left standing. Tradition associates it with the Armada as it is supposed to have been built by Spaniards who were grateful for being saved. The church is, however, of Norse origin. The waters around Sand are now full of salmon cages, as one of the major fish farms is located there.

Further along the western shore is Reawick. It is dominated by a well-preserved laird's Haa House, which was the family seat of the Umphrays and later the Garricks, who established the cod-fishing station and boat-building near Skeld. Reawick House was the residence of A. I. Tulloch, the late convener of the Shetland Islands Council from 1974 till 1986. He will be remembered as the powerful leader who guided the council through the oil-development era. Today the red granite sands of Reawick are a very popular spot for bathing and picnics.

The southern coastline of Sandsting with its spectacular cliffs and the large rock of Giltarump sticking out into the sea, is striking when

St Mary's church, Sand. Tradition has associated it with the Spanish Armada, but it is of Norse origin.

viewed from the sea. The bays of Silwick, Westerwick and Culswick are open to the Atlantic and exposed. The beaches there are steep and covered with round stones. Along the burn in Westerwick the slopes are full of wildflowers. This area was the birthplace of the poet Vagaland, or T. A. Robertson. Near Sotersta Loch are the remains of the Broch of Culswick. It has a strategic position at the entrance of Gruting Voe and must once have been an imposing sight, but it was used as building material for the now derelict croft buildings close by, and there is not much left of it. The area around the ruined farm of Sotersta where horses roam free must surely be one of the most beautiful sites in Shetland, but it gives also an almost frightening sense of space and solitariness.

At one time there was a loch in Stead of Culswick, separated from the sea by a shingle barrier, but during a gale this was washed away by heavy seas, and the area turned into a dangerous swamp. Culswick itself is a deep valley that once had a flourishing township of 130 people. As there was no road, most of their comings and goings were by sea, and there are still remains of stone nousts on the beach. The little Methodist church high up in the hillside was built in 1894. The road and the school came in the thirties, but by that time many people had left. The Culswick people were known for their capacity for hard work. Today very few of the original inhabitants remain in the valley, but new people have come in.

The island of Vaila forms a natural bulwark against the sea, but slopes green and fertile towards Vaila Sound on the landward side. An entry dated 3 March 1576 in *Register of the Privy Seal of Scotland* confirms the sale of the lands of Vaila by Dame Gurweill Fatheris-dochter to Mr Robert Cheyne and gives him the right 'to big ane hous and fortrice upoun the saidis landis of Walay for sauftie thairof fra the Heland men, perattis and utheris invasiones'. A tower known as Mucklabery Castle was built at the entrance to Wester Sound. Today

The 86-year-old Erasmus ('Rasmie') Reid, one of the very few original inhabitants remaining in Culswick.

it serves as a landmark, but it may have been used at one time to keep an eye on fishing boats coming in to land fish.

From 1838 onwards Vaila was a bustle of activity, with fish drying on the beaches and foreign vessels anchoring in Vaila Sound to buy loads of it. The native Shetlander Arthur Anderson, who founded the P. & O. Company, leased the island from the then owners, the Scotts of Melby. In an attempt to break the fish trade monopoly of the lairds he set up the Shetland Fishery Company which would give the local fishermen a fair deal. It seems to have prospered, but was wound up some time in the 1840s when Anderson could no longer devote time to it. In 1888 Vaila was bought by Herbert Anderton, a wealthy Yorkshire millowner, who spent a fortune on improving the house and grounds. The original house was made into the baronial hall we see today, and nothing was spared in furnishing it. By the harbour in Ham there was even a Buddhist temple.

The island still belongs to the Anderton family, although they now find the upkeep of the house difficult. Still it is a unique period piece of the past and should be preserved for the future. It is the largest house of its kind in Shetland and one of the few that can still be saved. It represents no bad memories of exploitation and eviction as so many of the other old houses, and even a simplified version of the original would be a wonderful tourist attraction. Therefore the indifference of the authorities is surprising. Directly across Wester Sound lies Burrastow House, which belongs to the same period as the older part of Vaila Hall, and was once in the same family.

The village of Walls is named for the surrounding area. The name derives from Vágar, plural form of the Norse word *vágr*, which has become 'voe' in Shetland usage. The same name occurs as Vågan in the Lofoten Islands. The name is equally fitting for the coast of Aithsting, where the narrow winding voes seem to merge with the small lochs. It is an area for the walker and the angler, who will have a difficult choice, for, as the local poet Vagaland says:

> Fair is mony a Wast Side toon—
> Dey're no little wirt;
> Gairden is a boannie place,
> An sae is Fugrigert.
> (*Reestit Mutton at da Althing*)

In the lovely township of Fugrigert, or Fogrigarth, at the head of West Burra Firth, lived Robert Doull, who seems to have been one of the last great ódallers. In his book on Shetland Samuel Hibbert describes how he visited him around 1820:

The smoke arose from a low house, built of unhewn stones, after the most ancient fashion of the country;—it was the *Head Buil* or Manor-house of a small landed possessor of Aithsting, named the Laird of Fogrigate. On opening the door, I passed through a double range of servants of both sexes, who occupied forms disposed along each side of the room, and made suitable obeisance to the *hoy saedet* or high seat of the house, filled by the laird himself, with all the patriarchal dignity worthy that primitive state of manners described in an ancient poem of the 8th century. (*A Description of the Shetland Isles*, Edinburgh 1822, p545)

On the holm of Helinster in West Burra Firth are the remains of a broch which was still fairly intact when visited by George Low in 1774. He found that it differed from other brochs he had seen, as it had a single wall and contained 11 small compartments to be entered from within. They had a diameter of 1.6 m (5 ft), and Low was unable to establish their purpose.

The islands of Vementry and Papa Little have both been inhabited, but are now empty. On top of the 90 m (295 ft) high Muckle Ward in Vementry is a specimen of the heel-shaped cairn, a kind of chambered tomb not found outside Shetland. Because of its isolation the site is better preserved than most, at the same time it is more unusual in its character. There is no entrance to the tomb, so it is possible that it was closed after the last burial. In the northwestern part of Vementry, at Swarbacks Head, are gun emplacements from the First World War.

Northeast and North Mainland

Along with Whalsay and Out Skerries, Nesting and Lunnasting make up one parish. Many archaeological remains point to this area as having been populated in prehistoric times, but so far little or no excavation has been done. One such prehistoric site was important in Norse times also: near Eswick was the large and fertile farm of Borg, now Brough, which in the fifteenth century was left to Munkeliv monastery in Bergen by Thorvald Henriksson, a descendant of Thorvald Thoresson of Papa Stour. After the Reformation the land became crown property, and was granted by King James VI in 1587 to Hugh Sinclair. His descendants called themselves the Barons of Brugh and their estate was huge, even including large holdings in Orkney. When Samuel Hibbert visited the area *c.* 1820 there were only the ruined walls of their chapel left standing. Later nearly the whole of Nesting became the property of the Bruces of Symbister.

A very romantic as well as interesting site is that of Lunna House, which is now a hotel. It became famous as the centre of Norwegian resistance during the Second World War through David Howarth's *The Shetland Bus*. It was for a long time the home of the Hunter family. Robert Hunter appears to have tried to introduce better tenures free from the obligation to fish for the laird. He also fought to have Shetland represented in Parliament, before this right was obtained through the Reform Bill in 1832.

The lovely old Lunna Church, so strikingly different from most

Shetland churches, was first built in 1753, but has been rebuilt twice since then. A small opening in the outside wall is said to have been a leper hole, but other explanations have been suggested as well. There are still unnamed Norwegian war graves in the churchyard. On top of a large mound beside the church are the remains of another old church, with an entrance to the south-west. The impressive gateway leading to this mound is very puzzling, as is the road, still clearly visible, leading from the gateway up to Lunna House itself.

Delting is an area of voes and valleys; apart from the valley that perhaps gave Delting its name, there is also the lovely little Skelladale. Crofting alone could never support the population, and fishing was always important, as in other parts of Shetland. On 21 December 1900 seven crews from North Delting set out for the winter haddock grounds in the 'East haf' of the notorious Yell Sound. There they set their lines. Then without warning they were struck by fierce winds of 120 miles an hour. Before they knew what was happening two boats went under. A northwesterly wind forced the remaining boats to head southwest, but only three of them made it, and 22 fishermen in all were lost. The Toft and Firth districts were especially hard hit by what became known as the Delting Disaster.

Sullom Voe is the longest voe in Shetland. During the Second World War a Coastal Command base was established at the southern end of the voe at Scatsta. Graven had accommodation for some 1200 R.A.F. men as well as 700 Norwegian fleet airmen. From here Sunderland and Catalina flying-boats patrolled the North Sea in all kinds of weather—a bleak and bitterly cold task. Testimony to the importance of the sea base is shown by the German reaction to it: in one of his broadcasts the British voice in Berlin popularly known as 'Lord Haw-Haw' promised that German planes would soon come to 'clean up that nest of vipers in Shetland'.

Today Sullom Voe has been taken over by the oil business, and this has naturally brought a lot of change to the Delting area as a whole, but perhaps the village of Brae shows it the most. Because of its position it had long been a centre of commercial activity. The name derives from the Norse *breið eið*—the broad isthmus—which would have been given to distinguish it from the narrow isthmus of Mavis Grind. Brae separates Sullom Voe from the sheltered waters of Busta Voe. These waters were at one time so important that the idea of connecting them by a canal was seriously discussed. The name indicates that Busta was always an important settlement, so that the voe was named for the farm and not the other way around. The fine old mansion of Busta was the seat of the Gifford family; they were the most important Shetland lairds, owning three-quarters of Northmaven and half of Delting as well as land in Yell, Aithsting and Walls, and also fish exporters. The story of the disappearance of the Busta sons in the Voe

The fine old mansion of Busta was long the seat of the Gifford family. It is now a hotel.

one night in May 1748, as well as the purloined marriage lines, reads like the plot of a Gothic novel. A law-suit about ownership dragged on for half a century and impoverished the estate. During the First World War Busta House was used as headquarters by the admiral in charge of the Tenth Cruiser Squadron. This was responsible for the blockade of German ships and was based in Swarbacks Minn. Unfortunately the Busta estate papers that were of such importance to Shetland history were destroyed during the Second World War.

The island of Muckle Roe was also part of the Busta estate. It is fertile and well cultivated along the eastern and north-eastern shores. The magnificent pink granite cliffs in the north-western part— especially in North and South Ham where they form a contrasting backdrop to white sand and green grass— should be seen from the sea. This was once a favourite breeding-place of the great sea eagle.

The northernmost Mainland parish of Northmaven is also the wildest and most striking. It is entered through the narrow Mavis Grind, a name meaning gateway of the narrow isthmus and aptly fitting for the low neck of land with high and forbidding rocks on either side. Mavis Grind used to be a convenient short-cut for fishermen going from one haf to the other—the boats could be dragged from the Atlantic to the North Sea. Today the fishing boats are too heavy to be handled like that, but it was still done as recently as the 1950s.

Mangaster, which may be a distortion of Magnussetter, was at one time an important farm. It gave its name to the voe as well, and was possibly the original name of the large bay known today as St Magnus Bay. Further along is Hamar, which was one of the largest farms in the district. It is described in a will of 26 April 1403 as 'Hamar sem liggir firir nordhan Mæfeid'—Hamar which lies north of Mavis Grind. In this will Thjodhild, the daughter of the priest Sira Helge, left Hamar to Munkeliv monastery in Bergen.

The parish takes its name from the district south of Ronas Voe. It is an area abounding in the most spectacular coast scenery. The action of the sea has worn away the softer, stratified rock and left rugged peaks and precipices in fantastic forms. About half a mile from shore rise the Drongs—isolated granite rocks looking like a castle or a phantom ship, depending on the light and the angle. Further west is the Dore Holm with its great natural arch.

The natural centre of this area has long been Hillswick with its interesting old hotel and the public house Da Bød dating from Hanseatic times. It also has a big old church that was built in 1869 to hold 600 people. At one time there was an old church known as the Cross Kirk at Breckon in Eshaness. This was considered a holy place and remained a place of pilgrimage long after the Reformation; this is said to have so enraged the zealous Protestant minister Hercules Sinclair that he had it razed to the ground in 1664. Traces of the old church can still be seen, and the churchyard around it has some interesting tombstones. This is a famous inscription, to one Donald Robertson:

He was a peaceable quiet man, and, to all appearance, a sincere Christian; his death was much regreted, which was caused by the stupidity of Laurence Tulloch in Clothister who sold him nitre instead of Epsom salts, by which he was killed in the space of 3 hours after taking a dose of it.

Also buried in this churchyard is John Williamson, who fought his own private war against smallpox, the epidemic that was the scourge of eighteenth century Shetland. He appears to have preceded Edward Jenner, who is generally credited as the originator of inoculation against smallpox. Born in 1740 at his father's croft in Hamnavoe, where he stayed all his life, he had no formal education as there was still no school in Northmaven at that time. He was a weaver by profession but could turn his hand to anything. When struck by an idea he would fall into deep concentration, almost a trance, and for that reason he was nicknamed Johnnie Notions. He is still remembered

Dore Holm, with its great natural arch, seen from Esha Ness, with the sea-mark which was put up by the Northern Lighthouse Commissioners in the 1920s.

by that name in Shetland. At the time orthodox medicine seems to have held that smallpox was the breaking out of bad blood, and bloodletting was therefore a common cure that only the most robust would survive. John Williamson worked on his theories for years; to obtain a serum he inoculated a Shetland pony with pus from a patient with smallpox.

He dried the serum to powder in peat smoke, taking care to protect it from the effects of the smoke, wrapped it in camphor and buried it underground. He was most careful to see that the serum was at least seven years old before being put into use. This, he said, was to lessen the reactionary effect on a very weak and highly-fevered patient, but it seemed that the physicians, peeved by scepticism, did not agree. (Thesis of Dr Thomas Cowie, 1871)

The medical profession grew increasingly hostile to him, but no case was ever recorded where the inoculation failed to take effect within a few days. In the Shetland Museum there is a head he modelled in wood of his first patient, an old crofter from Burn near Hillswick. There is also a plaque to his memory on the wall of the house which was later built at the site of his birthplace in Hamnavoe.

Eshaness has a lighthouse built on the edge of a precipice where stones have been flung so high out of the sea that the windows have been broken. The name Eshaness probably derives from *esja* which refers to rocks that split easily. There are still remains of fishing-booths in the old station at Stenness nearby, and along the coast north of Eshaness the Atlantic has cut passages through weak parts of the cliff wall and shaped eerie places like The Holl o' Skraada and The Grind of the Navir. *Nafarr* in Norse was a drill or an auger. It is this coast north of Hamnavoe which is the scene of the novel *Thin Wealth* by the young Shetland writer Robert Alan Jamieson.

The 7 miles (11 km) long Ronas Voe has been a haven for trawlers surprised by bad weather. During the third Dutch War 1772–74 the outward bound Dutch East Indiaman *Het Wapen van Amsterdam* in December 1773 chose this voe as an anchorage while waiting for a fair wind. She was a ship of about a thousand tons, and like all merchant ships at the time, was heavily armed. Relations between the Dutch and the local people had always been friendly, and the war was very unpopular in Shetland. The Dutch vessel seems to have been windbound for some time, for on 11 February 1774 she was attacked by three British frigates, and probably taken as a prize to England. At Hollanders' Knowe on the southern shore of Ronas Voe is the grave of the Dutch sailors who were then killed in action. During the First World War Ronas Voe was an anchorage for the navy.

It is possible to climb straight up Ronas Hill from the voe. It is the steepest route but it gives the best view. Ronas Hill is, in fact, easily accessible from many directions, for in contrast to the rugged scenery around it and in spite of having the same granite structure, it is softly rounded with a smooth surface. It is 450 m (1475 ft) the highest hill in Shetland. On the highest peak of the hill is one of the most complete specimens of a chambered cairn in Shetland. The name Ronas Hill is a modern distortion of the earlier Roenes Hill, which probably derived from Rauðanes, the red promontory. This name would have referred to the whole area, making the word hill superfluous.

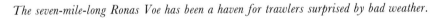

The seven-mile-long Ronas Voe has been a haven for trawlers surprised by bad weather.

The remains of another cairn are found at The Beorgs of Housetter. It is watched over by two standing stones, and the site is known as The Giant's Grave. Nearby are the remains of a chambered tomb called Towie Knowe, and as the names indicate, both sites are part of local folklore. There are also many broch sites, but unfortunately most of them have been levelled.

There are obvious remains of a prehistoric house also at Fedaland, the northernmost part of Mainland, but the interest of this area is connected with more recent Shetland history—this was the largest of the haf fishing stations. Today the long ness of Fedaland is quite empty. The main road ends at the farm of Isbister, but a few years ago when the lighthouse was being constructed at the Isle of Fedaland a road was built right across the hill. This is not open to cars. There is also a track which was made by the fishermen who for so many years worked the haf from Fedaland. The huts of the fishermen and the nousts for their boats can still be seen on the stony beach between Easter and Wester Wick. Even today it is not hard to imagine what the scene must have been like in the summertime here. It is a place of incredible beauty on a calm summer day, but the worn coastline all around speaks for itself of the violence let loose upon it in a storm. Life there was hard. Christian Pløyen describes it vividly:

I went into several of the huts and asked leave to look how they were furnished, and I was received by these poor hardy fellows with the utmost civility. The whole was like a great ship, for there were none present but weatherbeaten seamen, not a woman was to be seen in the hamlet. The inside of these huts corresponds with the outside. You will find nothing but some beds made of rude boards, nailed together, containing straw and coarse blankets. On some of these lay men, who had thrown themselves down in their clothes and enjoyed sweet sleep. (*Reminiscences of a Voyage to Shetland, Orkney & Scotland*, p39)

The nearby Kleber Geo is so called because of all the steatite, or soapstone, it contains. The local word for this is kleber; it was used to good effect in Shetland as an external application for the cure of burns. Out to sea are the inaccessible and dangerous Ramna Stacks.

Nearby Sandvoe was the birthplace of James Inkster, who wrote *Mansie's Rød* in Shetlandic, a description of the old crofting life. Westwards along the coast is Uyea with its beautiful green pasture. At the time of the 1851 census this was a community of 15 houses containing 92 people. On the beach of Burrier Wick there was once a haf-fishing station. At certain states of the tide it is possible to walk across to the island of Uyea which is well worth a visit. Not only rich in copper ore the island is said to have the richest grass in Shetland. The Kettlebaak Cave in the southern part of the island is shaped so that a person hiding there is not easily found, and it was therefore a popular refuge in pressgang days.

22 THE NORTH ISLES

Till recently the islands that make up the northern part of Shetland were in many ways a world apart. For a long time the main link with Mainland was the inter-island vessel *Earl of Zetland*, which until 1974 made regular calls at the main ports and was perhaps the quickest but not the cheapest way of getting to the North Isles. In many of the places where she called there was not a good enough pier, so passengers and cargo would have to go ashore in a flit-boat, which was usually an old sixern. She travelled a dangerous coast, in all kinds of weather. The story goes that one captain would pay a woman at the north end of Bressay to put an oil-lamp in her window on stormy nights, so that he would be able to find the north entrance to the Lerwick harbour.

Since then a very good car-ferry connection has made Yell, Unst and Fetlar almost extensions of the Mainland. Still these islands are all very different and all worth a visit.

Fetlar

> Surrounded by the Hammers green,
> With Houlnastoura in the rear,
> The homes lie snugly all serene,
> *The Garden of Shetland*, Catherine Mary Isbister of Fetlar

The island of Fetlar is a contained world of its own, sheltered as it is by the long hill of Lambhoga. A place of breathtaking beauty, it has often been called The Garden of Shetland, as it is green and fertile; in agricultural potential it compares with Unst and Dunrossness. More than 200 different species of wild flowers have been recorded on the island. Indeed, tradition has it that Fetlar was the first island to be colonized by the Norsemen, because of its good farming land. They landed at Funzie, as did King Harald Fairhair a century later when he thought their descendants needed to be taught a lesson. He moved on to Unst, because then as now, there is no safe harbour in Fetlar—its one drawback.

The only road to speak of stretches from west to east, and today it is along this road that people live. But in old times the island was divided into ten skattalds, and each of these was a taxable unit and

The ferry-geese at Gutcher. A very good car-ferry connects Yell, Unst and Fetlar, making the islands almost an extension of the Mainland.

The island of Fetlar is a contained world of its own, sheltered as it is by the long hill of Lambhoga. It is a place of breathtaking beauty.

The Finnigord or Funzie Girt, a prehistoric stone dyke which divided the island of Fetlar into two almost equal parts.

probably had its own chapel. One such narrow band of skattald, known as Houbie, ran down the island from the north coast at East Neap to the south near the Tresta broch. On the west side of this was a prehistoric stone dyke called the Finnigord or Funzie Girt—the Finns' dyke—which divided the island into two almost equal parts. This may explain why the name of Fetlar ends in the Norse plural–ar. The dyke is 1 m (3 ft) wide and can still be seen; a good view can be had from Vord Hill. It is very well defined from the north shore till it straggles and disappears near Whilsa Pund. A dyke emerges south of Skutes Water and meanders through meadows and marshland till it crosses the Vallahamars and ends by the Stack of Billaclett; this may be the continuation of the Finnigord.

Today the northern part of the island is left to the birds. Between Urie and East Neap is a nature reserve with a RSPB warden resident in the summertime. It is closed to visitors for two and a half months in the summer to protect the birds breeding there. The site became famous in 1967 when a pair of snowy owls nested there and bred chicks. They were the first recorded pair of these Arctic birds to nest in Britain, and their breeding site became a place of pilgrimage for ornithologists.

In the steep hillside east of the bird sanctuary a dramatic rescue took place around 1700, and the story about it has been told to this day in Fetlar. An erne, a white-tailed eagle, stole a baby from the croft of Stutaft, on the south side of Balta Sound in Unst, and brought her back across the sea to its eyrie in the Fetlar cliffs. According to tradition young Robert Nicolson was lowered by rope to bring up the baby, who was restored to her parents without a mark on her. The story ends romantically: Robert later met and married Mary Anderson, the girl he had rescued, and they settled in Yell, where they lived happily the rest of their lives. They have descendants living in Fetlar to this day.

At the time of this story there were still many crofts along the northern shore. During the Napoleonic Wars more than 120 men were pressganged into the navy from Fetlar alone. Only about 20 of them came back again. There were more than 900 people living in Fetlar at that time, and it was indeed a green island with many kinds of crops. In the early nineteenth century practically all the land belonged to two major landowners: Sir Arthur Nicolson and Sir Thomas Dundas, who later became Lord Zetland. Only two centuries earlier there had been a large number of odal landholders in Fetlar.

In 1822 the first crofters were evicted, in order to make room for sheep. The crofts on Lambhoga which were the first to go, were marginal, but it was a serious loss to the crofters of Tresta, Toon and Velzie to have their skattald on Lambhoga taken away from them. Instead Lambhoga was filled up with Sir Arthur Nicolson's own sheep.

The evictions set a pattern: a high, beautifully worked stone wall was erected from Papil Water right across Lambhoga to the south-western cliffs. When the wall was finished the crofters were given 40 days to leave the land. By 1840 the wall around the Grutin district was completed and the 14 holdings there were taken over by Sir Arthur. With the stone from the croft houses he had his 'folly' built—a three-stories-high tower that served no purpose and today seems like cruel mockery. According to old Fetlar tradition, Grutin was the first part of Shetland to be settled by Norsemen, and there were many interesting old place-names; later it became deserted. By 1858 the northern and western parts of Fetlar were empty, after 16 more townships had been cleared. Since then the grass has covered the ruined walls of the houses, and ironically Brough Lodge, the home of the laird, will soon share this fate.

Among those who had to leave Fetlar was the family of the Shetland scholar Laurence Williamson, who was one of Dr Jakobsen's best helpers in his northern studies. He traced his family's occupation of North Dale in Fetlar back to 1540, when the land was still odal. As he was very intelligent, he was sent at seven to Mathewson's school in East Yell—at that time considered the best school in Shetland. He early began collecting Fetlar place-names, and was able to give Jakobsen a list of some two thousand names. Among these were names from Grutin and other areas affected by the evictions, where the old names were no longer needed. Most of these names can now be found in Jakobsen's *The Place-Names of Shetland*. Laurence Williamson is buried in the churchyard of Fetlar.

Another Fetlar emigrant to be buried in the same churchyard, is the famous surgeon Sir William Watson Cheyne. For many years he assisted Lord Lister in his pioneer work in antiseptic surgery, and went on to become president of the Royal College of Surgeons. After he had retired from medical work he served as Lord-Lieutenant of Orkney-Shetland for 11 years. His house at Leagarth was quite a showpiece in its time, with spacious grounds, exotic plants, and a private electricity supply.

Too many followed the pattern of emigration. After the haf fishing was abandoned there was nothing but farming left, and crofts often were not relet because the owner wanted to use the land for sheep or to breed ponies. The men left for whaling or the Merchant Navy; whole families emigrated. Thus the family history of Catherine Mary Isbister who wrote *The Garden of Shetland* illustrates the recent story of Fetlar. Her family name has died out in Fetlar but is very much alive in New Zealand where so many of them went. In Fetlar the population fell to about one hundred and many were elderly or unmarried. The island was no longer so green.

The daily roll-on-roll-off ferry from Yell to Oddsta has brought some changes, and hopefully the tide is now turning. Concern for the future made the Fetlar Community Council take the brave step of advertising in the national press for incomers to repopulate the island. Most of all they wanted young people with vitality and ideas who would bring children and new life to the island.

Unst

The isle of Unst ... is the pleasantest of the Shetland Isles ... (Martin Martin, *A Description of the Western Islands of Shetland, c* 1695)

Unst is the most northerly of the islands and has its own records: Britain's most northerly post office can be found at Haroldswick; the most northerly dwelling is the croft house at Skaw on north-east Unst. It was at Skaw that Walter Sutherland lived—the last man in Shetland to speak the Norn language.

Past wild waters lies Muckle Flugga Lighthouse. It was completed in 1858 at the then staggering cost of £32,000. Building the lighthouse on a 61 m (200 ft) high, almost inaccessible rock in those days was no mean feat of engineering. It must have also been backbreaking and dangerous work. Still, it was not high enough, as the lightroom had

Britain's most northerly post office. Post-mistress Doris Gray at Haroldswick, Unst, will stamp your cards with a special postmark proclaiming this fact.

to be raised another 15 m (50 ft) to be safe from the sea. The lighthouse was constructed by the famous engineer David Stevenson. He was an uncle of Robert Louis Stevenson, the Scottish writer, whose signature can be seen in the old visitors' book. Surely it can be no coincidence that the layout of his imaginary Treasure Island bears a distinct resemblance to the map of Unst!

Further out to sea is the Out Stack where Lady Franklin in a symbolic gesture went to pray for her husband Sir John Franklin who never returned from an expedition to find the Northwest Passage. His ships the *Erebus* and *Terror* disappeared in the autumn of 1845, westbound into Lancaster Sound. She was very brave to climb it, as there is always a dangerous swell. Due north there is open sea to the ice of the Arctic.

The north coast is craggy and rugged with caves and fantastic rock formations. The Out Stack, or Ootsta as it is called locally, also figures in folklore—it was the haunt of the mermaid loved by the giants Saxi and Herman who guarded the entrance to Burra Firth. They would quarrel and throw stones at each other as giants do, but by racing them to the North Pole she got rid of them both.

Today the 284 m (932 ft) high Saxa Vord is the home of a different kind of giant—a radar scanner operated by the R.A.F. Hermaness is now a sanctuary for thousands of seabirds, run by the nature Conservancy Council. There is another nature reserve at Keen of Hamar, near Baltasound.

Unst is an exciting place not only for the bird watcher but also for the geologist because of a rock variety seldom found in such a small area. The name of Clibberswick, near Haroldswick, tells us of a place where the Norse settlers found kleber, or soapstone. A rare rock type, the serpentine, extends on the east side from Haroldswick to Uyeasound. Unst and Fetlar are the only places in Scotland where it is found in any quantity. It is a quite porous rock, and this explains why peat has not formed in this part of Unst. One of its components is chromate of iron, which was quarried north of Baltasound in the nineteenth century, giving employment to about 50 people. The mineral was used for producing yellow paint. Talc quarries are still in operation.

History has left its mark on Unst. There are ancient ruins from prehistoric times through the broch-building period to Viking times. A ninth century Norse longhouse recently excavated at Underhoull was found to be built on an earlier, probably Pictish, site. A later Norse settlement has been found at Sandwick. More intact than the earlier remains, but still a ruin, stands Muness Castle as a symbol of the Scottish period.

In the Middle Ages the farms Hundagerdi and Munes (Hannigarth and Muness) in the south-eastern part of Unst, were the property of Munkeliv monastery of Nordnes in Bergen, one of Norway's richest

Muness Castle, Unst, built by Laurence Bruce, stands as a symbol of the Scottish period.

and most important monasteries. In 1598 Lawrence Bruce of Cultmalindie in Perthshire chose Muness as the site of his northerly stronghold.
He was a half-brother of Earl Robert Stewart who made him
Underfoude of Shetland in 1571, but he was deprived of this position
after a few years because of his oppressive practices. He lies buried
near the mediaeval chapel of the now derelict Framgord township on
the far side of Sand Wick.

Muness Castle was designed by the same man who built the castle at
Scalloway. Although rather stark-looking today it must at one time
have been an impressive building. It appeals to the romantic imagination and not surprisingly several legends are connected with it. The
Muness heir kept Helga, an odaller's daughter, in the castle against
her will. A resourceful young lady, she climbed out from an upper
window to join her lover and escape with him from Unst. But it was
a stormy night and their boat was small—they were never heard of
again. Another legend tells how the castle was burnt in the seventeenth
century by 'Hakki of Dikkeram'.

Unst is a fertile island and in the manner of the nineteenth century,
many landed proprietors built great houses around the island. The
Mouat Cameron family lived at Belmont where the ferry terminal is

today. At Buness in Unst lived the Edmondston family who are still famous for their cultural effort on Shetland's behalf. The Hall in Uyea was the home of Sir Basil Neven-Spence who was the Member of Parliament for Orkney and Shetland till he was defeated by Jo Grimond in the 1950 election.

Fishing was also important. Hanseatic merchants set up their stores at Westing and Uyeasound, where one such bød can still be seen. In Woodwick the huts of the haf-fishing station survived until recently. But Baltasound was always the centre of fishing: a natural harbour, it competed with Lerwick as main herring port. At the peak of the herring season its population would grow from 500 to 10,000, and there were so many fishing boats lying there that it was possible to walk dryshod from one end of the voe to another.

There are Arctic alpine plants in Unst and the wild honeysuckle grows by the Loch of Cliff.

Yell

... Yell stands on its own. For me it *is* Shetland. It stands for kindliness and remoteness, for wildness and yet for peace. (G. K. Yeates, *Bird Haunts in Northern Britain*)

At first glance Yell seems barren compared with Fetlar and Unst—the overall impression is of miles and miles of peat hills. The Scottish historian Buchanan wrote that it was 'so uncouth a place that no creature can live therein, except such as are born there.' He was hardly entitled to an opinion as he had never set foot in Yell; besides he wrote in the sixteenth century when natural beauty was synonymous with the pastoral and the fertile. There is a bleak grandeur that can be appealing about the blackish-brown hills of peat stretching away on all sides. There are also idyllic spots, but they have to be sought out—the hills around the Lochs of Lumbister, the coast north of Cullivoe and the village of West Sandwick.

Yell is almost split in two by the deep voes of Whale Firth and Mid Yell Voe; less than a mile separates them. In the inter-war years there was a herring station in Whale Firth, otherwise it is a very secluded spot. The Germans themselves have said that during the First World War their submarines would sometimes seek refuge in Whale Voe, where they ran little risk of being discovered. It is sheltered against the Atlantic by fine cliffs, and today it is a nice walk from the Stuis of Graveland, at the mouth of the voe, along the coast to West Sandwick.

Another deep inlet is Gloup Voe in North Yell; it has an 'edge of the world' feeling about it. A visitor in 1832 put it like this:

Gloup Voe is certainly one of the wildest and most retired spots in Shetland. The head of the voe is a narrow gorge, and the banks rise precipitately on

The deep inlet of Gloup Voe in North Yell, has an 'edge of the world' feel to it. Until tragedy struck in 1881, Gloup Voe was one of the best fishing stations in Shetland.

either side to a very considerable height. A small stream steals down the narrow valley, and abounds with the finest trout; (*Journal of Edward Charlton, M.D.*, p187)

Until tragedy struck in July 1881 Gloup Voe was one of the best fishing stations in Shetland. In the days of the sixern the fishermen of North Yell were, according to the same visitor, 'proverbially known over the rest of the islands for their daring spirit and recklessness in the hour of danger'.

The north-east coast shows traces of having been inhabited through many different cultures. In the sands of The Wick of Breckin skeletons have been found, indicating an old graveyard. There may have been an ancient settlement, similar to the one at Jarlshof. The name of Papil Ness does of course point to the early priests, and it is not surprising that a Norse church dedicated to St Olaf is found close by. The Norsemen were wont to build their churches on old sites of worship, both pagan and Christian. The church at Papil survived the Reformation and was the parish church for North Yell until *c.*1750. No fewer than 15 chapel sites are known in Yell. There are also about a dozen identified broch sites.

Today the village of Mid Yell is the natural centre of the island. It has an excellent harbour, protected as it is in the east by the island of Hascosay, and is a popular place for sailing regattas. There is today

217

Burra Ness Broch, one of a dozen identified broch sites in Yell. The surviving remains still reach a height of over 3.6 m (12 ft).

a fish factory at Mid Yell. Any employment possibilities are welcome, as the island has been threatened by depopulation. The ruined crofts show that the island has carried a lot more people than there are today. Agriculture has long been secondary to fishing, which now is no longer labour-intensive. New alternatives must somehow be found to make it possible for the young people to stay.

Sites of old chapels are found also in the small, uninhabited islands of Balta, Uyea, Linga, and Hascosay; perhaps pointing to a different population pattern in older days. The chapel in Balta was dedicated to the Norse saint St Sunniva. The grass is green in Balta and makes very good pasture land, but the east side of the island is under constant attack from the North Sea which slowly carries away the land.

Further south lies Haaf Gruney, which used to be an important haf fishing station. It is a very fertile grazing island, and is famous for its serpentine of a superior quality. This serpentine, which was used for ornamental stonework in the Town Hall in Lerwick, has an unusual colour almost resembling the antique green.

218

Linga is associated with an old tale, one of the few tales preserved in Shetland from Norse times. A green ring on Linga used to be called the Bear's Bait. Legend says that Jan Tait of Fetlar fell out with and killed the King's man, and was duly summoned to Norway to answer for his sins. He so impressed the King with his calm courage that he was offered his freedom if he could capture a bear that was terrorizing the area. Jim brought the bear to the King, who told him to take it away, so he brought it to Linga, where it wore a ring in the ground by its restless pacing around a stake.

Like Eynhallow in Orkney the small, low island of Hascosay, between Fetlar and Yell, is supposed to possess soil of a magic quality so that mice stay away. This soil was even taken away and used as a mice-deterrent—with what success though no-one knows. There are fine caverns on the island, which today is left to the herons. In 1841 there were 42 people living on 6 crofts; at the time of the next census in 1851 only 13 remained and by 1861 it was empty. Hascosay was bought by Sir Arthur Nicolson; even so the people were not evicted but left of their own accord, perhaps because there was only one rather inferior well. The island used to belong to a branch of the Edmondston family, and in 1645 one James Edmondston is mentioned as laird of Hascosay. They had left by 1800, but at Housa Wick the walls of their old hall are still standing: 'The ancient house of Hascosay has been deserted for a long, long time...' (Jessie Saxby: *Shetland Traditional Lore*, London 1932, p187)

Rapid tides run through Yell Sound. Right in the tidal race lie the small islands of Bigga and Samphrey which were inhabited not so long ago. There are said to be mostly women and children buried in the small graveyard on Samphrey, as 'Samphrey men are taken by the sea'. The crew of a sixern from Samphrey made it to Norway in 1832 when they were overtaken by the great gale while at the haf. In the following spring they returned home where they had been given up as lost.

23 THE NORTH SEA ISLANDS

Out Skerries

Far out in the North Sea lies the cluster of islands known as Out Skerries or just the Skerries. The name may refer to their distant position or derive from *austr*—easterly. The islands lie about 5 miles (8 km) from Whalsay and 10 miles (16 km) from Mainland. The twice weekly car-ferry *Filla*, named for one of the smallest skerries, takes between two and three hours to get there from Lerwick, depending on its ports of call.

From the sea the islands seem bleak and inhospitable, the coastline even dangerous. But no matter how wild the sea is, to enter the harbour in Out Skerries is to reach a natural haven, with a wonderful calm. There are two entrances to the harbour. The main entrance is through the South Mouth, but there is a narrow passageway through the Northeast Mouth that is just as good. In rough weather it is even better unless the wind comes from the north-east. The North Mouth also leads to a safe anchorage. It is to their safe harbour that the rocky

A serious water problem in Skerries resulted in an interesting channel system being built in 1957, leading rain water down the 52 m (171 ft) high Bruray Hill to a reservoir.

islands of Out Skerries, said to be one of the happiest communities in Britain, owe their prosperity. It was used by fishermen from all over Shetland when they worked the nearby fishing grounds, and was especially important at the time of the deep-water ling fishing.

Crofting, by comparison, is relatively unimportant. A belt of limestone makes parts of the island quite fertile, and the soil was improved upon over the years through careful fertilizing with fish offal and seaweed; the turf was also scraped from the hillside and taken to the fields. But in stormy periods the seaspray is everywhere. Before the new bridge was built it might even have been impossible sometimes to cross between Housay and Bruray. And strange as it may sound, there is a serious water problem in the Skerries. In 1957 an interesting channel system was built, leading the rain water down the 52 m (170 ft) high Bruray Hill to a reservoir. It is rather like the Roman aqueduct system in miniature. Even so water tankers have to be called in during dry summers.

Some 90 people live in the Out Skerries today. At its peak in 1891 the population numbered 165, so it has remained fairly stable. This is perhaps because the fishing, which is the mainstay of the islands, started doing well in the period between the two world wars, and has brought prosperity ever since. There are at present four vessels fishing out of Out Skerries. Whitefish from the Skerries sells well, and the islanders also used to run their own factory to freeze it. It was a great success while it lasted and established a reputation for having excellent products. As time went on the price of whitefish became too high for the factory to keep going, so the Skerries fishermen branched out into

Winter dawn over Housay, Bruray and Gruney, the three main islands of Out Skerries.

salmon farming, keeping cages in West Voe and using the old factory for cleaning salmon at the killing seasons. Whatever they do, most enterprises will be shared: Out Skerries is famed for its energy and community spirit.

The main islands are Housay, Bruray, and Grunay. Housay, from the Norse *Húsey,* has the most people, as well as the church and the community hall, where all kinds of indoor games like snooker, badminton and darts can be played. The bridge joining Housay to Bruray was built in 1957. Bruray comes from the Norse name *Brúarey,* meaning bridge island; seeing one island as a bridge between others was not uncommon in Norse times. The third island is Grunay—'the green island'. For a long time the lighthouse-keepers were the only people living on Grunay, and the good pasture-land there made fine grazing for their sheep.

The lighthouse itself is on Bound Skerry, which is about as far east as it is possible to go in Scotland. It was constructed by David Stevenson, who later built the famous lighthouse at Muckle Flugga. It is one of the largest lighthouses in Shetland and its light can be seen for some 20 miles out to sea. The lighthouse was bombed twice during the war by the Germans who insisted on believing that it was a munitions factory. Today the lighthouse has become automatic, like so many others. It was an awkward place to get to from Grunay when the weather was at its stormiest, so there were always two keepers on duty at the same time. Their old living quarters on Grunay were sold along with the whole island some time ago.

There is about a mile of road in Out Skerries, and at times it seems positively congested! There are cars going back and forth to the two shops or to the nice new pier, and passing can be a problem. But a road is not necessary as the ground is firm and good for walking. This is perhaps because there are no peat-hills. The Skerries people have old peat-cutting rights in Whalsay, but the dried peats had, of course, to be transported back by boat, so this custom died out some time ago. Few houses have open fireplaces today, but old habits die hard and people still collect the driftwood brought in on the beaches by winter weather. It is stacked in piles, and there it stays. Of course, venturing down in geos and gullies looking for 'rack' is an exhilarating pastime in a place like the Skerries. With luck one might even find old coins washed ashore from one of the numerous wrecks.

The scenery is varied. The southern part of Housay is known as Mio Ness, a name deriving from the Norse adjective *mjór,* which means narrow. This can only be reached by crossing a gully known as the Steig. It used to be a cave, but the roof collapsed some time ago. Sheep are taken across on a rope, but people have to climb it with care. The shy sheep take fright and scatter up the slopes of the Ward when strangers approach. But the affronted shags at the far edge do not yield an inch. On a stormy November night in 1711 the Dutch East Indiaman *De Liefde* hit the rocks on Mio Ness.

Whalsay

More than in any other place in Shetland life on Whalsay is bound to the sea. As soon as a young boy leaves school he hopes to get a place on a boat, and when he does he has made it; he has entered the brotherhood of Whalsay. The island is the natural place for a fishermen's training centre as it has long been a nursery for sailors. When the Whalsay men were permitted by the laird to do so, they joined the merchant navy or went whale or seal fishing; some also chose the navy. In the old days the navy chose them against their will, when in times of war the pressgang hunted high and low all over the island for able-bodied men. It even happened that the pressgang took men off the sixerns while they were at the haf-fishing. Many never returned.

In a community whose chief dependence was on fishing, the disaster of 1832 was bound to take more of a toll than in most places. Probably the words of this Whalsay woman could have been said by others with as much reason:

... my father, my two uncles, and other friends were lost in the great storm in 1832, and when one boat after another came home I and the other children

More than in any other place in Shetland, life on Whalsay is bound to the sea. A closer look at this washing line revealed that the 'socks' were, in fact, fish!

of the place used to go day after day to the top of the Setter Hill, and watch to see if our boat would come back. After sitting there for hours, and when we had cried till we could not cry more, we had to go home when it grew dark. But the boat never came back, and we had to stop gaen to the hill; but though its mair than forty years since syne I have never forgotten the sorrow and distress. (Rev. John Russell, M.A., *Three Years In Shetland*, p190, London 1887)

By the turn of the century the sixerns of haf-fishing days were replaced by decked sail-boats, which in their turn were followed by motor-boats and steam drifters. The Whalsay fishermen have been a vanguard in most of the changes taking place in Shetland fishing in this century. They have taken chances which most of the time have paid off, so that today a large and thoroughly up-to-date fishing-fleet operates out of Whalsay. It is owned by the men who work it, and almost all of these live in the island. The British fleet of purse-seiners consists of some 50 vessels, and 9 of these belong to Whalsay. Most of these are steel built. They go for mackerel and herring anywhere they are allowed to fish.

In addition to the purse-seiners there are 14 smaller boats going for whitefish or scallops. All of 190 full-time fishermen are now working from Whalsay, almost five times as many as there were a few decades ago. There have been developments on shore too. A pier has been built and another is planned at Symbister. There is also a whitefish factory employing around 90 people, but processing facilities for pelagic fish, that is herring and mackerel, are needed as well.

In the nineteenth century Scots fishermen called Whalsay the Bonnie Isle, and it is indeed a lovely island. Today it seems curiously closed to outsiders, but this impression may be caused by the natural reserve of the islanders. Still, it may not be without reason that Whalsay people seem to turn their backs on the rest of the world, after all they made it on their own, with no help from oil. And the Scottish writer Hugh MacDiarmid certainly found a refuge there when he needed it most.

Later MacDiarmid wrote about his stay which lasted from 1933 to 1942:

... it was a great relief when my friend Dr. David Orr, who was Medical Officer for the Northern Islands of the Shetland Archipelago, suggested we should join him on the island of Whalsay. How we survived virtually penniless I do not care to recall; but in many respects this Shetland sojourn, which lasted till after the outbreak of War in 1939, was an excellent experience. I got a lot of writing done, and advances on various books—The Golden Treasury of Scottish Poetry, Lucky Poet, The Islands of Scotland—served to keep the pot boiling. (*The Company I've Kept*, 1967)

At Sodom, in the hill above North Voe, MacDiarmid rented a cottage

Hugh Macdiarmid's cottage at Sodom, now a ruin, which he rented for 27 shillings a year.

for 27 shillings a year, and there he lived with his wife Valda and son Michael. From there he looked directly across at the island of West Linga and its raised beach at Croo Wick. In *The Uncanny Scot* MacDiarmid tells us how he went even further than Robinson Crusoe when he once had a boatman leave him on West Linga with orders to look for him after three days. He brought only his thick black tobacco, plenty of matches, Rilke's poems and a book on Paul Valéry. He managed to catch four sillocks with a pin and a piece of string, and he slept in a cave in the rocks.

Although he describes this incident ironically, MacDiarmid had been going through a period of serious self-searching. This is reflected in the now famous poem he wrote, *On a Raised Beach*:

> I am no more indifferent or ill-disposed to life than death is;
> I would fain accept it all completely as the soil does;
> Already I feel all that can perish perishing in me
> As so much has perished and all will yet perish in these stones.
> I must begin with these stones as the world began.

His sojourn on West Linga takes on a different dimension when we learn that the whole story is a matter of poetical licence! MacDiarmid was only over for the day with the owner of the sheep grazing there.

For a political rebel like MacDiarmid it was hard to see the exploitation the Shetland people had been subjected to for so long, and he expresses a deep and caring understanding of them:

225

In the old days they lived under conditions of virtual slavery; the laird had to get his share of all the fish they caught, then the minister had to get his, and between them these two gentlemen got the best of the fish. The Shetlanders had to live on the balance and the similarly-taxed crops of their small crofts. (Life in the Shetland Islands, *The Uncanny Scot*, London 1968)

He also flayed the landowners in his lines *To Any Scottish Laird*.

In Whalsay all the land was acquired by a branch of the Bruce family. Although they were mostly absentee landlords, they still ruled like petty kings, and anybody who refused to toe the line would have to leave the island. Today fantastic stories about their dealings are part of the island lore. One of them is the tale of how the odaller of West Linga was tricked out of his land. While he was out at sea his son got his head jammed in a jar. His frantic mother let herself be blackmailed into signing over the land to the laird in return for his help. His men then calmly broke the jar. This is surely a myth, but that there was greed for the land as well as some sleight of hand on the laird's part is probably true enough. The land on West Linga figures in another strife as well. On the 7 August 1485 a meeting was held at Korskirken in Bergen to look into an illegal purchase of land in Shetland, and of the land listed the most important was the ten merks of land on 'Liungøuo i Hwalsøyo'.

One of the Bruce lairds built Symbister House—a large square house built entirely of granite—perhaps the largest mansion in Shetland. Tradition has it that the laird built the house at enormous expense to spite his heirs. Since the 1950s it has served as a school, but it is cramped and unsatisfactory for today's requirements, and a new school for Whalsay has long been sorely needed.

Bressay

A'm been awa, bit A'm come hame ta bide:
did is da place, an here da hamely tongue,
an da lights o Lerick fae da Bressa side,
sam as whin I wis young.
Da Lights o Lerick fae da Bressa side, Stella Sutherland.

Bressay is often described as the island which gives Lerwick its wonderful harbour or as the land to be crossed in order to get to the Isle of Noss with all its birds. Few see what Bressay itself has to offer, even with the ferry running so often few Lerwegians for example have really explored their close neighbour. And yet the view from the Ward Hill is one of the best to be had in all of Shetland, in good weather giving a wide sweep of all the islands. Its southern slope The Ord Head ends abruptly in perpendicular cliffs, making the southern entrance into Bressay Sound very impressive. For guiding ships safely into harbour the lighthouse was built on the point of Kirkabister in 1858.

If the historian P. A. Munch is right in his belief that Bressay Sound is the Breiðeyjarsund of the saga, then this is where King Hakon Hakonsson's large fleet lay at anchor in 1263 while gathering their forces for the Scottish campaign, which ended in the battle of Largs and Hakon's death in the Bishop's Palace in Kirkwall. It was also in Bressay Sound the Dutch fishermen would gather every year while waiting for the herring fishing to begin. Indeed it was said locally that Amsterdam was built 'oot o'da back o'Bressa'.

To the Dutch Bressay Sound was known as 'the Grotta bay'. Probably they would have been familiar with the cave which today is popularly called The Orkneyman's Cave, but is also known as the Cave of the Bard. It has an opening wide enough to let several small boats in at the same time, but the passage narrows before it opens up into a spacious room about 18 m (60 ft) high. Tradition has it that an Orkney sailor was pursued by the pressgang and tried to hide in this cave. He scrambled onto a ledge but forgot to secure his boat, which drifted away with the ground swell. He sat on this ledge for two days, waiting for the sea to calm down. Then he swam to a point where he could climb ashore, and in this way he escaped. According to Sir Walter Scott, however, the name is due to an Orcadian boat having run into the cave to escape from a French privateer.

Bressay is an island of contrast between low-lying fertile farmland, vast empty hills and sheer cliffs. The lonely Loch of Grimsetter is the haunt of waders and whooper swans. A wild and remote place like

Looking east from The Ord, Bressay, over the wild and remote area around Sand Vatn.

Sand Vatn is a natural home for the bonxie, and the north coast is deeply indented by voes which form long narrow nesses. Although chiefly composed of old red sandstone, the island also has volcanic outcrops and some slate quarries. The stone from the quarry at Aith was at one time much in demand for housebuilding, and was also used to pave the streets of Lerwick.

Not so very long ago most of the population lived on the east side of the island, with townships at Beosetter, Gunnista, Aith, Culbinsbrough, from the Norse *Kolbeinsborg*, Noss Sound and Wadbister by the Loch of Grimsetter. Most of these small communities went the way of so many others in Shetland—they were cleared in the 1870s by the laird, Miss Mouat of Garth, to make sheep walks, or were left because the tenant emigrated or died in the war. Today many of them are just heaps of rubble; by walking around inside them we may still get an idea of what living there was like at a time when each township was largely self-sufficient.

On top of Ander Hill a well-built but derelict lookout tower is another relic of times past. It was built by the Admiralty just before the First World War. On a low promontory at the foot of the hill lies one of the most interesting church ruins in Shetland—that of St Mary's Church. It is the only cruciform church known in Shetland, and may date from Norse times. Within the arch-diocese of Nidaros small churches were usually rectangular, and only churches of some import-ance and size had a transept. Thus St Magnus Cathedral in Kirkwall is the only other cruciform church in the bishopric of Orkney, of which Shetland was a part. The transept was possibly a later addition. St Mary's also had a manse and glebe close by, but St Olaf's at Gunnista seems to have served as the parish church. There was also an early church dedicated to St John at Kirkabister on the west side. Until the nineteenth century Bressay, Quarff and Burra formed one parish. It was an awkward parish to work in, as a visit to parishioners in Burra meant 'aucht myles of land and twa ferries, quhilk makis greit chargeis' (Proc. Soc. Antiq. Scot., xliv, 306). It was also one of the poorest parish benefices in Shetland; only Fetlar brought in less revenue.

Probably St Mary's Church was built on the site of an older chapel, as a Pictish symbol stone with an ogam inscription written down both edges was found there in 1864 by the local minister. The beautifully carved monument is known as the Bressay stone and can be seen at the Scottish National Museum of Antiquities in Edinburgh. It is interesting because it shows Scandinavian influence, and as some scholars believe it was made late in the ninth or early in the tenth century, it points to a peaceful co-existence between Picts and Norsemen. Thus the two points used to separate the words were common in runic inscriptions. Norse elements in the inscription has made a tentative translation possible:

Crosc : Nahtvdads : Datr : Anbenises : Meqdroan.
'The cross of Naddodd's daughter here
Benres the son of the Druid here.'

This may have been the Naddodd mentioned in Landnámabók, the Icelandic Book of Settlement, as the first Norseman in Iceland. Outlawed in Norway, he was driven off course by a storm in AD 861 and ended up in Iceland, where he went ashore but found no people. He is known to have had a grandson named Benir, who might be the Benres of the inscription.

In 1727 the parish council was moved to the west side, which gradually grew in importance. This development was taken further when the crofts on the east side were cleared. Some of those who were evicted hacked out new crofts in the west hillside, but many people left the island, and the population dropped from 904 in 1841 to 269 in 1961. One reason for this was Bressay's merchant navy traditions and the proportionate loss of life in two world wars. Since then it has risen again, to just over 350 in 1987.

The ferry has made it possible to live in Bressay and go to work in Lerwick every day. The fishmeal factory at Heogan has been in operation since 1888 and is still the main local employer. There used to be another fishmeal factory at Aith, but there is no full-time commercial fishing carried on from Bressay anymore. Many of the crofts are still actively worked; there are also three fair-sized farms: Maryfield, Setter and Hoversta. Maryfield used to be the home of the laird's factor, but is now farmed by the laird, who lives at the mansion house of Gardie. It was built in 1724. Another landowning Bressay family were the Bolts of Cruister, but their estate was bought by the Mouats of Garth, and the Haa of Cruister is now a ruin.

Noss

One of the most popular places to visit is the Isle of Noss with its thousands of seabirds. It was declared a National Nature Reserve in 1955, and is an important site for the monitoring programme of cliff-nesting seabirds carried on by the Nature Conservancy Council.

Noss rises gradually in an inclined plane towards the east where it plunges steeply into the sea. The highest point is the 181 m (594 ft) high overhang cliff of the Noup. To the Dutch fishermen it was known as the Hang-lip. The sea and the wind have worn the red sandstone cliff into horizontal ledges and scooped out hollows where innumerable seabirds nest and bring up their young. The whole east side of Noss is a breeding ground for colonies of puffins, gannets, fulmars, herring gulls, kittiwakes, guillemots, razorbills and others. Both great and arctic skuas nest in the broken ground along the cliff edge and are quick to charge when they feel their rights impinged on by too eager visitors.

The whole east side of the Isle of Noss is a breeding ground for colonies of puffins, gannets, fulmars, herring gulls, kittiwake, guillemot, razor bills and others. The puffins are certainly not camera-shy!

In order to see the Noup at its most impressive it should be approached from the sea. Close by lies the 50 m (164 ft) high Holm of Noss, a huge solid rock cut off from the island by a chasm which used to be wide enough to give a good berth for a small sailing boat, but was blocked up by a fall of stones some years ago. Today the Holm is quite inaccessible, but for some 250 years it was bridged by what was known as 'the cradle'.

Communication with the Holm was first suggested by the birds' eggs and the rich pasture. The offer of a cow was sufficient to tempt a cragsman from one of the fowling families of Foula to scale the cliffs sometime in the seventeenth century. Tradition has it that he climbed a ship's mast to take him part of the way. He fastened stakes and flung a rope across, but he was killed trying to descend the way he had come up. For some 250 years the cradle was slung in June and dismantled in November every year. Since the island is higher than the Holm, the rope would slope a little, and the cradle would come down by its own weight, but the returning passenger either had to work his way across or get friends to help. The so-called cradle was an oblong box which was swung on two cables and held a man and a sheep at a time. Today this seems a very desperate way of getting pasture, however rich, for a dozen sheep, as a fall would have meant certain death. It must have seemed so to Mr Walker, the laird's factor, too, as he had the cradle removed in 1864 and a wall built along the precipice.

The other approach to Noss is from Bressay across Noss Sound. At its narrowest point this is only about 200 m (656 ft) wide and is also very shallow. There is often a strong tide which makes crossing the Sound very chancy even in the summertime; the last tenant was Noss-bound for up to three weeks in the winter. Nevertheless old *shatt* records show that there were as many as five settlements along the south-western coast in Norse times. Today the traces of settlement include the ruins of Setter and its still green pastures. The old road along the shore ends there.

For a long time the only inhabited house on Noss has been Hametoun. It is a very old homestead, known to go back over 400 years. In the early nineteenth century it was famed for producing the best milk and butter in Shetland. The tenant farmer James Copland had an unusual lease for Shetland at the time as he also had fishing rights. He became a rich man who built his own house in Lerwick, just where Commercial Street now begins, as well as a pier below it. But it is his son of the same name who has a claim to fame today. Dr James Copland, in his day called 'the most learned of modern physicians', in 1832 published *Dictionary of Medicine*.

In the 1860s the island was entirely laid down to pasture, and Hametoun became occupied by a shepherd and his family. Then for a period of 30 years Noss was used by the Marquis of Londonderry for breeding ponies for his Durham coal mine, as child labour was no longer legal. The mares were kept at Maryfield Farm on Bressay and the stallions on Noss; thus the sheltie was scientifically bred to produce an ideal pony with 'as much weight as possible and as near to the ground as it can be got'. Since 1900 Noss has been the home of some 400 sheep. At one time there lived as many as 24 people on the island, but since 1939 it has been inhabited only in the summer. Today Hametoun is lived in by the warden and his staff.

In 1633 Robert Monteith referred to a small chapel in front of Hametoun, as sometime built by 'shipwrakt' persons. In 1774 only the walls of this were still standing, though the burial ground around it was in use until the middle of the nineteenth century. The site is eroded by the sea, and is due to be excavated by Dr Barbara Crawford, the well-known historian, who wants to find out whether there was a pre-Norse establishment on the site. There is fairly strong evidence that the Noss chapel site was originally Celtic because of a small stone cross found in the graveyard some years ago. The *papa* name nearby would seem to sustain this theory.

Mousa

> This broch has stood for twice a thousand years
> And watched men come and go.
> *The Broch of Mousa,* Vagaland

One of the main tourist attractions in Shetland today is the unusually well-preserved broch on the small island of Mousa. Together with the now ruinous Broch of Burraland directly across on the other side of Mousa Sound it must have been a sight awe-inspiring enough to have kept intruders at bay for a long time. It is still 13 m (43 ft) high, the diameter tapers from 15 m (45 ft) at its base to 12 m (39 ft) at its top, it is made of old red sandstone, which is the common local stone. The broch is very well constructed and built—as it would have to be to withstand two thousand years of wind and rain and human curiosity.

Today the broch is a romantic sight. Perhaps it seemed so to the Norsemen too; according to the Icelandic sagas it served as a hideaway for beleaguered lovers on two known occasions. The story of Bjørn Brynjulfsson and Thora Roald's daughter provides the beginning of the love theme in the often harsh but also stirring Saga of Egill Skallagrímsson, which besides Njál's Saga is considered the best of the family sagas. In the early tenth century Bjørn's father fitted him out with a ship and a crew of 12 to go from Aurland in Sogn to Dublin on a trading mission. This was a ruse to keep the lovers apart, but it failed as Thora joined Bjørn on board. They ran into bad weather and came off course.

The winds were bad and they were tossed and driven about in the waves for a long time, for they were determined to keep as far away from Norway as they could. Then one day when they were sailing up the east coast of Shetland before a strong gale, they damaged the ship as they tried to put in at Mousa. They carried the cargo ashore and into the broch there, then beached the ship and repaired the damage. (*The Saga of Egill Skallagrímsson*, trans. Pálsson and Edwards, Penguin Classics, 1976)

Bjørn married Thora as soon as they reached Shetland, and they spent the winter in the broch. But from a passing ship Bjørn learnt that he had been outlawed in Norway for abducting Thora, and he began to fear for their lives. As soon as spring weather came and the sea became calmer they set sail for Iceland.

Bjørn and Thora sought refuge with Skallagrím at his farm of Borg, and from then on the lives of the two families were intertwined. Thora gave birth to a daughter, Ásgerðr, who stayed behind in Iceland when her parents were allowed to return to Norway. She grew up with Egill Skallagrímsson, greatest of the Norse skalds, and became the love of his youth. But she married his brother, who died before she married Egill. Their granddaughter Helga is the heroine of Gunnlaugs Saga

Today the broch of Mousa is somehow a romantic sight. Perhaps it seemed so to the Norsemen too. According to the Icelandic sagas, it served as a hideaway for beleaguered lovers on two known occasions.

233

Ormstunga—Saga of Gunnlaugr Serpent-Tongue—perhaps the best constructed and definitely the most romantic of all the sagas.

The story is repeated more than two centuries later. Earl Erlend Ungi wanted to marry Margarét, who was the widow of Maddad, Earl of Atholl, as well as mother of Harald Maddadarson, Earl of Orkney who forbade the union. Assisted by his men Earl Erlend brought Margarét to Moseyjarborg, as the broch is called in the sagas, and for the second time it became the home of an abducted bride. The furious Earl Harald set off in pursuit, fully intending to kill his mother's suitor, but the broch proved too strong for him—'it was difficult to take it by assault' says the saga writer. Surely it must be one of history's little ironies that the strength of the broch in a siege was put to the test and proved adequate so long after the people who built it were forgotten. The broch was probably given up as a defence structure around AD 200, when a wheelhouse was built within its walls to make a family dwelling.

Today a breeding colony of storm petrels, the smallest of British seabirds, have their nests within the stones of the broch wall, and the small loch beyond the broch is a popular bathing place for many kinds of birds. Arctic terns have several colonies on the island. Usually there are many seals watching with curiosity the boatloads of tourists coming over from Mainland to West Ham in the summertime. They are strangely unafraid considering that for most of the year they have the island to themselves. Botanists may also find the unusual mixture of moor and saltwater plants of interest.

Today Mousa is uninhabited. Low tells us that in 1774 the island was inhabited by 11 families and tolerably well cultivated. The census of 1841 shows 12 people living there, but they were all gone by 1861, reputedly because of the isolation caused by the difficult Mousa Sound. On a lovely but exposed site above the loch are the remains of farm buildings. A ruined water mill of a type commonly used in Shetland for grinding grain can be seen closer to the eastern shore. There is also a simple two-storey old building called The Haa. On the same side of the island is an old quarry where many of the flagstones used for Lerwick streets were produced.

24 THE ATLANTIC ISLANDS

Papa Stour

In 1970 the small school in Papa Stour was closed when its last pupil went on to school on Mainland and there were no young children to take his place. The island was dying from depopulation. The 16 people still living on the island were all past childbearing age, and it might be only a question of time before they would have to be evacuated like the inhabitants of St Kilda in the 1930s. In the middle of the nineteenth century the island supported a population of 382.

The word spread that in Papa Stour anyone could have a croft and five sheep, and young people wanting an alternative lifestyle came from all over Britain in answer to the call. Papa Stour became known as the 'Hippie Isle'. Sweat, tears and back-breaking labour awaited the newcomers, along with a life more away-from-it-all than they had believed possible; many consequently gave up and went back after a short time. But a hard core of the incomers stayed, did up old houses

The small school on Papa Stour has reopened after closing in 1970. Luke and Naomi, two of the three children attending, proudly displaying their indoor garden.

Midsummer sunset over Papa Stour. The island is separated from Sandness in West Mainland by Papa Sound.

and raised families. They brought Papa Stour back to life, so that today there are some 30 people living in the island, and the school has reopened.

The name of Papa Stour derives from *Papey hinn stóra*, which means the big island of the priests. It is separated from Sandness in West Mainland by Papa Sound. Although this is only a mile wide, it can be very difficult to cross because of the strong tides, so that the island is often isolated for days at a time. In times of self-sufficient communities this was not necessarily considered a drawback. The men for whom the island was presumably named would have sought the island for the sake of this isolation, but also for its beauty and fertility.

The Norsemen would have coveted the island for the same reasons but also because it had a position which would have been strategically important for them, as well as good harbours where their ships could be beached. The nature of the farm-names seems to indicate that in Papa Stour, as in Papa Westray in Orkney, Norse settlement came quite late. The Norsemen may have respected the presence of priests and considered these islands out of bounds.

Papa Stour first appears in written records in 1299. The earliest Shetland document extant is a statement made by the lawmen about crown property in Papa Stour. Duke Hakon, the younger son of King Magnus the Law-Maker, held Faroe, Shetland, as well as Rogaland, Oppland and Oslo as ducal property, and he ruled his domain quite independently. He became King Hakon V Magnusson in 1299, the year of the Papa Stour document. When he died in 1319 without male heirs, the old line of Norse kings died out with him. King Hakon introduced a more orderly system in financial matters, one of his reforms being an annual inspection into how his sysselmen carried out their duties.

Against this political background the Papa Stour document seems extremely interesting. It deals with the accusation of corruption made by Ragnhild Simunsdatter, probably one of the tenants, against Lord Thorvald Thoresson, who appears to have been Duke Hakon's sysselman in Shetland. She made these accusations twice in the presence of witnesses, both outside and in the *stofa* of Hakon's farm on Papa Stour. It seems a logical conclusion that this letter had a direct bearing on Hakon's later decision to check up on his officials.

The kings of Norway owned much land in Shetland, some of which had been forfeited by the islanders when they were defeated by King Sverre in the naval battle of Florevåg in 1194. The reference to a stofa in the Papa Stour letter is unique—no other royal building in Orkney or Shetland is mentioned in Norse sources. The word stofa would be used of the 'notched log' type of timber building which was adopted at the end of the Viking Age. The wooden framework was constructed inside the stone walls. There were wall benches running along three sides of the stofa, which would usually be panelled and have a wooden floor.

The letter greatly intrigued Dr Barbara Crawford at the University of St Andrews. She reasoned that Papa Stour must have been a place of importance at the time, with some kind of crown estate.

We therefore have a historical reference to a house of the kings of Norway on a small island where it might be traced; the only place in the Scandinavian settlements around the coast of Britain where this is so. (Northern Studies 11 (1978), p27)

On the strength of the letter Dr Crawford therefore carried out excavations on Papa Stour during four summers between 1977 and 1982. After careful consideration the farm known as Da Biggins was chosen as a most likely site of an important settlement.

The excavations revealed the foundation of a mediaeval Norse house lying at right angles to the derelict croft house known as Da Gørl, which is probably derived from the Norse *garð-höll*, the farm of the hall or great house, and thus also points to the earlier importance of the site. That this must have been a dwelling-house of some standing is shown by the remains of a wooden floor close to the wall of the croft house. This is the only one of its kind in the Northern Isles, but a similar one has been uncovered at Tjornuvik in Faroe. Among the artefacts found are textile fragments of what may originally have been quite a fine garment.

Dr Crawford also points out a circle of at least 46 stones enclosing an area roughly 40 m (131 ft) in diameter just behind the beach at Housa Voe. This may have been the site of a Norse Ting or assembly. There was also a local oral tradition of there having been a royal castle and a tingstead on the island. If this is indeed so, then the letter probably refers to a meeting of the ting for the west side of Shetland.

The stone circle appears in later island lore, as recorded by George Low in 1774:

On a small level green, near the middle of the cultivated part, observed the marks of a circular enclosure, in which tradition says a Lord Terwil fought a duel with another gentleman, on some dispute or other, and afterwards accompanied by his eleven sons, went down on purpose to rob his neighbours, but together with his whole family perished on a rock, since called Terwil's Ba' or rock.

In his *Description of the Shetland Islands* from 1822 Samuel Hibbert throws some more light on the story of Lord Terwil:

There is a rock near Mavis Grind, named Tairville's Baa, connected with the name of an ancient Norwegian settler, who slew in a duel, fought at Papa Stour, a gentleman of rank, and resisted all the attempts that were made to bring him to a trial for the act, living by the depredations of the country.

There is also a place called Turvalds Head on the west side of Mavis Grind.

The Lord Terwil/Tairville of the duel is no doubt the same person as the Lord Thorvald Thoresson whom Ragnhild Simunsdatter accused of corruption. He is known in an earlier Norwegian document as Thorwaldum de Shetland. Through two influential marriages in Norway he became an extremely rich man. Somehow Papa Stour became his private property where he spent most of his time. The story of how his sons perished may have some foundation in fact, because on Lord Thorvald's death his estate was inherited by his daughter Herdis. She seems to have stayed on Papa Stour for at least part of the time, and according to P. A. Munch she lived on a grand scale. When she died her land in Shetland passed to the prominent Sudreim-family, who also owned Giske, the old home of the first Earl of Orkney.

In 1490 Lady Herdis' lands in Shetland were split up and Papa Stour with attached estates in West Mainland, Northmaven and Yell passed to the Rømer family. As Dr Crawford points out, the third strong-minded and colourful woman to become part of the story of Papa Stour was Inger Ottesdatter Rømer (*c.* 1475–1555), who lived at the castle of Austråt by the Trondheimsfjord, and already owned vast estates in Norway. She is the main character of Henrik Ibsen's *Lady Inger*, one of his early plays. He sees her as a person with a historical chance of saving Norway in her darkest hour. The shadows and darkness of the sombre mediaeval castle somehow give to the play a feeling of destiny, but the picture Ibsen draws of Lady Inger is not historically correct.

Thus the 'lairds of Norroway' held onto their estates in Papa Stour long after the pledging, but at some point the land was let to a Scottish incomer, Andrew Mowat. He established himself at North-house, where Hibbert in 1822 saw 'the gateway of an old mansion that belonged to the Mouats of Bauquhally, in Banffshire, where the arms of the family can be seen with the inscription 'Monte Alto'. It was a member of this family who later founded the Rosendal barony in Hardanger, Norway's only barony. Later two of the merchant lairds of the eighteenth century, Thomas Gifford of Busta and Arthur Nicholson of Bulyster, divided Papa Stour between them. The island is still part of these estates.

There are no signs today of the earlier importance of the island. The cultivated land lies east of a massive turf dyke, which in the south ends in Gorsendi Geo—from the Norse *garōsendi*, the end of a dyke. On the western side of it the land has been stripped till it resembles a mountain plateau in its barrenness—somehow a herd of wild reindeer would not seem surprising. The turf was taken to improve the land already under cultivation, it was also used for bedding the animals for the winter, but first of all it was used for fuel.

The lack of peat became a serious problem in the 1870s, when the turf was all gone. It was possible to go to Papa Little for peat, but the men were busy fishing every possible day. Many tenants left, and in ten years the population dropped from 351 to 253, a decrease of more than a fourth. North-house was left quite empty, and there was even talk of moving everybody to Fetlar. But in 1885 a herring curing station was built in Papa Stour for the firm of J. M. Adie & Sons of Voe, and this seems to have stemmed the tide of emigration for some time.

At one time there was settlement also west of the dyke, and the derelict township at Miley Punds, between Culla Voe and Dutch Loch, is still green. There is a stone-built road leading to it, one of the so-called meal roads—built for a hand-out of oatmeal during the famine of the late 1840s. Evidently the township was past saving even then.

Around Gorda Water are the ruins of huts that according to tradition were the final refuge of lepers. Food would be left for them by the dyke. At one time Papa Stour received lepers from the whole west side of Shetland. There are remains of 'Leper Houses' on the top of the Brei Holm as well. Today it is thought that these poor people may not have suffered from an infectious disease at all, but from malnutrition and vitamin deficiency.

Although Papa Stour is not a big island its coastline is so heavily indented that it measures some 21 miles (34 km). A walk around the many geos, caves and natural arches on a fine summer day is a wonderful experience. Close to Virda Field, the highest point in the island and from the name clearly used for a beacon in times past, lies Akers Geo. It is a fairly easy and rewarding climb down to the bottom, where it widens out to become a natural Atlantic cathedral whose wall of old red sandstone has been richly carved by the onslaught of sea and wind. A natural arch forms a wall to the sea. It is the home of shags whose indignant guttural cries are the only jarring note. In the sea bob the heads of seals in placid curiosity. And beyond them are the notorious Ve Skerries—over the centuries a graveyard of shipping. On a calm summer day it is difficult to imagine the force of a winter storm on this coast. But in the great storm of 1953 the well-known landmark the Horn of Papa—a curious horn-shaped rock formation on the south side of Akers Geo—was swept into the sea.

This old landmark is remembered in the chorus of a song of haf-fishing days, 'Da Sang o' da Papa Men', written by the Shetland poet Vagaland (T. A. Robertson) and set to music by Dr T. M. Y. Manson:

> Oot bewast da Horn o Papa,
> Rowin Foula doon!
> Ower a hidden piece o water,
> Rowin Foula doon!
> Roond da boat da tide-lumps makkin
> Sunlicht trowe da cloods is brakkin;
> We maan gang whaar fish is takkin
> Rowin Foula doon!

'To row Foula down' was to row so far west that the high cliffs of Foula were no longer visible on the horizon. But the Papa men were in no danger of losing their way—'Fir da scent o flooers in Papa/Leds wis aa da wye'—the scent of the clover and wild flowers in Papa Stour would waft out to sea and lead them all the way home.

Foula

> As sunset light makes the waters golden,
>   Away to seaward Utrey lies:
> A five-leafed flower at eve unfolding
>   Purple against the Western skies.
>   *Utrey*, Vagaland.

Between 15 and 20 miles (24–32 km) west of the Mainland the five large hills of Foula rise dramatically against the sky. The Noup, Hamnafield, The Sneug, The Kame, and Soberlie all seem to lean in the same direction—to the north. When seen in the golden light of a summer sunset the island is a fairy-tale land 'east of the sun and west of the moon'.

When Agricola, a Roman governor of Britain, sailed around Orkney in AD 84, he saw land in the northwest: 'despecta est et Thule'—seen

The spectacular north end of Foula, with sheep coming down the hills to Ristie. The Gaada Stack is in the background.

is also Thule. Thule was the name given by the ancients to the most northerly part of Europe, an island discovered *c.* 310 BC by the Greek traveller Pytheas, and variously identified with modern lands. It has been a popularly held idea that what Agricola saw from Orkney was Foula.

Some have also been struck by the similarity between the names of Foula and Thule, but this is entirely a coincidental similarity. The dative form of the name appears in a document from 1490 as 'i Fugle'. The original name may therefore have been just Fugl, the Norse word for bird. Such a comparison name was not uncommon in Norway; it would have been given because the island looked like a bird when first sighted. Still the more down-to-earth name of Fugl-ey, used to describe an island full of birds, seems more probable. Another known name is Uttrie or Utrey, the outer island.

Only St Kilda, west of the Hebrides, has higher cliffs or was more isolated than Foula. In 1930 the St Kildans wanted to leave their island, and this evacuation caused a lot of interest in life as it was lived on the remote islands. It was felt that this should be recorded before it was too late. The classic *Edge of the World* was filmed on Foula in 1936; the main characters were professional actors, but the supporting cast were all Foula people. The great funeral scene was filmed at Ristie in the north end, and all the islanders took part in it. For an added touch of realism the film crew were weatherbound on the island for some weeks! In the film the name of the island was Hirta, which was the Norse name for the main St Kilda island.

The opening caption of the film spoke of the 'slow shadow of death' falling over the outer Scottish islands, but nothing could be further

241

from the truth in Foula! The people of Foula are passionately attached to their island; they make up a very robust community who would not willingly share the fate of the St Kildans. Perhaps it has been till now a life without electricity, running water or shops, with winds strong enough to sweep the hay into the sea and the roof off the house, but it is a life that has many compensations and can be beautiful for those with eyes that see.

All the fertile land in Foula faces east. The island is said to have some of the best arable land in Shetland, but there is not much of it. The two main settlements are Hametoon in the south and Ham, the only place where landing is made, and then with difficulty. Earlier there was also the now derelict tun o' Harrier as well as the settlements at the north end, which used to be known as the oot-ower-tuns. Birds, eggs and fish therefore used to play an important part in the island economy. A trade in live birds could at times be done with collectors:

I told him that I wanted *lyra* (or Manx puffin), the *tystie* (black guillemot) and the *mootis* (or stormy petrel), along with *bonxies* (skua) and their eggs and that I did not wish for either *lomwies*, *tamienories*, *brongies* or *laarquhidins*, in plain English guillemots, puffins, cormorants or shags. Hearing this he drew forth a *lyra* from beneath his jacket, and with it shewed me its egg, a rarity indeed, he had taken it he said, upon the Noup about 50 yards below the top of the precipice, the bird was dreadfully savage, and bit his horny fingers most unmercifully. (*The Journal of Edward Charlton*, M.D., 1834)

Today there are 15 inhabited houses in Foula where about 50 people live, of whom one-third are children. Old people remember when there were more than 200 people living on the island, but two world wars took their toll.

According to popular tradition the first Norse settler in Foula was Guttorm, who made his home in the south of the island and ruled it from there. His farm was still supposed to be named after him when George Low visited there in 1774. But this story does not ring true, for uncompounded personal names were not used as Norse place-names. The name has also been spelled as Goteren or Guttrum. It is derived by Jakobsen from *Gaut-ár-heimr*, the homestead on the banks of the river Gaut. Heimr-names are very old; they had gone out of fashion by the time the Viking Age started, and there are none of them in Faroe and very few in Iceland. Much therefore indicates that this is the primary farm, and that the essence of the tradition is right.

The southern settlement is known as Hametoon. Toon, from Norse *tún*, was used about a fenced, cultivated area. Probably the first part of the name refers to the ending—heimr in Guttorm and means the land belonging to the home or dwelling there, as this was the first settlement. But it is also possible that the whole name literally means the home fields, in contrast to the skattald.

The fact that this is where Low recorded the Ballad of Hildina from the singing of William Henry makes it holy ground to the Norse scholar. When the Faroese linguist Jakob Jakobsen stayed in Foula in 1894, one of his best sources and storytellers was David Henry, a kinsman of William Henry. In the evenings Jakobsen would gather the people of Hametoon in one of the croft houses to question them about lore and names and old words. He thought the people of Foula were lively and intelligent and of better memory than in any other place.

Records of past history in Foula are sparse. The island consisted of 57 merks of cultivated land. Two-thirds of the island, or 39 merks, belonged to the old earldom estate. Sometime between 1628 and 1716, probably in 1666, the earldom estate was sold. The remaining portion of 18 merks was still ódal land in 1716–1717, as is shown in the *Zetland Scatt Rental* for that year. There is a persistent tradition in the island connected with a laird known as the Queen of Foula, who lived in the second half of the sixteenth century. She is known both as Katrine Asmunder and Katrine Kirkleog; probably she was called both, as Asmunder would have been the patronymic. The site where her house stood is still known as Kru Katrine, and today it is just a mound of grass-covered stones beside the church. The soil has been scraped away, so it is not possible today to tell what her land would have been like.

The story of Katrine is romantic and sad, with echoes of the island's doomed fight for its future. Her suitor was Hakki Manson, who lived at Guttorm in Hametoon. He seems to have lived up to the saga ideals of young manhood, for he was a daring and skilful sailor and a good athlete. In the year 1590 he set out on mid-summer day with four other Foula boats for the fishing grounds. He never returned. Katrine refused to believe that he was lost, as he and his crew were too good sailors for that. Some 30 years later her faith proved justified—she received a letter from Hakki's son. He told her that Hakki and his crew had been taken by a passing ship to the West Indies and sold as slaves. But Hakki had later been freed, had married and done well. Katrine had remained true to him and never married; one tradition has it that she drowned while on a ship trying to save the island with money sent her according to Hakki's will, but there are many variations on this last theme.

In 1720 an epidemic which was known as the muckle fever, but probably was smallpox, almost emptied Foula of people. According to tradition only three people were left in the island, which had to be resettled from Mainland. The islanders' legendary fear of infection is said to have been caused by this.

According to another tradition in the island it was towards the end of the eighteenth century that the remaining odallers on the island were tricked out of their deeds by one of the Scotts of Melby, a man they trusted. The Scotts remained lairds of Foula till the end of the nineteenth century, but they were rarely there, the Haa in Ham being lived in by their factor.

A more recent laird of Foula was Professor Ian B. S. Holbourn who took over the island in 1901. He took a fancy to it when sailing by and later bought it at an auction in London. He collected the island lore in his book *The Isle of Foula*. His family grew strongly attached to the island, and today three of his grandchildren are crofters in Foula.

Foula is surrounded by rich fishing grounds, and in the haf-fishing days good catches were taken on the Regent's Bank, which lies west of Foula and stretches south to Orkney, as well as on the eastern cod-banks known as the Shaalds o' Foola, where the wreck of the ocean liner *Oceanic* lies. There used to be booths and nousts in Ham, and a fleet of sixerns fished from there during the summer months. The coming of the trawlers killed the fishing in Foula, as in most of the small islands, and especially in those with difficult, exposed harbours. And as the old self-sufficiency disappears and the island comes to depend on outside services, the lack of harbour facilities becomes felt more and more. The islanders are hoping for pier improvements which will let the island boats lie safely in harbour throughout the summer. The mailboat could then be replaced by a bigger one which would make the connection with Mainland more stable.

The lack of a good harbour increased the natural remoteness and isolation of Foula. Old customs lived on. Thus the Foula people still live by the old Julian calendar and celebrate Old Yule on 6 January and New Year on 13 January. Therefore it may be that children go to school as usual on the 23 December, but it also happens that they get the best of both worlds—two Christmases and two New Years!

It has also been possible to keep unwelcome guests out. The story goes that when a doctor first came to vaccinate the Foula people, an old man made the men believe that he was coming to geld them. They would not let him get ashore, and he had to sail back again. When next he came he had brought the police, but their boat fared no better:

> He takked nord, he takked sud,
> he takked ost an west.
> Bit fir aa it he could budge and blaa,
> da noris kept dir nest.
>
> (From an old verse)

Nori was the nickname given to the Foula men by other Shetlanders.

In 1934 the Norwegian folklorist Einar Seim from Sunnfjord spend some time in Foula, and found to his surprise that he heard Norn words that Jakobsen had not noticed: 'I knew previously that the Norn speech had survived long in Foula, but I had no idea that a mass of

The high hills of Foula form a dramatic backdrop for the fertile croft land. The only opening in this massive western wall is through Da Daal. The Noup rises 248 m (813 ft) high to the south.

Norn words would still be in use'. At the home of an old woman he also got a kind of food that he had heard tell about at home as 'drøsta'. It was burstin: dried beremeal mixed with milk. They often used this in Foula. Although Seim had never tasted it, he had heard a story about this food. An old woman had served it to a pedlar, who refused to eat it. She then said: 'Is the man daft? He won't eat drøsta!'—and this became a local expression. But not so Seim: 'If the meal is dry and good one need not turn up one's nose at this dish nor look at it like the pedlar. I finished what I got.'

The high hills of Foula form a dramatic backdrop for the fertile croft land. The uncultivated land is known as 'de hogins' and is grazing land for the 1500 sheep in the island. It rises sharply towards the west,

245

and is a large untamed area. The only opening in this massive western wall is Da Daal—a valley which goes from Hametoon to Da Sneck ida Smaallie, which is a deep and very strange fissure in the cliff face. This was once the site of a terrible wreck. From there it is possible to see the Atlantic at its most beautiful, as well as its most awesome. The wind sprays the water from the burn on Wester Hævdi high up in the air, and forces the birds to fly backwards.

The western cliffs are the home of enormous colonies of seabirds. The island truly lives up to its old name, as the population of breeding birds is estimated at around 500,000. This includes the largest breeding colony of bonxies—great skuas—in Britain. Walking around in the hills is made difficult by the swooping attacks of furious bonxies. In the north-west The Kame plunges vertically 372 m (1220 ft) into the sea. This steep cliff is responsible for the whirlwinds known as 'flans' which sometimes howl down the hills with tremendous force.

In Hamnafield are still the remains of the Catalina which crashed there in the autumn of 1944, carrying a number of servicemen who were going away to receive their gallantry medals, killing all but one passenger. Close to the top of Hamnafield is The Lum of Liorafield, said to be a kind of chimney descending to sea level some 1100 ft below. In Norse Liorafield meant the mountain of the lum, or chimney. It is described by Sir Walter Scott in his novel *The Pirate*. All kinds of stories grew around it, but at some time it was covered with a cairn, and is now difficult to find.

25 FAIR ISLE

> ... A lonely island
> Looms forth between Shetland and Orkney
> Raising high to heaven its bold, proud head.
> The Fair Isle—belonging to Shetland,
> And of like origin, and by like race
> Inhabited at first. A mere insect
> It seems, from a thick swarm disjoined,
> And here alone into the sea cast down.
> (*Fair Isle*, Wilhelm Jensen 1837–1911)

Fair Isle is a stepping stone set in the sea between Orkney and Shetland, some 25 miles away from each. In clear weather it is possible to see both island groups from Ward Hill, the highest point. Traditionally Fair Isle has had links with both Orkney and Shetland. The story goes that when the Orkneyman Stewart of Brough in Sanday became the new laird of Fair Isle in the 1770s, it was because he had won it at brag, a card game rather like poker, from Sinclair of Quendale. The Old Haa, the largest house in Fair Isle, is built in an Orkney style. It was used by the Stewart lairds to house their factor, and Sir Walter Scott dined there in 1814. Fair Isle was bought back to Shetland in 1866 by Bruce of Sumburgh, and is now a part of the county of Shetland.

It might be said that the fertile southern part of Fair Isle resembles Orkney just as the northern hills are Shetland. All the crofts are found in the southern part where the land slopes evenly down to the sea at Skadan and Meoness. The cultivated land is separated from the hill by a prehistoric turf dyke going right across the island; this used to be known as Gonnawark, a name still remembered in the geos where it ends. According to tradition the name referred to a troll or giant. Today it is known as the Feelie-dyke, and south of the fence there is a round mound called Holi Gonni. The name may derive from the Norse word *gondull*, which is used in Norse literature especially when a troll woman or her work is mentioned.

The north end of the island rises sheer from the sea like a wall, with grass growing to the edge. There are numerous caves, and the ongoing process of cave-making is plain to see. As layers of rock are washed away, rocks and stacks assume the most fantastic shapes. At Skroo the sea can be seen to eat away at the narrow ridge of land between the foghorn and the North Lighthouse—an awe-inspiring site.

Fair Isle is the Friðarey of the Orkneyinga Saga. In 1135 it played a part in the conflict between Earl Paul and Earl Rognvald Kalie Kolsson. The 'varða'—or beacon—on Ward Hill was an important link in an alarm system of beacons throughout Orkney and Shetland. Through a clever stratagem on Earl Rognvald's part it was not lit at the crucial moment to warn Earl Paul of his coming. The first modern version of the island name occurs as 'insula de Fairyle' in 1572. (Orkney and Shetland Records I, p179.) Locally the island is spoken of as 'da isle'.

Through the centuries Fair Isle with its dangerous crags, geos and stacks was feared by those who for some reason sailed close to its coast. Some came too close. The wreck of one of the flagships of the Spanish Armada on Fair Isle in September 1588 has become legendary. The whole story of the Armada is fantastic in itself, and the way it came to affect this small island is no less so. After their plans of invading England failed, the surviving ships of the Armada were on the run up the east coast of Britain, with the north coast of Ireland as their only escape route. Not even the Vikings had tried going west against the prevailing wind, in waters they did not know.

At first luck was on their side. The channel between Shetland and Fair Isle known as 'the Hole' was downwind, and the fleet sailed through. Somewhere northwest of Scotland the wind changed. The fleet was thrown into disarray. *Gran Grifon*, flagship of the squadron of transport ships known as urcas, beat against head winds for weeks. She was a German ship of 650 tons from the Hanseatic city of Rostock, and was named after its heraldic emblem the griffin—a fable creature with the head and wings of an eagle, but with a lion's body. The ship had the original German crew, and carried many soldiers as well as survivors picked up from a sinking ship. On board was also Don Gomez de Medina, commander of the squadron of urcas.

Because of the heavy load and the wild seas the ship's seams opened up: *Gran Grifon* could stay afloat only by bearing off with the wind, and had to sail wherever the wind would take her. After six weeks they were back in Orkney, completely lost, with rocky shores all around. A diary recording the last voyage of the *Gran Grifon* has survived. Nobody knows who wrote it.

Truly our one thought was that our lives were ended, and each of us reconciled himself to God as well as he could, and prepared for the long journey to death. To force the ship any more would only have ended it and our lives the sooner, so we gave up trying. The poor soldiers too, who had worked

North West side of Fair Isle. Through the centuries, Fair Isle with its dangerous crags, geos and stacks, was feared by those who sailed close to its coast.

incessantly at the pumps and buckets, lost heart and let the water rise... At last, when we thought all hope was gone except through God and His holy Mother, who never fail those who call upon them, we sighted an island ahead of us. It was Fair Isle, and we anchored in a sheltered spot we found, this day of our great peril, 27th September 1588.

They had found a bay in the southwestern part of the island known as Sivars (Swarts) Geo. According to tradition the ship was taken by the tide and wedged into the Stroms Hellier where it sank, but not before all the three hundred men on board got safely off ship and even saved most of their equipment. The wreck was found by divers in 1970. The *Gran Grifon* had carried 38 guns, and among the finds was a long-range gun which was fully loaded—one of the few Armada guns still preserved.

There were 17 occupied crofts in Fair Isle then, and it is said that some of the crofters thought the Day of Judgment had come when they saw all the strange men in armour. In the opinion of the diary writer the islanders were dirty savages who could be called neither Christian nor heretic. Still he maintains that the Spaniards and the islanders got along extremely well. The Spaniards seem to have taken whatever food there was. Although they paid for it, the islanders must have been worried about the future, as they are said to have tried to hide their breeding stock in caves. And there have been stories in Fair Isle indicating that the relationship between the islanders and the strangers was strained, even hostile. This nursery rhyme was taken down by Einar Seim from an old woman at the croft of Kwi (Quoy):

> Haligelu came dunw fai Skru
> wi' knifs au rusti hwattels,
> te cut de throat o' wicked men
> dat eats manni's vettels (victuals).
> Jol i Sunnfjord, 1947

This seems like wishful thinking: a trow coming down from the hills to take care of the wicked men who are eating their island bare. Certainly mercenaries dying of starvation and disease would not have been the best of guests, but there are reports indicating that the islanders and the soldiers got on remarkably well. It took about six weeks before they could be taken off the island and during that time some 50 of them died and were buried in the south of the island at a place called Spainnarts Graves. For a long time the story has been told that the soldiers taught the women of Fair Isle how to make natural dyes and also how to knit the patterns that have since become traditional, but this has been discredited.

A later wreck has also become famous. The *Lessing* of Bremen, which was a new ship on her first passage and bound for New York, with emigrants from many European countries, was wrecked in Klaver Geo, beside Shaldi Cliff. The officers believed that they were some 50 miles past Fair Isle and set every sail to catch the breeze, so that she struck the cliffs when going seven knots. It proved hopeless to lower the boats as they became smashed to pieces by the breakers. This happened early in the morning of 22 May 1868. The cries of the shipwrecked roused the islanders who could see nothing because of the dense mist. Going by the sounds they came to help the shipwrecked through the narrow sea arch called the Hole o' Klaver. A young artist, John T. Reid, visited Fair Isle a few weeks later and told the story of the rescue:

> All were taken through that narrow tunnel—a work of great difficulty and danger. They were landed at the foot of cliffs three hundred feet high, at the top of which stood all the women of the island in earnest consultation; as there was scarcely any meal in the island at the time, gloomy pictures of famine filled their troubled minds. But soon sympathy for the shipwrecked ones overcame every other consideration; and one by one they descended the steep path to help up their unfortunate sisters, carrying their children for them, and welcoming them to the shelter of their humble cottages, and a share of such fare as they possessed. Every cottage in the island was

250

crowded, and the two little churches and a schoolhouse were turned into temporary dormitories. (*Art Rambles in Shetland* Edinburgh 1869, p 53)

This description also indirectly draws a picture of a life with no reserves to fall back upon—May would be a critical time in a subsistence economy. Crops in Fair Isle were never sufficient for the number of people living there, and fishing was long the main source of income. The islanders seem to have done fairly well at it too; in the early seventeenth century the laird traded in dried fish with Hamburg merchants from a booth in Fair Isle. There was also an export of feathers. But around the middle of the nineteenth century conditions deteriorated. A change in the climate limited the fishing and caused bad harvests. Bruce of Sumburgh, who wanted to buy Fair Isle, maintained that the island could not sustain its population of 380 people; and in 1862 the Board of Supervision for Relief of the Poor in Scotland organized a mass emigration of 132 men, women and children to New Brunswick in Canada. However, they may not have been as poor as he made out.

Fair Isle first became famous for its birds early in this century following visits by the two notable ornithologists the Duchess of Bedford and Dr W. Eagle Clarke of the Royal Scottish Museum. The latter was an international expert on bird migration. Some of the islanders also became very interested in bird identification. But it was really George Waterston who put Fair Isle birds on the map. He first visited the island in 1935. During the war he was taken prisoner at the fall of Crete, and the idea of building a bird observatory in Fair Isle was originally conceived in a German prisoner-of-war camp. When he fell seriously ill, he was repatriated on a Swedish hospital ship, and incredibly the first land sighted was Fair Isle and Sheep Craig. That settled the matter for him. He bought the island in 1948 and established an observatory in the old naval station at North Haven.

In 1954 the island was handed over to the National Trust for Scotland, and eventually the wartime huts were replaced by a modern purpose-built observatory. This has made it possible for both staff and visitors to work in comfortable surroundings. The island has a large breeding seabird population, but it is perhaps even more interesting for studying the migration of birds. Two main streams of migration meet in Fair Isle. One comes from the area around the Barents Sea down along the Norwegian coast, the other from Greenland, Iceland and Faroe. In Fair Isle they find a welcome resting place. The migration of birds still presents many unsolved problems; because Fair Isle is a small island it is possible to make daily observations of various species. Traps of wire-netting have been built along dykes and across the Gill o' Finniquoy, and many birds have been caught, measured and ringed.

In the 1950s the population of Fair Isle was down to 44, and the question of evacuation was seriously discussed. The lifeline of the island was then, as now, *The Good Shepherd*, which maintains the sea link with Shetland. But there were simply not enough men left to draw the boat up the slipway at North Haven. Through a combined effort of Zetland County Council and the National Trust the harbour was improved and the homes in the island had electricity and running water installed. In the eighties the population rose to 72. The harbour was then improved once again: a berth was excavated in the cliff side and an 80-metre two-railed slipway was built. It can be used at all states of the tide and has made it possible to use a larger ferry. *The Good Shepherd IV*, therefore, was launched. It is a steady and sturdy boat which takes the excitement out of crossing the Sumburgh Roost.

Today the island has many interesting features besides its birds and is a particularly close knit community. There is still a great reliance on community effort; it used to be all-important for the hauling up of *The Good Shepherd*, for unloading as fast as possible the coal that was brought into the island once every year, as well as for the many tasks in crofting and fishing. Among the more spectacular feats were the visits to Sheep Craig to catch, shear and bring down some of the sheep and lambs grazing there, but this has not happened for some time.

There are many tales told about the intelligence of the Fair Islanders and their interest in the world about them. It began even in Norse times, as can be seen from an incident in Njál's Saga. It describes how the Viking Kari Solmundsson came from Iceland to avenge the murder of Njál. He stopped for some time in Fair Isle with a man called David the White, who could tell him that the killers were staying with Earl Sigurd in Orkney. The Spanish diarist reveals that the Fair Islanders could also keep their own counsel: 'It is true that they confess that the doctrine that once a year is preached to them by people sent from an island nine leagues off, is not good; but they say they dare not contradict it, which is a pity.'

As early as the 1730s The Scottish Society for the Propagation of Christian Knowledge founded a school in the island, and in the Statistical Accounts of 1791–9 we are told that almost all can read, and many can write. There are many eye-witness accounts of how the islanders would go out to meet the steamers, to trade and hear news. This is one from the second part of the nineteenth century:

> ——our course is dotted over with ten or a dozen little boats, which seem in a fair way of being either run down by the steamer, or swamped by the wash of her paddles. The boatmen evidently have no such fear, for instead of avoiding the apparent danger, they pull close up, and amid the roar and rush of the steamer, which has not slackened speed, they are heard addressing the passengers hurriedly, but eagerly and clearly, with 'Throw a paper, throw a paper!' (*Half Hours in the Far North*, pp 197–8)

26 THE SEA

Nothing is as spacious as the sea, nor as patient. Like a good-natured elephant it carries on its back all the puny creatures who inhabit the earth, and in its large cool depths it has room for all the misery of the world. It is not true that the sea is faithless, for it has never promised anything: without demands, without obligations, free and pure throbs the great heart—the last sound element in a sick world. (Alexander Kielland, *Garman & Worse*, 1880)

It is a strange coincidence that the name of this writer, who better than most knew the people living by and from the sea, is known across the world because an oil rig bearing his name capsized in the North Sea. It was the most serious accident befalling the oil industry at sea, and it revealed man's vulnerability in spite of and because of advanced technology.

The North Sea is a small shallow ocean surrounded by the most highly industrialized countries in the world. Through the centuries these waters have been put to manifold uses, and conflicts between the nations were bound to occur, even taken to the point of war. As an active member of the North Sea community, Shetland was seriously affected by most of these conflicts. But Shetland could also benefit from being next-door to one of the richest sea basins in the world for seafood. There is an abundant variety of fish, and fishing is carried on all over the North Sea. This is also the most heavily trafficked ocean area in the world. Sails have filled the North Sea through the centuries, from the single square sail to the complicated rigging of the windjammers. Today oil tankers come and go near Shetland, and there are still enormous riches of gas and oil waiting to be taken out of the North Sea.

But one only has to see how an old banger is tipped over the cliff somewhere in Shetland to realize that for the people living by the sea it has always served as a dumping-place; quite literally it was used to hide 'all the misery of the world', as people just shrugged 'the sea will take it'. Shetland beaches are littered with the kitchen refuse of Europe dumped from ships: milk cartons in a variety of languages can be picked up everywhere. When the oil-tanker Torrey Canyon foundered in 1970, attention for the first time became focused on large-scale pollution from accidents at sea. Still, land-based industry is responsible

253

There are still enormous riches of gas and oil waiting to be taken out of the North Sea, and test drilling goes on all the time. The picture shows the semi-submersible drilling platform, Zapata Ugland, owned jointly by Norwegian and American companies.

for two-thirds of the marine pollution. The North Sea is not yet dying, but it is seriously threatened. Fish from the Baltic are too toxic to be fed to polar bears at the zoo; if this or worse is to be avoided the North Sea community of maritime nations must realize that there is no time to lose. The land is carefully nurtured, why not the sea too?

And yet the North Sea may have to give room to a kind of misery not even dreamed of by Alexander Kielland. For some time the waters around Orkney and Shetland have been considered as excellent dumping sites for high-level radioactive wastes from the nuclear power industry. This would mean a threat to whole communities who depend for their livelihood on the sea, as such wastes would need tens of thousands of years to decay sufficiently to become harmless. An expansion of the nuclear plant at Dounreay to enable it to receive uranium and plutonium from the EEC countries has been bitterly opposed by Shetland, Orkney and Norway, where the Chernobyl accident took a heavy toll.

The North Sea is actually a 600-mile extension of the Atlantic, and Shetland is strategically placed between the two oceans. The sea has shaped Shetland life. Houses were built by the sea, and a boat was the most highly valued possession—to most people it was their lifeline. According to an old Shetland saying there are three godsends: *a stranger, a wreck, and a caa of whales*. Common to these godsends is that they are all three brought by the sea.

In a community where all know of each other any stranger would have to come by sea. It must surely be their ingrained generosity which makes it possible for the Shetlanders to view any stranger as a godsend—they were often enough raided by pirates and privateers. In 1695 a minister's daughter was abducted from Norwick in Unst by the crew of a French privateer. One day in September 1779 two Cunningsburgh men were fishing in a small boat off Mousa, when they answered the call for a pilot from a strange vessel approaching from the south—not until they were on board did they realize that it was a French warship waiting to be piloted into Lerwick harbour. Somehow they made the Frenchmen believe that there were two heavily gunned British warships lying there. Still the French would not let them go, but kept them below deck with a lot of other British prisoners. By a strange coincidence they were freed when the French ship was later captured by one of the warships they had lied about as lying in Lerwick harbour. After about a year of seeing Europe against their will they returned to their families, who for a long time had mourned their death.

An incident in June 1958 placed a strain on Russian–British relations: a Russian ship had anchored off Wats Ness in West Mainland, making it possible for a young Estonian seaman to run off in the ship's motor boat. He made it to Footabrough and started walking inland. Some 20 Russians in hot pursuit scoured the area for him, but he was safely inside a croft house at Crookataing, relaxing over tea. In the House of Commons Jo Grimond called the Russian visit 'an intolerable intrusion of a type which the Russians would be the first to deeply resent if it happened to them'. And in *The Shetland Times* the cartoon character Tirval was pictured doing bayonet practice with a muck fork—'practising for da nixt invasion'. But over the years relations between the Shetland people and the visiting Russian trawler crews have become quite friendly. And when the Out Skerries ran out of fresh water in the summers of 1968 and 1971 the Shetland Islands Council chartered a Russian water tanker to help the island.

Wrecks

It is no wonder that the Shetland coast is studded with wrecks of all kinds, from Viking ships and whalers to frigates. A wild sea, the winter darkness and a storm are formidable opponents; to that is added a torn coastline full of baas and skerries. Until recently this was largely uncharted. Still the passage through the Hole, between Fair Isle and Sumburgh, as well as the way around the north end of Shetland were much frequented routes into the North Atlantic, and then on to North America or the West Indies. The latter was known as the north about route, to the Dutch who used it more than any other nation, it was their 'achterom' route. In the turmoil of the many European wars the English Channel as often as not would be out of bounds, so that to go past Shetland was the *only* route.

Much interest has been focused on the Spanish Armada, but the similar fate of a Dutch fleet in Shetland waters during one of the many wars between Holland and England is almost unknown. One August evening in 1652 Admiral Cornelius Tromp on board his flagship the *Brederode*, with 102 warships and 10 fireships, was in search of English ships, and met up with an English squadron of 62 ships under the command of the famous Admiral Robert Blake between Foula and Fair Isle. They were both preparing themselves for a naval battle when a storm came upon them quite suddenly. The Dutch fleet seems to have been worst hit: several ships were smashed against the Burra coast or were lost off the coast. Only about 40 Dutch ships managed to return to Scheveningen.

About a decade later another Dutch ship was dramatically lost at Out Skerries. This was the *Kennemerland* of Amsterdam, an East Indiaman outward bound for Batavia in December 1664. She was running before the wind when in the dark she ran full tilt into Stoura Stack in the south entrance to Skerries. The greater part of the shattered ship was carried out to sea; the stern parts were cast up on Bruray; and three seamen on the look-out in the rigging were the only crew members saved—because the fore-mast fell ashore. The body of the ship's drummer was washed ashore on Bruray and the place where he was buried is still known as the 'Drummer's Grave'.

Rumours ran wild of a treasure on board of several million guilders as well as chests of gold. In actual fact some 120,000 guilders worth in gold and silver coin was recovered at the time from the wreck. According to tradition, enough kegs and casks of spirits were washed ashore to keep the Skerries people on one long binge for weeks. The wreck is remembered in a local verse:

> The *Carmelan* frae Amsterdam,
> Cam' on a Maunsmas day,
> On Stoura Stack, she broke her back,
> And the Skerry folk got a prey!

At that time the Earl of Morton had the right to most wreck and salvage in Orkney and Shetland, because of a debt owed him by the Crown. This right did not, however, extend to any ships belonging to the enemy in time of war. The feud between King Charles II and Morton about ownership of the wreck was a drawn out affair. It ended with the Morton family being deprived of all their rights in Orkney and Shetland for more than 40 years. Steps were also taken to find the goods that had disappeared from the wreck. It must have been plundered by people from far and near, for in 1675 the late Gilbert Murray in Laxo was ordered to bring back a variety of goods he had taken, such as 'nyne hundred ells of ribbands', or pay a large sum in cash. But as the man was dead and his widow found to live in poor circumstances, nothing came of this claim.

Then in early November of 1711 the same drama was played once more in Skerries. During the War of the Spanish Succession the French maintained an effective blockade of all Dutch ships. In an attempt to break this blockade a large convoy of Dutch ships was to keep together till they were safely past Shetland. In the storm and the dark some of the ships came too far to the westward, and at least seven of them were lost without trace. Most of them probably foundered on reefs off Whalsay. The East Indiaman *De Liefde* struck Mio Ness, the south end of Housay. As with the *Kennemerland* all hands were lost except the man on the lookout in the fore-top. Apparently, he was found wandering around in shock by Skerries people on their way home from church the next morning.

The *Liefde* had gold and silver specie on board worth something like 227,000 guilders, and there were other Shetland wrecks as well that became legendary for their treasure. But in treeless islands the timber that floated ashore from some of the wrecks was also very welcome:

> ... very providentially a large vessel from Norway loaded with wood for Ireland, was put into Quendal bay by a cross wind and by a great storm driven ashore and wrecked below the Ness Kirk, which is never plenished with seats to this day, though the people would have cheerfully paid for them. The wood was sold off for profit. However, the Kirk of Sandwick and manse of Dunrossness were built with wood out of it. (*Diary of the Reverend John Mill 1740–1803*, Edinburgh 1889, p 8)

Probably the strangest accident to happen in Shetland waters was the sinking of the great liner *Oceanic*—for many years known as the 'Queen of the Seas'. When she was built in 1899 she was at 17,274 tons the largest ship in the world, as well as probably the most luxurious one. She could take some 1,700 passengers, and no expense had been spared to make their voyage comfortable. When war broke out in 1914, the ship was taken over by the Navy and became H.M.S. *Oceanic*. As an armed merchant cruiser she was sent off on the Northern Patrol to check the cargo and crew of passing ships.

In the morning of 8 September 1914 the people of Foula could not believe their eyes when a huge ship loomed up before them, heading straight for the jagged rocks of the Hoevdi Reef—also known as The Shaalds of Foula—about 2 miles (3 km) east of the island. The reef lies just below the surface and is not noticeable in a calm sea. The *Oceanic* was driven inexorably on to the reef by the flood tide, and from the moment she was stuck there she was beyond hope. The puzzling question was how it was possible to get there in the first place, in a mirror-calm sea. The answer seems to be that it was a navigational error; at the court-martial it was found that the navigator believed they were further south and west than they were. The fact that there were two captains in command also led to a confusion of responsibility:

> Smith told the naval captain that it was too dangerous, in a fog, to take a ship the size of the *Oceanic* where the latter suggested. The naval captain told Smith he was only a merchant ship master, and no longer in command of the ship, and that she would go where he, the naval captain, said she would go. And go there she did—on to the reef, breaking her back. (Simon Martin *The Other Titanic: Salvage of an Ocean Queen*, Newton Abbot 1980, p 30)

Everyone on board was safely taken off the ship. People on Foula said they would give her about two weeks before the sea and the storm would get her. And they were right; at the end of September that once so proud ship broke up and sank during a stormy night.

The tide-race on the Shaalds was notorious, and for a long time the site was considered undiveable. In 1973 the two divers Alec Crawford and Simon Martin found that it was possible to dive during slack tide times. While based in Foula they searched the wreck, weather permitting, over the next seven years for valuable scrap metal. During all that time they could dive on a total of only 200 days.

Interest was focused on the older wrecks. In 1964 the *Liefde* was discovered by the Royal Navy crew of H.M.S. *Shoulton*, and the following year Commander Alan Bax R.N. began the excavation. This was pioneering underwater archaeological work by a man who is still well known internationally as a marine archaeologist. In 1967 a company of divers calling themselves Scientific Survey and Location Ltd (S.S.L.) were permitted by the Dutch government to carry on with the excavation of the *Liefde* site in Skerries. Luck was with them and they found an intact chest which turned out to contain silver

Diver Richard Price shows his latest find of three gold ducats from the Liefde *to Shetland photographer Dennis Coutts.*

coins. Their finds that year comprised more than four thousand silver coins and some gold ducats. About half of them had been minted in Utrecht in 1711, the year the *Liefde* sank.

This was the kind of find that divers dream of, and a Klondyke rush to Shetland wrecks was to be expected. Tom Henderson, the late curator of the Shetland Museum, suggested that the Zetland County Council should lease from the Crown the rights to the sea-bed around the more important wrecks. Such an action had no precedent, but it has worked. This agreement has given to Shetland almost complete control over the 14 historically most important sites, and has preserved them for excavation by responsible divers and marine archaeologists.

The fate of the *Gran Grifon* has caused much romantic speculation over the centuries. She, too, was said to have carried treasure. In 1970 a team led by Colin Martin found the wreck at Stroms Hellier, and the contents were bought by Shetland Museum and can be seen there. One silver coin was all the treasure found.

In Skerries the wreck of the *Kennemerland* was found in 1971 by a team of divers from Aston University Sub-Aqua Club. During the seventies the excavation on this site was led by Richard Price, assisted by the laterine archaeologist Keith Muckelroy, and a very important collection of artefacts was gradually brought up to the surface. All the items were purchased by the museum, and the money thus raised was used to set up the Shetland Trust for Nautical Archaeology, whose trustees have made grants to other underwater excavations in Shetland. The finds make up a collection which gives a fascinating picture of life on board ship in the seventeenth century.In 1974 the same team also did some diving on the nearby wreck of the *Liefde*, and found that much still remained to be done there. With permission from the authorities they therefore in 1976 carried out excavations which resulted in over 1600 silver coins and some gold ducats being found. This made S.S.L. raise an action against Richard Price to prevent him from doing any more work on the wreck, as they claimed exclusive rights to it. There were important legal principles involved in the case, so that when the judge ruled in favour of Richard Price a precedent was set.

Whales and whaling

Although Shetland has never had any whaling industry of her own it has still meant much to the island economy. For more than a hundred years—from the middle of the eighteenth to the late nineteenth century—the whaling ships from English and Scottish fishing ports made up their crews in Shetland before they sailed for the Greenland Sea. By Act of Parliament the crew must be of a certain standard; thus a three hundred ton vessel had to carry six harpooners, six boat-steerers, six line-managers, ten seamen, six green-men and six apprentices, apart from the skipper and the ship's doctor. During the peak years from 1840 to 1860 it was sometimes difficult to recruit a qualified crew.

Both for the hunter and the hunted whaling was probably the hardest and most brutal marine activity ever pursued. As a training for seamen there was nothing like it. There was also adventure involved, for in their search for new whaling grounds the whalers became explorers; in their study of the whale's movements they learned about ocean currents and winds and became the first practical oceanographers. It was dangerous work; in one year alone 19 vessels were lost. In 1867 the Hull whaler *Diana* staggered into Ronas Voe with her crew dead or dying; only 2 of the 51 men on board were still able to stand on their feet; 26 of the crew were Shetlanders. For six months the ship had been trapped by the Artic ice, and they had suffered great hardship from the cold and lack of supplies.

For a short time whaling was also carried on close to the Shetland coast. At the beginning of this century Norwegian companies established stations at Ronas Voe, Olnafirth and Collafirth where the whales were brought in. This industry did not last long, as people objected to the smell and the pollution; the Council even appealed to the Prime Minister about it.

Late in the nineteenth century the Norwegians began Antarctic whaling. This was made possible by the invention of a harpoon gun with an explosive head. The whaling ships became floating factories with shore stations in places like Grytviken and Leith Harbour in South Georgia. The season extended from November through March, and whaling could therefore be combined with crofting. A great many Shetlanders went to the Antarctic every year, and until it came to an end in the 1960s whaling brought in much needed capital.

In the nineteenth century, especially, stranded whales were considered a godsend and the Shetlanders made much use of them. This was mostly a smaller type of whale travelling in schools, which could number as many as a thousand animals. At times they drifted into voes or shallow water and got trapped there. In a terrible free-for-all slaughter they would be killed for the oil and the bone. Whale meat— some of the most tender meat of all—was never eaten in Shetland. The blackfish or caaing whales as they were called in Shetland, were often driven ashore when men in boats cut off their way of escape. The same word is used about driving the sheep into the crö for marking or shearing.

The largest kill in Shetland is said to have taken place in Quendale Bay in September of 1845, when 1540 whales were caught. Whales appear to have become stranded rather frequently, but even so Shetlanders do not seem to have been prepared for the whale hunt, for they would use any weapon to hand, from hayforks to tushkers. And the whale hunt never had the sociological significance it has had in Faroe. The reason for this may have been that the Shetlander himself got to keep less than a third of the value of the whales, in spite of doing all the work. The Crown and the laird each took one third, of the remaining third the Church would take its share in teind (an ecclesiastical tithe).

Sometimes the Church even took an active part, judging by a story told in Dunrossness. The minister was in the middle of his Sunday sermon when he noticed several of his parishioners edging for the door. He realized that a whale hunt was on, and quickly finished his sermon by saying: 'I have only one final word to say, my brethren, and that is: Let us all have a fair start—just a fair start'. Then he, also, ran out of the church.

The famous Hoswick whaling case was fought about the ownership issue. When in 1888 more than three hundred whales were driven ashore in Hoswick in South Mainland, the local inhabitants whose efforts had caught the whales decided that they had had enough, and refused to pay the lairds their share. The matter was taken to the highest court in Edinburgh, and money came in from Shetlanders all

THE SEA

over the world to pay for legal assistance. Of course the Crofting Act
had set a precedent, and the case was won by the islanders. But times
have changed, and today a school of stranded whales are considered
merely a nuisance.

The knowledge of the sea acquired through generations made the
Shetlanders into natural seamen. Unfortunately, this skill has not
always served them in good stead. At the end of the eighteenth century,
when the Napoleonic Wars began, the Navy wanted experienced
seamen. In relation to the population Shetland was expected to supply
about a hundred men. Many more than that volunteered, but the
Navy was still not content, and sent a 'press-gang' who virtually
kidnapped anybody unfortunate enough to be at large where they
struck. There are numerous stories about how the men would try to
outwit the press-gang; even so an estimated 3000 men ended up in
the navy. Since then Shetland men have made disproportionate
sacrifices in two world wars—as a war memorial will tell us in even
the smallest community. No other county in Britain paid so heavily
in human lives.

'From their manner of life they are constantly exposed to the most
deplorable accidents', says a nineteenth century writer about the
islanders. Although for taboo reasons the women could never take part
in the fishing or other activities at sea, indeed just the sight of one on
the way to the boat could make the men turn around and go back
home, they were not always out of harm's way. In the early eighteenth
century two young girls from the island of Uyea off Unst went to Haaf
Gruney in a small rowing boat to milk some cows that were pastured
there. On their way home they were caught in a storm and driven
before the wind for days. Their boat was cast ashore on the island of
Karmøy in southwestern Norway. The people who found them got
over their initial fright at the sight of them when one of the girls made
the sign of the Cross. They both married in Karmøy, and their
descendants are still living there.

A better known story is the voyage of Betty Mouat in 1886—it
became front page news all over the world. Betty Mouat was at the
time of her ordeal 60 years old, and she lived on a croft at Scatness in
Dunrossness. She was born lame and walked with some difficulty; she
had also recently had a mild stroke. She was going to Lerwick to see
a doctor as well as sell her knitted shawls to the merchants. It was 14
years since her last visit there. She had no choice but to go by boat.
There was a weekly service from Grutness to Lerwick by the *Columbine*,
a 15 m (50 ft) long sailing vessel rigged as a cutter. Her neighbours
entrusted her with selling their shawls as well, so that she carried a
bundle of 40 shawls, along with some milk in a bottle and two biscuits—
after all the voyage was not going to take long. She went below deck.
There was a crew of three, but she was the only passenger.

262

When the *Columbine* was abreast of Voe there was a wrenching noise and the skipper shouted 'The main sheet's broken'. After that there was the mate's voice: 'Get away the boat', and then there was nothing but the noise of the sea. The skipper had fallen overboard, and while two men tried to save him the *Columbine* drifted off. Horrified they realized that there was no way they could catch up with her. By hanging on to a rope in the cabin, Betty Mouat prevented herself from being thrown against the walls and the furniture by the wild movements of the boat. She never slept at all during the eight days and nights her voyage lasted, and had nothing to eat except the milk and the biscuits she had brought. Five days later on Wednesday she saw a coast with snow-covered hills, but it disappeared again. On the Sunday morning the boat stopped moving. Some small boys playing on a beach in the island of Lepsøy, 9 miles (14 km) north of Ålesund on Norway's north-western coast, got the surprise of their lives when a woman's head suddenly appeared in the wreck, shouting for help. The *Columbine* had zig-zagged in between dangerous reefs, and it was a miracle she landed where she did.

Yet, for Betty Mouat the publicity that followed her plight was probably worse than the experience itself. She took a passage from Ålesund to Hull. The train ride from there to Edinburgh was a new experience, and the crowds waiting at Waverley Station to have a glimpse of her a nightmare. People came to look at her while she stayed in the town, and to ask her for hairs from her head. She was offered money to go on exhibition in various places, but she just longed to get back to the Scatness croft and carry on with her life as she knew it. When she got home, there was a letter from Queen Victoria waiting for her, with a sum of money. She never left her croft again and died there at 93; today her home at Scatness is one of the many empty Shetland croft houses.

The woman's place was on the croft where most of the daily work and responsibilities fell to her lot. Her task was an important one. Far too often she was left to shoulder the whole responsibility alone when her father, husband or son—sometimes even all three—was lost at sea.

> A storm overtakes the fishers, when many miles distant from land, and from the too common custom of members of one household forming the crew of the same boat, we often witness the pitiable case, of a wretched female losing, at a stroke, husband, sons and brothers,—and youthful widows left to mourn the short period of wedded happiness they had enjoyed,—while numerous helpless children are thrown on the charity of the neighbourhood,—a charity, by the way, never appealed to in vain. In these, and similar cases, long and bitterly do survivors mourn.'(Eliza Edmondston, *Sketches and Tales of the Shetland Islands* Edinburgh 1856, pp 17–18)

To the crofter-fisherman the sea might be both his place of work

Unknown grave at Lu Ness, West Burra. To the crofter-fisherman, the sea might be both his friend and his foe.

and his grave, but his life and the lives of his family were intricately linked with it. He lived in a community where the few resources had to be carefully husbanded. It was an egalitarian community, as it is even today when the trawlers have replaced the sixerns and the sailing smacks—the skipper is only the first among equals. By necessity the small fishing communities, which were surprisingly similar all around the North Sea, were flexible—they had to be when the interests of fishing and crofting collided or bad weather struck. Somehow man had learned to survive, even make a worthwhile existence, out of a marginal environment. This knowledge is dying out with the present generation of old people. It should be stored for the future; knowing how to survive in marginal communities might become useful to us all.

BIBLIOGRAPHY

General books

Robert Cowie, *Shetland: Descriptive and Historical and Topographical Description of that county*. Aberdeen, 1879.

Samuel Hibbert, *A Description of the Shetland Isles*. Edinburgh, 1922.

George Low, *A Tour through the Islands of Orkney and Schetland (1774)*. Kirkwall, 1879.

J. R. Nicolson, *Shetland*. Newton Abbot, 1984.

Anna Ritchie, *Exploring Scotland's Heritage. Orkney and Shetland*. Edinburgh, 1985.

The Shetland Book, A. T. Cluness (Ed.), Lerwick, 1967.

The Third Statistical Account of Scotland, Vol. XXB: The County of Shetland. Edinburgh, 1985.

John R. Tudor, *The Orkneys and Shetland*. London, 1883.

Chapter 2: Nature

A. C. O'Dell, 'The Shetland Islands. A Geographical synopsis.' The Viking Congress, Lerwick, 1950.

Articles in: Thomas Manson *Guide to Shetland*, Lerwick, 1932.

Alan Small, 'Geographical Location: Environment and History.' *Shetland and the Outside World 1469–1969*. Oxford, 1983.

Ursula Venables, *Life in Shetland. A World Apart*. London, 1956.

Chapter 3: Early History

Gilbert Goudie, *The Celtic and Scandinavian Antiquities of Shetland*. Edinburgh, 1904.

Articles in: *Shetland Archaeology*, Brian Smith (Ed.), Lerwick, 1985.

W. Douglas Simpson, 'The Broch of Clickhimin'. The Viking Congress, Lerwick, 1950.

Chapter 4: Norse Times

Articles in: *The Vikings*, R. T. Farrell (Ed.), London, 1982.

From *Essays in Shetland History*, Barbara E. Crawford (Ed.), Lerwick, 1984: Paul Bibire, 'Few know an earl in fishing-clothes'. Barbara E. Crawford, 'The Cult of St. Magnus in Shetland'.

Alan Small, 'A Viking Longhouse in Unst, Shetland'. The Fifth Viking Congress, Tórshavn, 1965.

BIBLIOGRAPHY

Chapter 5: In Scotland

From *Shetland and the Outside World 1469–1969*. Donald Withrington (Ed.), Oxford, 1983: Barbara E. Crawford, 'The Pledging of the Islands in 1469: the Historical Background'. Klaus Friedland, 'Hanseatic Merchants and their Trade with Shetland'. Gordon Donaldson, 'The Scots Settlement in Shetland.'

Anton Espeland, 'Norsk samband med Orknøy og Hjaltland'. Norsk Aarbok, 1928.

Chapter 6: In Britain

Brian Smith, 'Shetland Archives and Sources of Shetland History'. History Workshop Journal No. 4. (Autumn, 1977).

Brian Smith, '"Lairds" and "Improvement" in 17th and 18th century Shetland.' *Lairds and Improvement in the Scotland of the Enlightenment*. T. Devine (Ed.), Glasgow, 1979.

John J. Graham, 'Social Changes during the Quinquennium, *Shetland and the Outside World 1469–1969*. Oxford, 1983.

Chapter 7: The Shetland Bus

David Howarth, *The Shetland Bus*. London, 1951.

Heroes of Nowadays. London 1953.

Ragnar Ulstein, *Englandsfarten*. Bd I: Alarm i Ålesund. Bd II: Søkelys mot Bergen. Det Norske Samlaget, Oslo 1965–67.

Johanne Herlofson, 'Shetlands–Larsen.' Krigsseileren, No. 2, 1982.

J. R. Nicolson, 'Memories of the Shetland Bus I–III.' Shetland Life, 1984.

Chapter 8: People

J. R. Nicolson, *Traditional Life in Shetland*. London, 1978

James W. Irvine, *Up-Helly-Aa*. Lerwick, 1982.

Chapter 9: Folklore

John Spence, *Shetland Folk-lore*. Lerwick, 1899

Ernest W. Marwick, *The Folklore of Orkney and Shetland*. Batsford, London, 1975.

Halvdan Koht, 'Var 'finnane' alltid finnar?' Maal og Minne, 1923.

Inger M. Boberg, *Sagnet om den store Pans død*. Copenhagen, 1934.

Chapter 10: Shetlandic

Marius Hægstad, *Hildinakvadet*. Kristiania, 1900.

Jakob Jakobsen, *The Dialect and Place Names of Shetland*. Lerwick, 1897.

Oskar Lundberg, 'On the Shetland Sea Language as a Source of Old Norse Literature'. The Viking Congress, Lerwick, 1950.

J. Y. Mather, 'Dialect Research in Orkney and Shetland after Jakobsen'. Fróðskaparrit, Tórshavn, 1964.

Chr. Matras, 'Dr Jakob Jakobsen'. Norsk Aarbok, 1924.

David Murison, 'Scots Speech in Shetland'. The Viking Congress. Lerwick, 1950.

David Murison, 'Shetland Speech today.' Fróðskaparrit, Tórshavn, 1964.

A Corpus of Shetland English. Bengt Orestrøm (Ed.), Stockholm, 1985.

Laurits Rendboe, 'How 'worn out' or 'corrupted' was Shetland Norn in its final stage?' Nowele No. III, Odense University Press, 1985.

John Stewart, 'Norn in Shetland'. Fróðskaparrit, Tórshavn, 1964.
Ulf Zachariassen, 'Jakob Jakobsen og ritgerðir hansara'. Fróðskaparrit, Tórshavn, 1964.

Chapter 11: Place-Names
Frå hav til hei. Heidersskrift til Per Hovda. Oslo, 1978.
Per Sveaas Andersen, 'Peter Andreas Munch and the Beginning of Shetland Place-Name Research.' Essays in Shetland History. Lerwick, 1984.
A. W. Brøgger, Den norske bosetningen på Shetland-Orknøyene. Oslo, 1930.
Jakob Jakobsen, The Place-names of Shetland. London, 1936.
P. A. Munch, Geographiske Oplysninger om de i Sagaerne forekommende Skotske og Irske Stedsnavne. Christiania, 1853.
W. F. H. Nicolaisen, 'Early Scandinavian naming in the Western and Northern Isles.' Northern Scotland, 1980, iii, pp 105–21.
'The Post-Norse Places-Names of Shetland.' Shetland and the Outside World. Aberdeen University Studies No. 157, 1983.
John Stewart, 'Shetland Farm Names.' Fourth Viking Congress, York 1961. Aberdeen University Studies No. 149, 1965.

Chapter 12: The Cultural Heritage
Håkon Grüner-Nielsen, 'Den Shetlandske Hildina-Vise og Sophus Bugges Tolkning.' Heidersskrift til Gustav Indrebø. Bergen, 1936.
Knut Liestøl, 'Ei folkevise på norn-mål frå Shetland.' Maal og Minne, 1936.
Laurits Rendboe, The Shetland Literary Tradition. Odense, 1986.
Svale Solheim, 'Jakob Jakobsens folkeminnetekster på norn.' Fróðskaparrit, Tórshavn, 1964.

Chapter 13: Music
Peter Cooke, 'The Fiddle in Shetland Society'. Scottish Studies Vol. 22: Edinburgh, 1978.
Peter A. Jamieson, The Viking Isles. London, 1933.
Ronald G. Popperwell, 'Music in Shetland'. Essays in Shetland History. Lerwick, 1984.

Chapter 14: Fishing
C. A. Goodlad, Shetland Fishing Saga. Lerwick, 1971.
H. A. H. Boelmans Kranenburg, 'The Netherlands Fisheries and the Shetland Islands.' Shetland and the Outside World 1469–1969. Oxford, 1969.
Christian Pløyen, Reminiscences of a Voyage to Shetland, Orkney & Scotland in the Summer of 1839. Transl. Catherine Spence. Lerwick, 1894.

Chapter 15: Knitting
Helen M. Bennett, The Origins and Development of the Scottish Hand-Knitting Industry. Chapter VII: Shetland. PhD thesis University of Edinburgh, 1981.
Audrey S. Henshall/Stuart Maxwell: 'Clothing and other articles from a late 17th-century grave at Gunnister, Shetland.' P.S.A.S., Vol. LXXXVI, Edinburgh, 1951–2.
Anne Kjellberg, 'it par bundingshoser sorte'—Norsk Folkemuseum, Oslo, 1985.
Stickat och virkat i nordisk tradition Østerbottens Museum, 1984.
James R. Nicolson, 'Promoting knitwear with the Shetland lady.' Shetland Life, April, 1986.

Chapter 16: Crofting

S. H. U. Bowie F.R.S., 'Shetland's native farm animals.' Shetland Life, September, November, 1986.

A. D. Cameron, *Go Listen to the Crofters.* Stornoway, 1986.

J. R. Nicolson, 'Crofting since 1886.' Shetland Life, November, 1986.

Jonathan W.G. Wills, 'The Zetland Method.' *Essays in Shetland History.* Lerwick, 1984.

Chapter 17: Oil

Jon Naustdalsli, 'Shetland møter oljealderen.' Syn og segn No. 4, 1980.

Shetland Islands Council, *Shetland's Oil Era.* Lerwick, 1981.

The Shetland Way of Oil. John Button (Ed.). Sandwick, 1978.

Chapter 18: Local Government

Island Futures. Roy Grønneberg (Ed.). Sandwick, 1978.

Nevis Institute, *The Shetland Report: A Constitutional Study.* Edinburgh, 1978.

Magnus Olsen, 'Med lögum skal land byggja.' Maal og Minne, 1946.

John Stewart, 'Udal Law and Government in Shetland.' The Viking Congress. Lerwick, 1950.

P. N. Sutherland Graeme, 'The Parliamentary Representation of Orkney and Shetland, 1754–1900.' Orkney Miscellany. Vol. 1, 1953.

Edward Thomason, 'Shetland in the seventies: a Shetlander's View of Oil.' *Scandinavian Shetland: An Ongoing Tradition.*? Edinburgh, 1978.

'Towards Island Government. The Aims and Aspirations of the Shetland Movement.' Report from a seminar in Lerwick 1984.

Chapter 19: Lerwick

James R. S. Clark, 'A Hundred Years of Lerwick.' *Scandinavian Shetland: An Ongoing Tradition.*? Edinburgh, 1978.

James W. Irvine, *Lerwick–the Birth and Growth of an Island Town.* Lerwick, 1985.

J. R. Nicolson, 'Arthur Anderson—Shetland's Most Famous Son.' Shetland Life, Feb. 1986.

Chapter 20: Scalloway and its islands

Gilbert Goudie, 'A Gold Armlet of the Viking Time Discovered in Shetland.' P.S.A.S. Vol. XLVII.

Adrian G. Osler, 'Boatbuilding by the Duncans of Hamnavoe, Burra Isle.' *Scandinavian Shetland: An Ongoing Tradition.*? Edinburgh, 1978.

Chapter 21: Mainland

Mills Diary. Shetland 1740–1803. Edinburgh, 1889.

Ian Morrison, *The North Sea Earls: The Shetland/Viking Archaeological Expedition* London, 1973.

Rolf Nordhagen, 'Når et vertskap vil bli kvitt sendrektige gjester.' Maal og Minne, 1969.

Chapter 22: The North Isles

Laurence Bain, 'A Fetlar Hamefarer.' Shetland Life, July, 1985.

The Island of Unst, Shetland. Geographical Field group, Nottingham, 1964.

Robert L. Johnson, 'The deserted homesteads of Fetlar.' Shetland Life, November, 1981.

Charles Sandison, *Unst—My Island Home and Its Story.* Lerwick, 1968.

Chapter 23: The North Sea Islands

Richard Perry, *Shetland Sanctuary—Birds on the Isle of Noss.* London, 1948.

Rev. John Russell, *Three years in Shetland.* London, 1887.

Roland Svensson, *Ensliga öar.* Stockholm, 1954.

Chapter 24: The Atlantic Islands

Barbara E. Crawford, Reports on excavations at 'Da Biggin', Papa Stour in Northern Studies Nos. 11(1978) and 13(1979)

Barbara E. Crawford: 'The Biggins, Papa Stour—A multi-disciplinary investigation.' *Shetland Archaeology,* Brian Smith (Ed.). Lerwick, 1985.

Sheila Gear, *Foula. Island West of the Sun.* London, 1983.

I. B. S. Holbourn, *The Isle of Foula,* Lerwick, 1938.

Stella Shepherd, *Like a Mantle, the Sea.* London, 1971.

Roland Svensson, *Ensliga öar.* Stockholm, 1954.

Chapter 25: Fair Isle

David Howarth, *The Voyage of the Armada—The Spanish Story.* London, 1981.

Roland Svensson, *Ensliga öar.* Stockholm, 1954.

Kenneth Williamson, *Fair Isle and Its Birds.* Edinburgh, 1965.

Chapter 26: The Sea

Tom Henderson, 'Shipwreck and Underwater Archaeology in Shetland'. *Shetland Archaeology,* Brian Smith (Ed.). Lerwick, 1985.

Simon Martin, *The Other Titanic.* London, 1980.

T. M. Y. Manson, *Drifting Alone to Norway.* Lerwick, 1986.

The North Sea. A Highway of Economic and Cultural Exchange. Bang-Andersen Greenhill, Grude (Ed.). Norwegian University Press, 1985.

INDEX

270